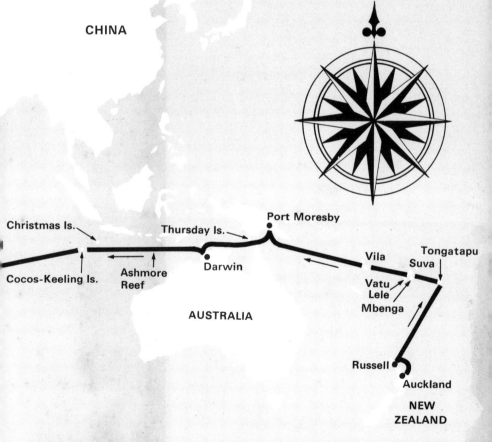

NORTH PACIFIC OCEAN

CHINA

Christmas Is.

Cocos-Keeling Is.

Ashmore Reef

Thursday Is.

Darwin

AUSTRALIA

Port Moresby

Vila

Vatu Lele

Mbenga

Suva

Tongatapu

Russell

Auckland

NEW ZEALAND

SOUTH PACIFIC OCEAN

CHILDREN OF THREE OCEANS

David Lewis

CHILDREN OF THREE OCEANS

*

COLLINS
St James's Place, London

This book is dedicated
to the four daughters of the wind,
and Granny

First Impression   September 1969
Second Impression   November 1969

Printed in Great Britain
Collins Clear-Type Press
London and Glasgow

CONTENTS

ILLUSTRATIONS

DIAGRAMS

MAPS

INTRODUCTION

THIS is the story of an adventure; of the first voyage round the world in a catamaran; of the youngest children to make the journey in a yacht of any type. The tale is completed here. The outward trip through Magellan Strait and the fierce wilderness of Patagonia and on to New Zealand is described in *Daughters of the Wind*.*

The beginning was the single-handed transatlantic race that started from Plymouth in May 1964, in which I sailed our catamaran *Rehu Moana* alone to Newport (R.I.). There I was joined by my wife Fiona, with the little girls then one and two years old, who had made a more perilous passage of the Western Ocean than mine, aboard a venerable tramp steamer. A year later, realising that the children needed one adult's full attention, thus leaving the boat to be sailed virtually single-handed by the other, we asked a friend from England to come with us. We also needed a second navigator for an experiment to test the navigational techniques of the prehistoric Polynesians. So Priscilla Cairns joined us in Valparaiso and has since continued in our company.

This book describes how we sailed from New Zealand round the north of Australia, across the Indian Ocean to weather what the Portuguese navigators picturesquely labelled the 'Cape of Storms', then by fog-bound deserts in Southern Africa and the stifling humidity of the Congo, to England again. It also tells of our continuing researches into ancient navigational methods.

Ranging free over a world normally impossibly compartmented and documented, has been something more than a similar itinerary by plane or liner would have been, for there was the immediate entrée into the local community where we *shopped* in the crowded markets instead of *looking* at them as tourists might. In this sense

* Gollancz, London, 1967.

9

we were part of each place. I have no ambition to produce a book of geographical facts that could be looked up in any reference library, so when I do write about strange lands that we visited, it is because I believe there to be a certain *validity in first impressions*, which are often more vivid and revealing than later ones.

A port came to life for us after this fashion. A conglomeration of shoreline and soundings on the chart was all we knew of it during the time it was our next objective; then suddenly we had arrived and in a few hours those lines and symbols had become places of interest and beauty, already peopled with firm friends. I use the term 'friends' advisedly because, appearing as we did in a small boat, all manner of people moved by a sense of adventure befriended us. Indeed the all too frequent goodbyes to them has added the one note of poignancy to our wanderings.

As to ourselves, I shall not write about the children here because the effect of their experiences on their evolving personalities is a major theme of the book. Where we have broken new ground perhaps, has been in taking our family circle *with us* into environments and experiences usually regarded as only suitable for athletic young men. I shall also postpone introducing Fiona and Priscilla until they have made their appearance in the story.

I am a forty-eight year old New Zealander of Welsh descent, a doctor who practised in London for eighteen years before our voyage. I have a married daughter Anna and a nineteen year old son Barry, by a former marriage. As a boy and young man I was adventurous in the sense of needing to come to grips with nature. I cared little for organised games, which I found oppressive and restricting in a land full of bush, mountains and wild rivers.

At seventeen I celebrated my last days at boarding school by building a canoe and informing the headmaster that I was going home in it at the end of term—450 miles across New Zealand by river, portage, lake and sea coast. His prompt veto was undermined by my parents' written permission. At what a cost to their peace of mind, since I was an only child, I only realised after becoming a parent myself. Since no one would come with me I set out alone.

It was on this trip that I first experienced the fulfilment of enforced self-reliance in struggling towards a goal. There were times, like a capsize in the icy Tongariro river that had only been once shot before, that I came close to losing heart. To haul the light craft on long portages I constructed a trailer with bicycle wheels. Anticipating the frequent wettings, I carried no blankets and slept wrapped in a ground sheet. But when I did reach my home in Auckland I had an empty feeling, as if an essential ingredient of endeavour was missing—left behind somewhere in the rapids of the Tongariro.

I re-discovered it while taking part in the ascent of several unclimbed peaks in the South Island where I went to Medical School. (One of these mountains I called Mt. Carinna after my mother, a name that we saw on the map on my return to New Zealand in *Rehu Moana*.)

But then followed further years at Leeds Medical School in England and, after qualification, war and adventure of a different sort. When I settled down to practise in East Ham I did my best to put aside thoughts of the free wind and the open spaces. Yet even here they intruded from time to time, increasingly taking on the mantle of an element I had rather taken for granted in New Zealand. Lying in bed on foggy nights I could not sleep for the hooting of steamers' sirens that came clear across two miles of sooty house-tops, through the frosty air. I tried to ignore their message that the sea was there waiting, still untamed and free and aloof as it always had been, as beautiful and as terrible in its impersonal anger. There were tentative approaches to it, like a sailing dinghy I built myself and a twenty-seven foot, sixty year old barge yacht in which I became acquainted with most of the sandbanks of the Thames Estuary. In general, however, I did succeed in overcoming these irresponsible longings.

A personal crisis some ten years back forced me into self-examination and the belated realisation that the link connecting the first canoe through mountain and forest to the old barge yacht was in fact the very essence of my character. I thereupon bought a pair of climbing boots and a ship's lifeboat. Those climbing boots led indirectly to my meeting Fiona—on a mountain in Wales—but long before then I had become embroiled in another kind of love affair—with the sea. (It and women have much in common of course, both being subject to unpredictable change—and boring if they were not.) The particular challenge that fascinated but also appalled me, was the single-handed transatlantic race of 1960.

Ultimately I sold the lifeboat, bought the five ton sloop *Cardinal Vertue* with the aid of a bank loan, and made New York in fifty-four solitary days from Plymouth, to come third behind Chichester and Hasler. The story is told in my first book, *The Ship Would Not Travel Due West*.* Another cherished ambition, to write, had also begun to be realised.

After this experience it was inevitable I suppose, that the call of distant seas should become irresistible. Eventually Fiona and I built *Rehu Moana*, sold our home and set out to sail round the world with our children, free of all encumbrances including a regular income.

* Temple Press Books, London, 1961.

Chapter 1

KIWI AND FLYING FOX

PREPARATIONS IN NEW ZEALAND

EARLY in 1966 the travel-stained *Rehu Moana* was drawn up at Westhaven under the shadow of Auckland Harbour Bridge. It was midsummer in New Zealand and we were staying with my cousins Bobbi and Fred Parsons who, at no small inconvenience, had put us all up. Bobbi's mother had even lent us her car which was garaged under the chocked-up *Rehu Moana* aboard which Fiona and Priscilla were wielding electric sanding machines.

"Where's the joker with the beard?" a passing yachtsman asked rather disapprovingly. Fiona explained that I had barricaded myself in an empty flat, where I was writing a book.

"That sander of yours sounds crook," remarked the questioner critically. "Wait till I get mine and I'll give you a hand. You're not doing a bad job though! Good on you, girls!"

We were continually reminded that this was a land where people do things for themselves, and perhaps for this reason are always ready with offers of assistance. I will be describing how we were helped to refit and carry out the alterations that 20,000 miles of voyaging had indicated, but before doing so it might be best to describe the vessel herself.

The name *Rehu Moana* is Maori and means 'Ocean Spray'. The more technical parts of the description have been concentrated in the following two paragraphs, especially the first, to allow anyone who wishes to skip to the part on accommodation and layout that follows.

The catamaran's overall length is 40 feet, length at water-line 35 feet 6 inches, beam 17 feet and width of hulls at the water-line 2 feet 9 inches. Since alterations in New Zealand the draft has been 3 feet, and she displaces about 8 tons. She was designed by

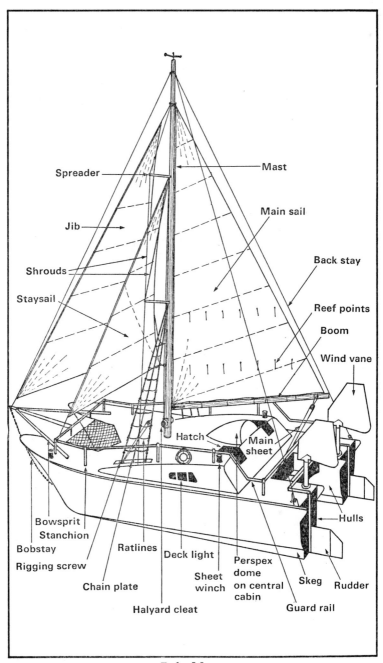

Rehu Moana

Colin Mudie and built by Prout Brothers in Essex in 1963. She was constructed of plywood, specially made by Bruynzeels from two hard West African woods, gaboon and utile. The bottom is ⅞ inch cold moulded and deck and topsides double skin with a total thickness of half an inch. The frames are laminated mahogany. The 47 foot mast is of metal. The rig is Bermudan cutter with points reefing. The sails 10 ounce synthetic cloth; area on departure from New Zealand 950 square feet, including the light weather ghoster.

Particularly successful in the design have been: the widely *flared bows* that prevent burying when running before gales; *arched* shape of deck in a transverse plane that confers flexible strength and offers minimal resistance to boarding seas; the high vee under the centre section that avoids pounding forward. Apart from such purely constructional features, there is the *covered-in steering* position which is not in the cockpit but in the centre cabin—which thus does duty as a kind of ship's bridge and family living room combined. The self-steering gear, about which more later, is adjusted from the same place, so avoiding unnecessary exposure to the elements. Finally the yacht is rendered virtually unsinkable by 7,000 pounds of buoyancy in the form of expanded Polystyrene behind bulkheads fore and aft in each hull.

We cooked on two standard Primus paraffin pressure stoves that could easily be replaced when they wore out after about a year of continuous use, and a Rippingilles paraffin wick stove with an oven. As the catamaran sailed level, none of these needed to be gimballed nor did we need fiddles round the table to prevent meals from flying into the scuppers.

The galley is on the inner side of the port hull. The Rippingilles is nearest to the hatch from the central cabin, forward of this is a fibreglass sink unit usually covered by a removable working surface, and beyond this again are the Primus stoves. There is full standing headroom in the galley in common with the rest of the hulls. The narrowness was an advantage. When Fiona was cooking at sea she braced herself against the food shelves behind her (made out of the former centre-board cases), and so had both hands free. Within reach on shelves or in netting, were most of the implements and ingredients she needed. Shelves above the

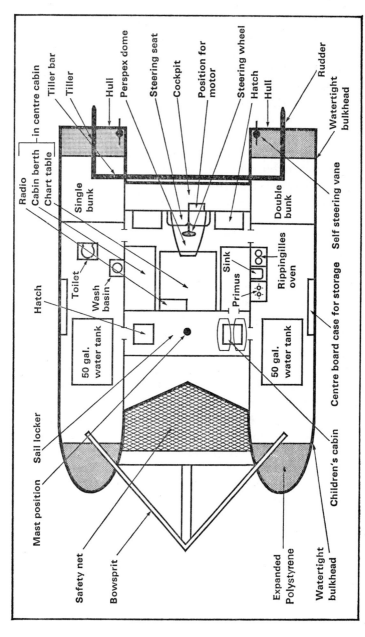

Radio
Cabin berth — in centre cabin
Chart table

Tiller bar
Tiller
Hull
Perspex dome
Steering seat
Cockpit
Position for motor
Steering wheel
Hatch
Hull
Rudder
Watertight bulkhead

Single bunk
Double bunk

Self steering vane

Hatch
Toilet
Wash basin

Sink
Rippingilles oven
Primus

Sail locker
Mast position
Safety net
Bowsprit

50 gal. water tank
50 gal. water tank

Centre board case for storage

Children's cabin

Expanded Polystyrene
Watertight bulkhead

Plan view of *Rehu Moana*

sink carried herbs and spices, garlic, matches, coffee, Primus prickers, sugar and saccharine in deference to my waist-line. Mugs hung on one side, saucepans on the other; there was a plate rack beneath the sink. Behind the cook's right shoulder were butter, crispbreads, biscuits, jam, a roll of kitchen paper and so on. Under her feet, between the two layers of floorboards, was another eighteen inches' depth of storage space, usually occupied by tins and bottles.

Lighting is by Aladdin Pressure Lantern and hurricane lamp, both of which use paraffin, electricity being reserved for navigation lights and the Marconi Kestrel radio transmitter. Battery charging is by a Wroxham Minor portable generator.

The diagram at the beginning of this section and the plan on this page give a general idea of the accommodation. There are two passage berths in the centre cabin, a double bunk for Fiona and me in the port hull, and Priscilla's cabin in the starboard. The children's cabin opens out of the front of the central one and was formerly part of the sail locker. Washing and toilet facilities are on the opposite side to the galley.

There is ample stowage space under the bunks and floorboards, in shelves in the old centre-board cases and centrally, beneath and behind the steering seat. A pair of fibreglass tanks fitted into the hulls hold 100 gallons of fresh water between them, supplemented by fourteen or so in plastic cans.

The sole motive of this 40 foot yacht apart from sail, is a $4\frac{1}{2}$ h.p. Seagull outboard motor that gives a speed in still water of $1\frac{1}{2}$ to 2 knots!

The refitting process was so lengthy that I can only mention a handful of the many people who assisted us, among the busiest of whom were members of the Auckland Multi-hull Association. One of them arrived with a very large saw one morning, cut out most of the cockpit floor and went away. For days we were in peril of falling through the floor. Eventually we discovered that he had gone on his summer cruise, forgetting to tell his friend who was to make the new floor. Liaison was re-established, the higher floor was soon installed and a trunk constructed down which to raise and lower the outboard. This was a vast improvement on its former position at the stern, from where I had been wont to retrieve it at the cost of much effort and strangled profanity when the boat speeded up leaving sheltered waters.

With the help of relatives and more friends, we stripped the yacht down, overhauled all gear and equipment, painted inside and out, fitted new guard rails, aired the water-tight compartments, constructed a composite aluminium and wood bowsprit, and made a pole for the second-hand spinnaker we acquired. New locker berths were constructed on either side of the central table.

I exploited some rather tenuous connections with Auckland University. These began disastrously enough, for after successfully finding the way over 1,600 miles without instruments, I failed to locate the lecture hall where I was to take the chair for Thor Heyerdahl, the hero of the *Kon Tiki*, and arrived dishevelled and panting and very late. However, I was able to recruit some helpers and supplement their numbers later on when giving lectures on ancient Polynesian navigation, with the odd result that much of our refitting was the work of the Archaeological Society.

This fitting out was interrupted by having to film sequences on board for television, and there was always the book. These were necessary activities because our savings were shrinking, and pouring money into the ocean only differs from spending it on a yacht in that the ocean at least has a floor somewhere! Priscilla was paying her share of the food, £10 a month, but it would have been unfair to expect her to shoulder any part of the costs of the refit since her contribution would have been absorbed in a boat that remained ours. Nevertheless she was continually offering to do so and unselfishly sacrificed her leisure.

Several firms helped us. International Paints gave us all the paint we needed and Crookes Wire Rope Co. re-rigged us, replacing our galvanised wire standing rigging and sheathing the new shrouds in plastic hose to prevent sails and sheets from chafing against them. The vigilance of their chief rigger, Cedric Chambers, disclosed an unsuspected crack through the stainless steel fitting at the mast head to which both our forestays are attached. But for him we should inevitably have lost our mast at sea.

Two major modifications, the only ones to be done professionally, were the replacing of drop keels by permanent skegs 17 feet long and tapering from 1 foot 3 inches deep aft to nothing forward and bolted beneath the after part of the hulls, and the fitting of strong steel rudders without swivelling drop blades. Weak keels and rudders had been the catamaran's only failing, though a serious one, during the first part of the voyage and we were determined to be free of such troubles in future.

The running rigging, including halyards and the steering and self-steering lines which are all of Terylene, were in perfect condition and indeed remain so to this day. This is all the more surprising as they have been in continual use since 1963, when British Ropes supplied them for our Iceland trip on which they survived two dismastings.

All was not well with the sails however. We had bought the materials at some expense after my offer to 'test it out' had been turned down with the withering reply that the makers needed no confirmation of its being the best in the world. Now with half the world still before us, we found the fabric had so deteriorated from the effects of tropical sunlight as to render the sails barely serviceable. Not being able to afford replacements we had to make the best of the situation. A less serious sail problem was that none of our headsails had been cut for our present rig and so set badly going to windward.

To our great regret we were too busy to accept all invitations but Priscilla, whose appetite for salt water is insatiable, did manage to go on a fortnight's cruise with Gordon Kells and his wife. These are very old friends of mine, and it was Gordon who had first taken me sailing as a boy. On his advice I had joined the Sea Scouts where the elements of seamanship were drummed into me. I still remember the 'Rule of the Road at Sea' rhymes we were taught—and the impressive nautical vocabulary we acquired one day from the Naval Petty Officer Instructor who was steering our whaler when a gull scored a direct hit on his eye! What a strange sensation it was, so many years later, to find that the place where I was to give a lecture was the very hall where the scouts used to meet!

The southern summer wore on. The children were mercifully out of our way at kindergarten and we were living aboard again. This would have hardly been practicable with no functioning cooking facilities on the dismantled catamaran had it not been for the 'Take Away' shops from which well cooked and cheap dishes were available. Among our own favourites were fried oysters, curries, fried chicken and chow mein.

"How do you like being a Kiwi again?" I was asked often. I liked it very much. New Zealand is an overwhelmingly outdoor country where the cities empty on Friday afternoons and the population goes camping, yachting, fishing, skin diving, tramping among the heavily bush clad ranges, canoeing or skiing. 'Make it yourself' is very much the order of the day. A typical forty foot yacht would be home made, and her owner/builder in all probability an engineer, electrician or welder, for the skilled manual trades rank high on the income scale.

One more generalisation about New Zealand; while prejudices between national groups exist as they do everywhere, there is no colour bar. When the Governor General presented me with the New Zealand Yachtsman of the Year award for 1965, he was disappointed to learn that while I have Maori cousins I myself have no Maori ancestry, a fact that I too regret.

The Maori part of the New Zealand population is increasing today and is being augmented by steady immigration from the Cook Islands and Samoa, so that New Zealand is now the 'heartland' of Polynesia, where by far the greatest concentration of Polynesians live. This fact, and her generally good record in the island territories, renders her the natural industrial, technical and cultural centre of the Polynesian world, a role well within the limits of her resources.

Once *Rehu Moana* had been launched again, the work of provisioning began. Canned food formed the bulk of our long distance supply since we lacked refrigeration. New Zealand is a place where it is readily available and not too expensive and, since the language is English, shopping is not too difficult. Even so, think for a moment how hard it is to provision a household for a long weekend, then consider what it implies to stock a family yacht for even a month—often to allow for emergencies we had to carry three months' stores—for there are no shops in mid ocean in which to buy anything that has been forgotten. We loaded up with enough tinned meat, vegetables and fruit to last us to the free port of Suva in Fiji. Then there was an assortment of concentrated fruit juices and cordials, dried fruit, crispbreads, cereals, tinned milk and margarine which keeps much better than butter. Bread, sliced and sun-dried, remains palatable for a long time; really fresh eggs will last for several months untreated; onions keep very well. We also put aboard potatoes, rice, flour, sugar and, at the last moment before leaving, a good supply of fresh fruit, green vegetables and tomatoes. Very important were such necessities as matches, Primus prickers, torch batteries, sweets for the children and well-concealed new books and toys to be brought out on birthdays and special occasions or times of crisis or periods of monotony and boredom. Reading this paragraph over I realise that to write 'we' is misleading. Nearly all the list making and shopping was done by Fiona, sometimes assisted by Priscilla, while my role in relation to food remained that of an appreciative consumer. Determined to try to catch something more than pieces of seaweed this time, we hopefully purchased new fishing lines, hooks and spinners.

After leaving Auckland we planned to call at Russell in the Bay of Islands, about 140 miles up the coast to the north, and thence take our departure for Tonga. When the day arrived for the official send-off, 5th May 1966, it found us ready for sea and cleared by customs (for there is no Customs Officer in Russell), but with the book still unfinished. So we hoisted sail, waved goodbye, and came to rest after a passage of some eight miles, in a secluded cove known to yachtsmen as Drunken Bay, between the rugged extinct volcano Rangitoto and the adjoining green island Motutapu. Here we spent a peaceful three days while I completed the manuscript.

Only then did we say goodbye to 'Uncle Alf' the Naval Storekeeper, and Joe, two kindly semi-retired men who lived on Rangitoto, and to the wallabies who came out of the bush at dusk to eat the bread they put out for them, and rounding the eastern side of Motutapu, we began stealing gently northward before the lightest of zephyrs.

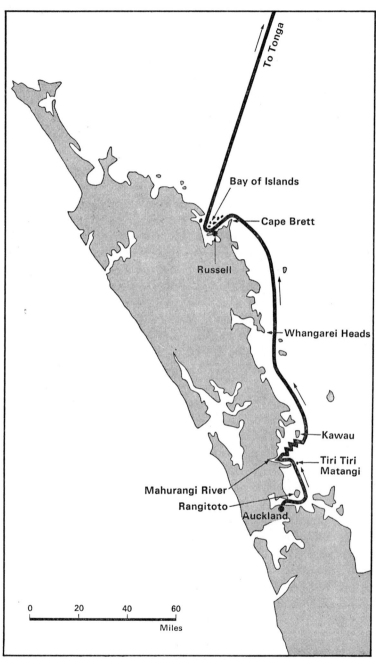

To Tonga

Bay of Islands

Cape Brett

Russell

Whangarei Heads

Kawau

Tiri Tiri Matangi

Mahurangi River

Rangitoto

Auckland

0   20   40   60
Miles

North Auckland

BAY OF ISLANDS

The Voyage Begins

Motoring in flat calm or with the spinnaker whenever there was breeze enough to fill it, we passed the peninsula Tiri Tiri Matangi, and soon after dark cautiously felt our way into the mouth of the Mahurangi River, where we anchored, and there we remained all the following day while cloud wrack drove by and rain drummed on deck and even those sheltered waters were whipped into foam.

By the next morning the wind had steadied in the South East and dropped to a strong breeze, force 6, so we beat out to sea against the flooding tide, pitching into the steep seas until we had Kawau Island abeam, when we turned northward and eased our sheets.

Kawau, incidentally, is a lovely wooded island deeply indented by sheltered inlets, the largest of which has the distinction of being so popular with yachtsmen that it is said to have become completely floored with brown glass so that an anchor no longer digs in but slithers uselessly across the expanse of beer bottles on the bottom.

Soon we all began to feel queasy and it seemed to us that the catamaran's motion was far more jerky and erratic than we remembered, while she seemed much harder to steer. Then at 8.30 that night in a cross sea off Whangerai Heads a wave broke against the starboard quarter, jarring the whole yacht. So steady is the catamaran usually that we had left the lighted Aladdin lamp unsecured on the table. It was catapulted across the cabin and struck Vicky's naked shoulder. She screamed with anguish and Susie with fright and anger.

"Naughty Daddy, you must tie up the lamp next time!"—Good advice that we followed strictly after. We treated the burn, which was about an inch long I suppose, with a soothing antiseptic cream and gave her a soluble aspirin and sweets. Even so, Vicky whose tolerance of pain is remarkable, awoke whimpering with pain from time to time during the night.

23

This unfortunate accident really did convince us that the ship's motion was worse than it used to be. The most likely explanation and one that proved to be correct, was that she was trimmed too far down by the head, so in the course of that night we laboriously began to move heavy weights further aft, and were heartened when we noted an immediate improvement. At the next port we took the opportunity to re-stow the rest of our heavy gear.

The damage to Vicky having been accomplished, the wind began to grow lighter and lighter as the night advanced until morning found us wallowing almost becalmed in a heavy lop off Cape Brett, the southern boundary of the Bay of Islands, an area which must offer some of the best cruising and game fishing in the world. Once round the promontory we threaded our way between grassy islands whose ravines were choked with heavy bush, past stacks and stratified cliffs and deep sandy bays, to anchor off the town of Russell in the early afternoon. Once New Zealand's first capital, it is now an attractive sleepy little place which must have been even smaller I reflected, when my great-grandfather James O'Neill landed there in 1839, before the country was a British colony.

An event had taken place at some time during our seclusion at Drunken Bay or on the coastal passage that was to bring us notoriety. When our rubber dinghy grounded on the shingle at Russell, we were startled and not a little dismayed to be greeted with cries of:

"There they are! You can see they're the same ones!" What could have happened? We were not left long in doubt.

"Those two little girls are the ones that were in the *TV* film!" Never had we experienced such an enthusiastic reception as this. Clearly the very extensive coverage that the press in New Zealand had given to our adventures had not made anything like the impact on the public imagination as had the half hour television film we had taken on the journey.

THE OPEN OCEAN

Toward Tongatapu

We left Russell three days later on 15th May, a still autumn day, exactly five months after we had landed in Auckland. Both children had had New Zealand birthdays, Susie reaching four at the end of December and Vicky three in April. We had seen pitifully little of my own country which I had badly wanted to show Fiona.

"At least I did manage to go to the races," she reminded me, and I smiled remembering how puzzled and fascinated the girls had been by the whole proceeding. The inevitable "Why can't we come?" had been followed by a rather charming remark from Susie.

"The man will say 'what a pretty hat' and let you ride his racing horse, Mummy."

Then Vicky in more practical vein—

"Will the racing horses give you money?"

Unfortunately they were unimpressed by the elegant hat and failed to oblige.

Fiona was born in Johannesburg, but studied and afterwards taught dancing and physical education in England. As a legacy of her South African girlhood she is a very good rider herself. The unco-operative racing horses apart, she did have the opportunity of riding a little in New Zealand. (I cannot help regarding horses as unnecessarily large animals, well able to gauge a rider's inexperience.)

"Another good thing that happened in New Zealand," said Fiona, "was finding the hand sewing machine. I had given up hope of ever getting one." She added pointedly, "But you haven't even bothered to look at it, you're only interested in boat things!" I indignantly denied the accusation. The machine was a beautifully finished piece of craftsmanship that she had bought for £2. She had been making (and designing) the children's dresses and many of her own all through the trip but had to sew everything by hand—no wonder she cherished her acquisition. The absence of electric power was no drawback she soon found, because the girls vied with each other for the privilege of turning the handle.

More than once in the sewing machine era when we had a special event to go to in the evening, I would find Fiona looking thoughtfully at a piece of material she had just bought or had been keeping.

"What is that for?" I would ask.

"My dress for tonight of course," would be the impatient reply, and sure enough she would appear in due course wearing something striking.

As the hills of New Zealand faded into the haze astern, the children began to ask excitedly, "what island next?" spinning their globe around and apparently identifying Tonga with China. As yet they had little idea of time so were expecting Tonga to appear at any moment, rather than in a fortnight or so. We were a little anxious lest their long and enjoyable sojourn ashore should have rendered life at sea less attractive but no, as always they seemed to relax and become calmer and more settled once we had put to sea. It was as if the circumscribed but familiar world of their floating home enclosed them protectively, giving comfort and a sense of security. Their months in kindergarten seemed to have provided them with more resources to occupy themselves so that sometimes now they would spend hours painting, drawing and singing from their nursery rhyme books. We have been asked so often if they were not afraid, that it seems ironical to have to answer—

"Yes, once in a house in New Zealand!" They had run howling to their mother sobbing out a story of a great roaring thing in the next room—it was a vacuum cleaner!

At dusk we discussed our night watches for the passage. We varied our arrangements according to the proximity of danger (land), the presence of shipping lanes and in response to the sky signs predicting the state of the sea and wind and controlling our destinies like some daily Zodiac. The arrangement we decided upon was fairly typical. Since the children did not allow Fiona to sleep during the day and she did most of the cooking, I tried to spare her a broken night. At that latitude and time of year there were eleven hours of darkness, from 7 p.m. until 6 a.m.

So Fiona would take charge in the early evening, from 7 until 9 p.m. Then I was on from 9 p.m. to midnight, Priscilla from midnight to 3 a.m., and myself again from 3 to 6 a.m. Priscilla then took over for the onerous morning watch that involved persuading the children to keep quiet for as long as possible, feeding them and taking the morning sight. I had a sleep in the morning, Priscilla in the afternoon.

In practice none of this was very difficult because, thanks to the wind vanes, we did not have to steer, the most that was usually needed being an occasional glance at the compass followed by a tug at the steering wheel, some re-adjustment of the vane setting or the attachment of a length of shock cord to the tiller arm. Most of the watch would be spent writing at the table, looking up charts and sailing directions or simply lying on the passage berth reading, breaking off at intervals to get up and scan the horizon for ships.

The wind vane self-steering gear, without whose aid the trip would have been immeasurably more difficult, consists of two plywood vanes that can be set to steer the yacht, which they do by turning the steering wheel and hence the rudders in the usual way. A course is maintained in relation to the wind not a compass heading; when the wind direction alters they have to be re-set. The diagrams below will make their mode of operation clearer.

If the vessel is perfectly balanced, variations in the *strength* of the wind do not affect the functioning of a vane system but in cases like ours where a yacht has 'weather helm', that is turns *into* the wind as it increases, the vanes are only about 80% effective, especially when running down wind. We improved our gear's efficiency in New Zealand by fitting larger vanes.

We made no attempt to keep our electric navigation lights switched on at sea since we simply did not have the generating capacity, but we did use them when a ship was seen approaching. More important we lit the Aladdin pressure lamp ready to exhibit on deck, where its brilliant light, unlike twelve or twenty-four volt yacht lamps, not only blinded us but was visible for miles, showing the approaching vessel that there was *something* afloat to be avoided. There was nothing casual in our attitude; we took the risk of collision very seriously indeed; and if our pressure lamp

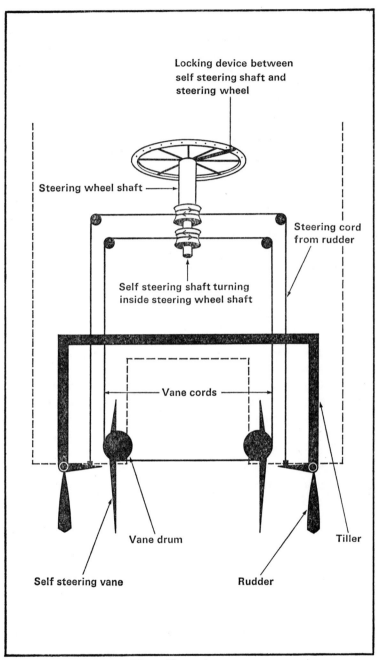

Locking device between
self steering shaft and
steering wheel

Steering wheel shaft

Self steering shaft turning
inside steering wheel shaft

Steering cord
from rudder

Vane cords

Vane drum

Self steering vane

Rudder

Tiller

The self steering gear

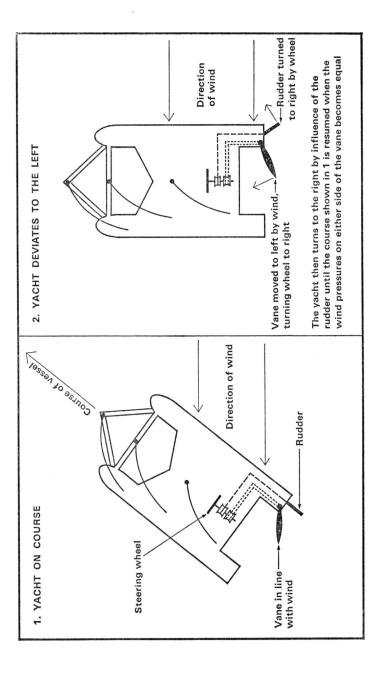

1. YACHT ON COURSE

Course of vessel

Direction of wind

Steering wheel

Rudder

Vane in line with wind

2. YACHT DEVIATES TO THE LEFT

Direction of wind

Rudder turned to right by wheel

Vane moved to left by wind, turning wheel to right

The yacht then turns to the right by influence of the rudder until the course shown in 1 is resumed when the wind pressures on either side of the vane becomes equal was not allowed for in regulations, we believed that ensuring we were unequivocally visible took precedence.

When no one was on watch at night, as during the single-handed Atlantic race, a pressure lamp on deck gave a fair measure of security. Another safeguard was our metal mast which acted as a radar reflector.

The demands of the voyage tended to form us into an interdependent team, each member having particular responsiblities. Fiona, for instance, naturally had special demands made upon her by the children. She was more intrigued with the country to which we were bound than the art of voyaging under sail as such, and took on almost all the catering and a larger share of the cooking. It is a tribute both to her and Priscilla that the two women were able to share a minute 'kitchen' for two years without noticeable friction.

Priscilla was much more interested in the actual techniques of sailing and navigation and had in fact won prizes in the latter subject. By profession she is a teacher of mathematics, which she gave up for two years and lived on her savings while she was on *Rehu Moana*.

During the first night out from Russell the wind fell so light at times that we had to lower the sails to prevent them chafing themselves to pieces as they flogged wildly to our rolling. The motion was so erratic that even the hardy little girls were rather subdued. The wind began freshening from the westward next day and became squally, so that by the third afternoon when we were about 200 miles offshore, we were sailing across a rough irregular beam sea. It was then that one of those freak accidents occurred that seem to make mock of the most meticulous of refits.

Our shrouds are attached to the mast tangs by stainless steel bolts that are kept in place by split pins. The split pin for the port lower shrouds sheared.

I was off watch and asleep when Priscilla awoke me, observing with admirable restraint that the port lower stays had fallen down and the mast was bending. I stumbled on deck and was horrified when I saw how it was whipping violently to and fro. We gybed hurriedly to bring the wind on the opposite side and thus transfer the major stress to the intact starboard shrouds, and then lowered

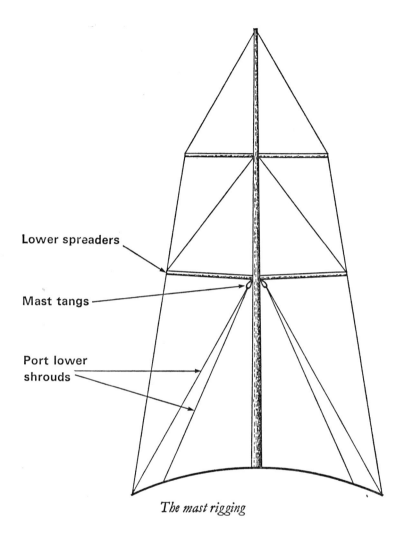

Lower spreaders

Mast tangs

Port lower shrouds

The mast rigging

sail. I scrambled up the alternately sagging and straightening rigging, gasping each time I was thumped against the mast and the breath knocked out of me, and, I fear, making a great to-do for I am never one to suffer in silence. I took two lengths of spare halyard with me that I lashed round the mast at the level of the lower spreaders. Meanwhile the crew had shackled blocks to the chain plates, and the moment the two ropes were fast

31

round the mast, they led one through each block to the sheet winches and hurriedly winched them in. . . . What a relief!

Though we were rather over-awed by the elasticity of our jury rope stays, the mast was now safe and we could hoist the headsails and resume our course. Headsails alone could be set until we could effect a more permanent repair, because the mainsail is hoisted up a mast track that was obstructed by our temporary shrouds.

The weather continued too bad for delicate work on a bending, partially stayed mast, so we had to content ourselves with cutting a bronze bolt to length and drilling it for a split pin. Next day we did succeed in replacing the shrouds in position, but as we were unable to insert the split pin and the whole contraption was only held in place by insulation tape, we dared not remove our jury supporting stays.

The children took the accident and the subsequent proceedings rather lightly I thought.

"What has Daddy got that ribbon for?"

"To tie the mast up with, Vicky." ·

"Is it falling down?"

The sea became rougher yet. Having to go aloft on the tenth day, I forgot the discomfort of clinging on, so wild and splendid was the scene. Soaring on impossibly long pinions above the crests whipped up by a rising westerly gale, was a great humpbacked, hook-nosed wandering albatross, and there dancing and fluttering about the foam itself were half a dozen of his fragile relatives the storm petrels, for the greatest and the smallest of the sea birds belong to the same family. My head was level with the lower spreaders 21 feet above the sea, yet many of the wave crests were being tossed up between myself and the horizon. This was astonishing. The wind was no more than force 7 as yet; the hurricane season which lasts from December to April in the South Pacific was well over, so a gale of about 11 must be blowing somewhere to the southward to have built up such big seas. That this was the case, we heard that night on the radio; 800 miles to the south off North Auckland, a well found coaster had gone down with all hands in a tremendous storm.

That strong gale never reached us but it continued very rough

Auckland: the start

Aboard *Rehu Moana*

Priscilla Cairns, David Lewis, his wife Fiona with Susie and Vicky

so that it was not until the day before we reached Tonga that we were at last able to secure our shrouds properly and hoist the mainsail.

As our landfall approached we had to adjust our clocks to Tongan time, a much more complicated process than usual for the International Date Line runs between New Zealand and Tonga. While the former country is 12 hours fast of Greenwich, once across the Date Line as we had done a week earlier, we should properly have been a whole day behind. But for convenience, instead of being 12 hours slow of Greenwich, Tonga is placed in a special zone 13 hours fast of Greenwich and 1 hour ahead of New Zealand.

If this seems complicated to the reader, let me admit at once that it is equally so to me, and that I could not have written the above without reference to the Nautical Almanac. In a sense our lives at sea were ruled by time even more than ashore. One needs to know Greenwich Mean Time to the nearest second for accurate navigation. Fortunately, any modern transistor radio that can be tuned to frequencies between 5 and 20 M.C. can pick up time signals anywhere in the world.

We approached Tongatapu from the south east in confident anticipation of meeting trade winds from that quarter, but to our chagrin the westerly winds persisted, so that while we sighted the high island of Eua on the morning of the 29th it took us another twenty-four hours to beat round to the western side of the low lying island of Tongatapu. On the way we were very nearly overtaken by tragedy.

To explain what happened I must touch on our navigational methods, considering sun sights only for simplicity. Two sights separated by sufficient time for the sun to move round substantially, worked out with the aid of the Almanac and simplified tables like the Navy's H.D.486, will establish one's position. (The art is not difficult. Starting from scratch I learned enough at fortnightly evening classes one winter to be able to cross the Atlantic alone the next year.) An inaccurate sextant naturally will disastrously affect one's results. We had checked ours after it had been serviced in Auckland to make sure it was still accurate. Unfortunately, we neglected to re-check it later to confirm that it was *still* all right, and as we were to discover to our chagrin, an index error to the tune of 15′ of arc or up to 15 miles had developed.

So all unwittingly on a moonless night we closed the southern shore of Tongatapu, which consists of an unbroken line of raised coral against which the Pacific rollers crash home forcing columns of spray through blow holes forty feet into the air—an attraction for tourists but not when viewed from seaward and not at night, for we were ten miles east of where we supposed ourselves to be. In our confidence that we were giving that dangerous coast a good offing, we were only puzzled at first when we made out a black line along the horizon right ahead. Was it cloud or a black squall? Surely no land could be there! Very watchful now we sailed on. It *was* land. Aghast at our narrow escape we came about and stood to seaward not daring to approach again until daylight revealed our true position.

Tongatapu is encircled on the west and north by a barrier reef that encloses a lagoon ten miles across in places. As we neared the thundering spouting reef line, we had reason to be glad of an innovation we had made in Auckland, the fitting of ratlines, in effect rope ladders up the lower shrouds. Out of the yachts that had lain near us in Tahiti the year before, six were now total losses, four at least having fallen victim to coral reefs. Since we lacked a powerful motor the danger was particularly real for us.

"When a boat bumps the rocks all the people have to swim," remarked Susie, eyeing the surf dubiously, "and I'm not big enough to swim."

This was where the ratlines came in, for with me perched aloft as a look-out, we were able to stand confidently into Tongatapu Lagoon through one of the lesser used reef passes, while I conned from the living chart spread out below me on which soundings were indicated by shades from pale blue to indigo, coral heads at various depths by orange or brown and sand fathoms deep a pale green. An hour later we were at the other side of the lagoon passing the picturesque wooden Victorian Palace of the late Queen Salote. Then a flurry of wind and rain swept over us, a few cables more past the deep water wharf and we rounded to and dropped anchor off Nuku'alofa, capital of the Kingdom of Tonga, on 30th May, two weeks and a thousand miles from

Russell. As we came to rest the wind dropped and the heat enfolded us like a blanket.

One hoists three flags on entering a foreign port; the national ensign astern, a courtesy flag of the country being visited in the place of honour at the starboard yard arm and the yellow quarantine flag to port. You then usually wait patiently to see what will happen, and if nothing does after some hours, go ashore to try to find the appropriate officials. Regulations are so varied that it is impossible to know beforehand what the 'correct drill' is going to be. But this time we had barely anchored before a launch with customs, immigration and health department personnel was alongside, and five minutes later they left, having completed forms giving us permission to cruise anywhere in the Tongas and advised us to move into the launch harbour. We had never before met such efficiency and dispatch.

TONGA

Starting the outboard we chugged down an artificial passage into a small harbour blasted out of the coral ledge that extends 200 yards out from the shore—the fringing reef. Inside was a varied collection of craft, a modern Seventh Day Adventist motor coaster, the derelict yacht of a Dane who had renounced civilisation for a hermit's life on an uninhabited island in the group, some small Tongan-built cutters and a big inter-island motor launch, whose skipper Kaloni was to become a firm friend. Several whale-boats were drawn up ashore. The Azores and Tonga are the only places where whaling is still carried on in the old intrepid way, in open boats with a hand harpoon. Next day the harbour became filled to capacity when we were joined by two New Zealand yachts, *Claire de la Lune* and *Vega*, and the American schoolboy Lee Graham in *Dove*, alone save for his cat.

A road along which three-wheeled motorcycle taxis puttered, ran by the waterside beneath lines of coconut palms that were bowing before the trade wind with that low boom that is the very music of the South Seas. Attractive palm frond houses (no doubt they let in the rain) and frame houses hideous with rusty corrugated iron, which probably did not, were scattered in clearings where they were half hidden in a blaze of scarlet hibiscus and were surrounded by rooting piglets.

We thought Nuku'alofa delightful; a busy rambling town of unpretentious buildings. At the time of our visit the kingdom was in deep mourning for Queen Salote who had died four months before. Everyone wore black with mourning mats round the waist, there was no dancing, music, cinema or noisy beating of *tapa* cloth. It was indeed a moving tribute to her memory. One is apt to forget, because the total land area of the Tongan archipelago is less than that of the Isle of Man, that the kingdom boasts about the oldest unbroken royal line in the world. We visited the megalith of one of Queen Salote's direct ancestors, A Tui Tonga who was himself the twenty-ninth of his line and was reigning at the time of the Norman Conquest of England.

Mr. Reid, the British Consul, who is an anthropologist in the tradition of Sir Arthur Grimble, was most hospitable. We were distressed to learn that he had been anxious about us. This stemmed we gathered from a misunderstanding as to when we had left New Zealand, the date we cleared customs in Auckland having become confused with our actual departure from Russell ten days later. We had arrived, much to the Consul's relief and our own, just in time to avert an air search. To our surprise, Vicky, who is normally the most sociable of children, evinced marked reluctance to visit the Consul's house, and when we did arrive insisted, "Susie go first." We found afterwards that she was confusing a consul with a dentist!

The Tongas are closely cultivated. Copra is the main crop but yam, taro, sweet potato, melons, avocados, known locally as Tongan butter, sugar cane, oranges, mangoes and so on are grown for subsistence and the local market—where incidentally, they are very cheap. Fish are plentiful as are shellfish on the reefs. Each man at eighteen is allotted a plot of land. An idyllic state of affairs apparently, and so it would be except for one problem— shortage of land. Having always been independent, Tonga escaped European rule that depopulated every other Polynesian territory to the verge of extinction. Now, with a growing population and the time honoured solution, conquest in Fiji, no longer respectable, the question of surplus population is a difficult one.

One evening we were invited to the home of a Tongan Member of Parliament, who with a skill that I am sure no British M.P. could match, had cooked us a traditional dinner, the food soaked in coconut cream and then wrapped in taro leaves having been baked in an *umu* or earth oven. (My assertion was incorrect. Dame Joan Vickers, M.P. for Devonport, tells me she has often cooked in an *umu* in Indonesia!) The centre piece was a distressingly life-like piglet, whose appearance so upset Susie that, after asking, "was that doggie burnt?" she refused to eat any of it. However, there were other dishes like chicken, corned beef wrapped in taro, breadfruit, plantain, yam, sweet potato and raw fish soaked in lime juice and coconut cream. It was a feast to remember.

There is a species of small fruit bat or flying fox in Tonga. In the village of Kolovai these have long been *tapu* or sacred, so that over the centuries they have become so confident as to have abandoned woods and caves as resting places in favour of the village ironwood trees, where they spend the day festooned in inverted clusters. When we went to pay our respects it was to-wards dusk and they were beginning to wake up. Still hanging upside down, some who had urgent business at the other end of their branch, were pushing and squeezing their way past the rest with much squeaking and squabbling, for all the world like a subway in the rush hour.

"I would like a flying fox for dangling in my cabin," Vicky sighed, then a new thought striking her, "but it might fly me away."

All Polynesians share an essentially similar culture and are physically alike, though the language of the western group (Samoa and Tonga) is now barely comprehensible in eastern islands like Tahiti. About 1870 a few itinerant drovers in the western United States were bringing great herds of cattle to the Kansas rail heads. In a decade the long drives were over and they had scattered but in that short span they had founded the whole mythology of the cowboy, his songs, his clothes, his free roving life and his six guns.

In much the same manner the Polynesians, who probably never numbered more than half a million all told, whose language is so poverty stricken as to be devoid of verbs and whose islands, far from being lotus lands, lacked in the beginning all mammals and all food plants save those they themselves brought with them in their canoes and introduced and acclimatised with prodigious labour and agricultural skill, have imbued the very words 'atoll' and 'South Seas' with their own special aura and legend. And quite apart from such romantic associations as their poetry and oratory, the sinuous dances of the western islands or the hula of Hawaii and Tahiti, there is reason enough for this. These resilient people have withstood the full impact of civilisation without it having eradicated their conviction that life was meant for enjoyment. They still possess a remarkable self confidence on the ocean that has been matched only by the Vikings. Indeed the old time Tongans did resemble the Vikings to no small degree.

Mounted by the consulate flagstaff at Nuku'alofa is a gift from the chiefs of the Tongan island of Ha'apai, one of the cannon from the *Port au Prince*. This ill-fated ship was taken at Ha'apai in 1806 and the crew slaughtered except for one youth, Will Mariner, who was adopted by a chief and spent the next four years in Tonga. Now Mariner left an account of the doings of one of the piratical Tongans that gives a very good idea of the nature and scope of Polynesian sea roving at a time when it was already in decline.

This navigator chief, Kau Moala by name, after fighting in the Fijian wars, left for home with his followers in a large double canoe, of course without charts or instruments. After sailing against the S.E. Trades, close hauled on the starboard tack for 420 miles, he sighted the Tongan island of Vavau but was unable to beat up to it. He then altered course for Samoa 310 miles further north but being unable to find it squared away back westward before the trades to Futuna 355 miles away. After considerable canoe building, marrying and fighting, he continued 240 miles to Rotuma and then circled south 250 miles to regain Fiji. More wars followed. His second and final departure for Tonga was celebrated by a feast at which were consumed 200 piles of yams, 200 pigs and 200 human bodies—not even Sir Francis Chichester was greeted with such a banquet!

The ancestral Polynesians had reached Tonga and Samoa from Asia by at least 500 B.C. and fanning out eastward became established in Tahiti and the Marquesas early in the Christian era, and in subsequent centuries, settled in Hawaii, New Zealand, Easter Island and the most remote atolls. The long saga of this migration across the Pacific, which after all is as big as all other oceans combined, must stand equally with the Homeric epics as part of the heritage of mankind.

There is no doubt that the Polynesian vessels, double canoes up to 100 feet long, were fully capable of covering the distances involved (I measured a steering paddle in Suva museum—it was 32 feet long), but what is needed to help interpret both traditional and archaeological evidence is a clearer idea of the usefulness and limitations of their navigational methods. That they were relatively efficient over hundreds of miles we know very well from Kau Moala's voyages and other sources but evidence is conflicting and scanty when we come to journeys of upwards of a thousand miles.

The Polynesian methods fall roughly into three categories; the use of stars and sun to indicate direction like a compass does, the determination of what amounts to latitude by certain stars and signs used to locate land.

As to the 'star compass' *KAVENOA* or Star Path, the trained navigator-priests knew by heart the names and bearings of upwards of 150 stars. Another instance, the Tahitians divided the horizon into sixteen named points identified from where the sun rose and set at different times of the year. When the heavens were invisible, course was maintained at a set angle to the wind or the more reliable swell lines.

The concept that the star that passes overhead at the same place during each twenty-four hours year in and year out is mystically connected with the island it passes over is an invaluable one for navigation, because one needs only to bring this star of the land overhead and keep it in one's zenith to remain in what we express as the latitude of that island.

The third set of skills, pertaining to the finding of land when it is below the horizon, depended on a number of clues. For instance, the direction of the flight in the morning and evening of those varieties of birds that rest ashore; the way ocean swells are curbed or thrown back on themselves by even distant islands; particular types of seaweed, fish, standing clouds over distant peaks or the reflection in clouds of big lagoons, all had their place.

The Polynesians used no instruments.

We had tried out these methods in practice ourselves, as far as one can learn such arts from the accounts of explorers and missionaries, and found them to work remarkably well. For instance, in favourable conditions from the deck of a catamaran, which after all is only a double canoe, we were fairly confident at judging latitude from the zenith star to within 30 miles. But was anyone left in Polynesia who was still heir to some part of this tradition? Did it still live anywhere or was the trail a cold one? There in Tongatapu we began to find the answer to this question—there were such people.

The Three Seas of Kaloni

Kaloni (the name is the Tongan form of the English 'Colin'), skipper of the inter island launch *Alai Moana* took us with him to the island of Eua. While he stood, steering with his foot, he began to tell me, haltingly, because he was searching for words in English, how he had sailed as a boy through the Tongan archipelago as far as Vavau and even to distant Samoa in his father's trading cutter. Yes, they did have a compass aboard he thought or perhaps not. In any case they did not use one. Why should they? His father took his courses from the stars and the sun and numerous sea signs and this had been the seamanship he had taught Kaloni.

The use of zenith stars, which always seems to have been part of priestly lore, was unfamiliar to Kaloni whose knowledge was essentially local, corresponding to a geographical range that had become even more restricted than in Mau Moala's day, albeit still covering a north/south distance of 500 miles, as far as John O'Groats is north of Land's End. Nevertheless, his store of facts was amazing. On subsequent nights aboard *Rehu Moana* he pointed out the stars that indicated this island or that reef or safe passage until my head swam and I was unable to memorise more than a fraction of what he told me.

He explained how the long ocean swell lines were distorted by land, being bent on each side of an island and ultimately joining beyond it in a complex interlocking pattern. On the windward side, an under-running back swell was refracted. If you knew how, he said, these effects could be detected and interpreted as much as twenty miles away from the smallest atoll. 'If you knew how'. This was the rub. I knew most of what Kaloni was telling me, in theory from books, but never having had practical instruction I had found the interpretation of wave patterns the hardest skill to master. Now at last I was to have a lesson.

"Three seas there are between us and Nomuka where you are going tomorrow," he said on our last evening. "I know you worry about those reefs of Ha'apai but do as I say. Sail in the afternoon in time to clear Tongatapu reefs by sunset, then follow that star——"

"No," I said firmly, "12° Magnetic by the compass."

"O.K. then," he agreed, "but Nomuka sixty five miles, how you know when to change course to miss Kelefesia reef? Remember the current is strong and changes all the time—your log won't help you."

He went on to describe in great detail the characteristics of three distinct types of sea we should meet the following night and exactly how they would affect the catamaran's motion, so that when this altered in a certain way we might be sure of our position.

And so it worked out. Two of the three 'seas' were easily identified during the hours of darkness and the advent of the third coincided with raising the feathery line of Nomuka's palms in the early dawn.

Now this third 'sea' was an irregular one and it extended right up to the island. I got ready the anchor as we approached and laid out the cable but carelessly neglected to make everything fast again. At a specially violent lurch the whole lot went overboard, only coming to rest when thirty fathoms of cable were hanging straight down below us. We had to heave to before, shamefacedly and with some effort, I was able to haul it aboard again.

The boat harbour, like the one at Tongatapu, had been blasted out of the fringing reef but this one was much smaller. We negotiated the entrance with more speed than control, swerving between three anchored cutters and letting go in about a fathom on to seagrass and white coral sand. The shallow draft trading cutters were being loaded with sacks of copra that were being ferried out to them across the choppy lagoon in outrigger canoes, one of which swamped amid delighted hilarity.

"Such a fine boat your yacht. All the women put on their lipstick and best dresses to see the captain," said a massively built lady whom we met ashore. Indeed her niece, another and very charming Salote, proceeded to adopt us forthwith—though when I suggested that the welcome was really meant for the skipper, Fiona put me firmly in my place!

The imposing aunt was about to leave for Tongatapu on one of the cutters. Not surprisingly she eyed the frail outriggers somewhat askance and asked me to row her out in our Avon rubber boat. I complied gladly until I saw to my dismay that she was not only bringing an enormous tin cabin trunk wrapped in matting and a pile of baskets and bundles but was accompanied by another lady quite as big as herself with her own baggage. We were beginning to ship water when, breathless and exhausted, I pulled up alongside the little 35 foot sailing boat. With much laughter, willing helpers hauled both passengers and luggage aboard and somehow squeezed them on to a deck that was already occupied by six passengers and all their bundles and trunks, a dozen sacks of copra and a family of pigs.

'Hello to you new visitor', began a letter that was handed to us that evening. 'Welcome you and your family to this remote island. I am a teacher. I and my students invite you and your family to come up to visit our school home tomorrow'. But next day Susie was in her bunk with tonsillitis and, for the sake of the island children more than her own, we dared not let her land. This was doubly unfortunate because a small niece of Salote's called Lah Vania had become her special friend, exchanging names and presenting Susie with a tortoiseshell necklace inlaid in silver with her name and date of her christening. We were both loth to accept such a valuable gift but to refuse would have given offence. We were very pleased however at how readily Susie entered into this fundamental Polynesian custom of gift exchange, and not only willingly gave her own best necklace in return but insisted on adding some other of her treasured possessions. I remarked on how pretty a name was Lah Vania, "But it is an English name!" exclaimed Salote in surprise, "You must know it, L-a-v-i-n-i-a."

But now the little island girl was sitting alone on the beach gazing disconsolately at the catamaran in the forlorn hope of seeing her friend. To try to cheer her up we persuaded her to show us some of the island and afterwards accompany us to the school. This was a palm thatch building with rows of desks, at which sat neatly dressed bare-footed boys and girls. The desks were set in the shining coral sand that formed the floor. I presented the teacher with my copy of *Vikings of the Pacific* by that great Maori scholar Sir Peter Buck (Te Rangi Heroa).

In the afternoon the adults went swimming with mask and snorkel along the edge of the fringing reef. There were fields of orange staghorn coral, I remember, among which flitted brilliant electric blue fish. Where the reef came to an end in a cliff face that plunged down nine fathoms into deep purple shadows, the dim shapes of larger fish could be discerned nosing among the coral. Fiona, who swims quite fearlessly among the reefs, too confidently perhaps, swam with me out to the reef pass, while Priscilla more cautiously stayed near the catamaran. Oddly it was the latter who found cause to be alarmed. Right beneath one of our hulls she had come upon a black and white sea snake. "It wriggled!" she said, sounding indignant, for some obscurely feminine reason.

We reluctantly left Nomuka the following morning, 13th June, for although Susie was a little better she was still probably infectious and we dared not risk spreading her infection ashore, for the effects of even the mildest European diseases may be catastrophic on remote islands. As we were being presented with gifts of yam, sugar cane, paw paw, tangerines, drinking nuts, avocado and water melon (bully beef and cigarettes were very acceptable in return), I remembered that this very lagoon had once been the scene of a famous dispute about coconuts. Like our predecessor 177 years before, we found ourselves passing the island of Tofus that afternoon but there the resemblance between the voyages ended. We carried on towards Fiji secure in our own vessel, while Captain Bligh and his companions had been marooned off Tofus in the open boat in which they sailed 3,600 miles to Timor.

We laid course to pass just north of the site of what was once Falcon Island, now marked only by a shoal of white sand six feet under the surface. There is no sign of volcanic activity now nor has there been since 1959, the last time the island sank. But there is little doubt that it will appear again as it has been up and down on at least five occasions since it was first seen as a reef in 1865. At times it has been several miles long and attained an altitude of as much as 300 feet.

Nomuka was the last island we would see in Polynesia proper. We were now bound for the Melanesian groups of the Fijis, New Hebrides and New Guinea. The distinction between Polynesia and Melanesia is more apparent than real. The darker skinned Melanesians have inhabited New Guinea for some 50,000 years and other groups for not much less, and over this long period their languages have evolved and become so diversified that even neighbouring villages may speak mutually incomprehensible tongues. Many linguistic roots however are the same as Polynesian. The pre-history of the whole area is vastly complicated and ill understood as yet. For instance, all or some of the Polynesian ancestors must have migrated through it during the first millenium B.C. but to complicate the search for traces of their passage, waves of Polynesians have moved *back* into Melanesia during the past 700 years. The Melanesian islands are bigger than anything further east and must have been attractive to land hungry Tongans and Samoans. One can imagine what desperate wars were fought against the fierce Melanesian warriors to secure these footholds. So today many chiefly Fijian lines are Tongan, a dozen or more of the smaller Solomon Islands are inhabited by Polynesians, while many of the Motu people of eastern Papua, New Guinea, might be taken for Tahitians or Tongans.

Chapter 2

CAPTAIN BLIGH'S ISLANDS

THE distance from Nomuka to Suva, capital of the Fiji Islands, is a little over 400 miles on a course slightly north of west. Our only navigational problem was to time our approach to the eastern or Lau chain of Fiji islands so that we passed them in daylight, for though high they were unlighted. We streamed the patent log, something we only do when an accurate record of distance covered through the water is required, since the spinning rotator astern has a far greater attraction for predatory fish than any hook or lure I ever possessed. 'Speed through the water' is the key phrase here because the log takes no account of tide or current set. Therefore, although according to the log we had covered 116 miles in the 23 hours since Nomuka and would still have ample sea room at daybreak, we might nevertheless be in the process of being swept more briskly towards the Laus than this indicated, so that evening as a precaution we took star sights.

We used on that occasion the most brilliant of all stars, the Dog star, Sirius, and Rigel Kent, one of the Pointers of the Southern Cross. Star sights can only be taken at dusk or dawn when both the stars and the sea horizon are visible. This limits their value as the sky is often overcast at the vital time but on the other hand, as several stars can be used almost simultaneously the result can be a very accurate fix. I must qualify this statement by adding that it applies to ships and marine sextants only. Aircraft can be held level and steady while even the largest ship can not, so aircraft bubble sextants incorporate their own artificial horizon which enables them to be used throughout the night.

Daylight revealed the first of the Laus, Ongea, a few miles away on the port bow. All day as island after island rose out of the sea we were tantalised by distant views but Suva is the only official port of entry and I did not want to embarrass my cousin Justin Lewis, who is Attorney General there, by having his disreputable relative make an illegal entry into the colony. So we resisted the temptation to tarry and sailed on. That night once again the early morning hours were wakeful and watchful ones because we had to leave another island, Totoya, to port before we could alter course and head direct for Suva. Moonrise was at 2 a.m. and we should be off Totoya by 4.30. Should it not have appeared by 3.30 we would have hove-to to await daylight but soon after three it took shape as a silhouette in the light of the tropical moon that, like the sun in the same latitudes, stands so much more nearly overhead than in Europe that it glows with a billiance unknown in more temperate climes.

We sailed another day and night in increasingly light airs and then the sun's rim broke over the horizon and the darkness rolled back like a drawn curtain to reveal that the whole of the southern horizon was broken by the hills of Kandevu while the even bigger island of Viti Levu on which Suva stands was visible some 24 miles ahead. The name of the whole group incidentally really should have been Viti rather than Fiji. Captain Cook, who only sighted a few of the outer islands, was told of their existence by the Tongans in whose language 'F' replaces the Fijian 'V', so the name Fiti or Fiji came to be incorrectly applied. Captain Bligh was the first European to see the larger islands when he traversed the archipelago so perilously in his open boat.

But Bligh, at least, had had his oarsmen and the war canoes that chased him, lusty paddlers. When, as the sun rose and the trade wind died away altogether, we were left becalmed on a glassy sea, we wished we had either of them. We rarely use our little motor in the open sea but as the hours passed and the wind still failed to materialise, we eventually set it going and motored across sinuous lines of yellow plankton that smelled slightly fishy and were scattered through the surface layers of the sea like pollen.

We do not often feel the heat of the tropics at sea because of the cooling effect of the wind. I mentioned earlier how we only became conscious of the temperature at Tongatapu after we had anchored. I didn't refer to it again, partly because we soon became acclimatised to the heat and also because all of Tongatapu and Nomuka are air conditioned by the Trades. But Fiji in any case is hotter than Tonga and now in the calm the temperature rose to 88°F. We rigged a white canvas awning over the Perspex dome to try to keep the centre cabin cool as we crept almost imperceptibly over the surface of what had become a burnished lake encircled by island peaks that shimmered in the heat haze.

It was nine that evening and the lights of Suva were clearly visible before the faintest of breezes allowed us to stop the noisy motor. Besides bringing relief after the stifling afternoon, it carried an almost overpowering scent of flowers. The children, who had been restless and fretful, soon went soundly to sleep—comfortably naked and without covering. When we had closed the land, we turned to port and skirted the coast of Viti, confused a little by the lights of the suburbs of Suva, but guided all the while by the muted thunder of the reef to starboard. By midnight although it was a little cooler, Priscilla was still wearing her bikini and Fiona and I the colourful sarongs that are variously known, according to locality, as *pareu* in Tahiti, *Vala* in Tonga, *Sulu* in Fiji and *lap lap* in New Guinea.

The reef pass into Suva harbour is wide and well lighted and one of the most straightforward in the Pacific. All the more reason therefore for being wary of over confidence and exercising all our usual precautions in preparing to enter. As the wind was very light and variable we started the motor again in order to have a 'second string' and catted the anchor ready to let go. Then we extracted the little girls from their cabin and potted them to obviate distractions during any nautical crisis that might ensue. In the event we entered on 20th June without incident, altered course to starboard and slid across the still water towards the lights of Suva waterfront close hauled to the flower scented land breeze, to bring up at what the chart indicated was the quarantine anchorage.

My cousin came out in the port doctor's launch next morning and patiently saw us through the formalities of customs, immigration and police.

Suva is a cosmopolitan and colourful city reflecting the enormous growth of the Indian population, which, descended from sugar estate coolies, has now come to comprise more than half the population—outnumbering even the native Fijians. Even among the graceful sari-draped women, a picturesque touch is added by the brawny and indubitably masculine Fijian policemen who are skirted in spotless white *sulus*. This uniform is so prized by local residents, that a recent plea by the police to be allowed to wear trousers, on the very reasonable grounds that hampered by their skirts they could not catch criminals, caused an indignant public outcry. A pleasant feature of Fijian life is ceremonial *kava* drinking. In the simplified form practised in offices, this consists of the visitor being proffered the *kava* bowl which he takes in both hands. While he drinks his host claps his hands and, on handing the bowl back, the procedure is reversed. *Kava* is a non-alcoholic mild stupeficient that, for some reason, was abhorred by the early missionaries. They succeeded in rooting out the habit of *kava* drinking in eastern Polynesia by introducing in place of that relatively harmless drink, a particularly virulent brew of palm beer. The drunkenness that resulted, in part at least from this cause, has been a major social problem in Tahiti and the central islands ever since.

Our stay in Suva was rendered particularly pleasant by Justin and his wife Kathleen. We were amused by the arrangement by which the bungalows of government officials were ranged in order of rank up a hill, near the summit of which Justin had attained an eminence only surpassed by the Governor. Among the people we met was *Ratu* or High Chief, Edward Cakobau. I must break off to explain that whoever devised the Fijian alphabet had not only a sense of humour but clearly wished to outdo English with its 'Cholmondely'—pronounced 'Chumley'—for Cakobau is pronounced 'Thakambau'. Similarly, the next island we were to visit is spelt Bqua but called 'Mbenga', which incidentally is how I will be writing it in this book. To return however to Ratu Cakobau; he is a handsome man, nearly seven feet tall, a distinguished soldier and an Oxford graduate with impeccable manners. At the time of our visit he was being tipped as the future Fijian representative in Sydney, where his sense of humour had endeared him to Australians in the past.

They still tell the story of how Ratu Edward was once seated

Preparing for departure

Yule Island,
New Guinea

at the Captain's table of a P. & O. ship en route to England and was being annoyed by a lady of prominent social position, who repeatedly insisted that Fiji must be uncivilised for that 'was where the cannibals came from'. At length, unable to stand it any longer, he turned to the steward who had just handed him the menu and ordered, "Take this away! Bring me the passenger list!"

The commander of the Fiji Military Forces invited us to the ceremony of Sounding the Retreat. The scene on the hill top parade ground as the flag was hauled down was full of colour in spite of the gathering dusk. The band, marching with the precision of guardsmen, stood out against the brilliant green of the tropical foliage in their scarlet tunics, *sulus* and bare feet. We were rather concerned lest the children should be alarmed at the detonation of the sunset gun. Not a bit of it! They enjoyed this most of all and kept pestering us with, "More bangs please, Mummy, Daddy—just one more!" while the band, in a rather back-handed compliment to ourselves, was playing 'For those in Peril on the Sea'.

Our host, who chose this tune, was well known for his sense of humour but it had been a different story when he had arrived six months earlier together with the new Air Force Commander and their wives. All had been strangers in Suva and nobody knew them. Taking advantage of this, Brigadier Morrison was able, by one stroke of masterly simplicity, to produce a scandal that rocked the colony for weeks. He merely introduced his own wife as that of the wing commander, and vice versa.

The Governor, whom we met at a reception, was impressive for his youthfulness and energy. It is typical of the attitude of senior British colonial officials today—though not in the relatively recent past when they administered a somewhat larger empire—that both the Governor and Justin insist on sending their children to mixed race schools. Some of the Europeans on the island still try to prop up a crumbling colour bar and will probably be genuinely puzzled and aggrieved should the Fijians and Indians later fail to set up a society with full equality for Europeans.

Not that Fijians could be easily repressed by colour discrimination or anything else. Their attitude is typically that of a cheerful giant of a man, very dark skinned, who said to us, "I have a little white man in me." We felt and probably looked, rather surprised but had no desire to offend such a colossus by contradicting him. Then with a shout of laughter and a flash of white teeth he explained, "My grandfather ate a trader!"

We were hospitably received at the yacht club which was recuperating after the departure of the hard sailing Kiwi yachtsmen from the Auckland to Suva race. Innumerable toads appeared on the club lawn at nightfall and these were a particular attraction for the children, who expended much of their excessive energy on fruitless pursuit of these animals.

There was one big gap, however, in the children's experience of the tropics. Although we have visited so many islands in the last two years, since neither Susie nor Vicky could yet swim, the underwater coral fairyland of the reefs had been hidden from them. So we became tourists and joined a party in a glass bottomed boat in which we spent a particularly enjoyable morning. After cruising to and fro over the marine rock garden of the inner reef, we anchored and some Fijians and the adults of our party brought up specimens of coral and sea creatures for inspection—a tiny octopus that clung to their fingers being the children's favourite. Fortunately, they are free from the general and irrational fear and dislike of certain animals—wolves or reptiles for instance—that must have originated far back in legend and pre-history.

Finding it necessary one day at the club to move our mooring, I started the outboard motor but omitted to remove the lashing with which I had personally secured the steering wheel the day before. The result which, fortunately, did not cause too much damage, was a head-on collision with the harbour wall before I was able to free the wheel. Now there is a universal law of nature that has never been studied by scientists as it deserves, that may be called 'the law of maximum cussedness'. It is this law for instance that determines which side up a slice of buttered bread will fall—butter side down needless to say. The law is specially applicable to small cruising yachts and never more so than in situations like this one. Undertake a manoeuvre with impeccable seamanship and it is always the dead of night and there is no one in sight for miles; do something such as I did and past commodores down to the third generation will be lined up watching. After a pregnant pause, the senior past commodore cleared his throat. "Those catamarans aren't very manoeuvrable," he remarked, with some degree of understatement, since I had approached the wall in a dead straight line. I shamefacedly mumbled agreement, cravenly blaming the ship for my own absurd error.

At the yacht club pontoon we found ourselves moored alongside our friends John and Ebo Littler in their 45 foot Prout designed catamaran *Doubloon*. While we had been visiting Tonga, they had sailed to Fiji direct from New Zealand, making the passage in a time that compared very well with the winner of the Auckland/Suva race. The unofficial Prime Minister, Ratu Mara, had just offered them what must have been the perfect job for any yachtsman. They were to transport government employees to the remoter parts of the archipelago and Captain Littler was also to survey certain reef passes. Seeing that both he and Ebo asked nothing better than to cruise among the outer islands, here they were being given official backing to do so and a generous salary to boot! I was consumed with envy until a year later we ourselves gained the promise of an equally exciting assignment.

Lest other yachtsmen head impetuously towards the Fijis, intent on emulating the Littlers, it should be realised that such opportunities as theirs are rare. Both in Fiji and in Australian administered territories there are punitive import duties on the yachts of even temporary residents. This hits would-be charterers hard. The Littlers escaped this import duty because their appointment was a government one. Moreover, it was only offered them because of the special features of their yacht—a catamaran—light draft, roominess and speed, coupled with seaworthiness.

We met an interesting friend of John and Ebo who was visiting them on *Doubloon*. She was a very aristocratic elderly Tongan lady of royal descent who had lived for many years in what had at first been enforced exile in Fiji because of an unfortunate marriage. It had not been the fact that her husband was a European that was disgraceful but that he was a commoner. He had been, in fact, a Swedish admiral!

Our visit to Fiji had its serious side, once again connected with the navigational pre-history of the island peoples. The Australian,

Harold Gatty, who was probably the foremost air or sea navigator of the first half of the 20th century, died a few years ago at his home in Fiji, where his magnificent reference library is now housed in the government archives. His best known work is not one of his bigger books but the famous *Raft Book*, a handbook on survival for airmen forced down at sea during the War. In it he drew extensively on Polynesian navigational methods. Naturally it would have been inappropriate in a publication of this nature to include references to original sources, so I had long been anxious to obtain access to Gatty's library to delve into the background of many of his statements. This, thanks to the courtesy of the Curator, was now possible and I spent several days among the archives. At once the scope of Gatty's reading and knowledge became apparent and its volume rather daunting.

Among much else that was informative and valuable, perhaps the most tantalising find was a translation he had made of a German paper. The original was missing, as were the vital first pages of the translation, which included the title and the author's name. I passed one whole day searching fruitlessly for the elusive pages but they were irretrievably lost. What could be done?

The paper explained in detail some zenith star techniques that were new to me but it was impossible to say from the part remaining what sources the author was quoting. Such Polynesian words as appeared in the text were Western Polynesian, Tongan or Samoan. The writer was clearly an experienced marine navigator addressing technically qualified readers, and the date did not seem recent. Could the article have been written, I wondered, by a German Naval officer who had served in what had been German Samoa before 1914?

On the chance of this surmise being correct I wrote for help to the Institute of Navigation in London, who in turn got in touch with their German counterpart. The latter were eventually able to send me what appears to be (for I have not yet been able to have it translated), a shorter or later version of the missing article. It is from a Naval Hydrographic review published in 1927.

Our meeting with Kaloni in Tonga had been our first contact since the previous year's navigational experiment with the trail of the ancient Polynesian seamen. This was the second, albeit an academic one. Later in our voyage, in New Guinea, we would be meeting direct inheritors of what was still a living tradition.

Time was pressing; odd though this must sound, it nearly always is on long yacht voyages, for if you miss this monsoon or run foul of that hurricane season, you may be delayed six months or more. In our case, there was a date by which we should be across the Indian Ocean if we were to be sure of avoiding the cyclone season, and we dared not trifle with this deadline. This was why we were forced to say goodbye to Suva on 30th June after less than a fortnight's stay.

We left the harbour by the wide reef passage, the safest we had encountered, under ideal conditions of calm sea and light favourable wind—and came nearer than ever before to ultimate disaster. 'Ultimate' is probably too strong a word because we could very likely have saved ourselves, since the surf that day was not heavy —but our lovely ship, our home, would have gone.

Rehu Moana was in mid channel and had almost cleared the entrance, when the breeze disappeared and we were suddenly gripped by a strong, unexpected current which rapidly swept us towards the northern horn of the reef. I flooded the motor in my hurry and agitation when I tried to start it, so that it would not fire. The depth was too great for anchoring and remained so right up to the reef which rose sheer from deep water. I caught up the spanner that was always stowed on the steering seat together with a spare spark plug whenever the engine was likely to be used; unscrewed the plug, hands trembling with haste, and substituted the fresh one. The others had only been able to watch helplessly and now I could feel the cockpit rise under me in the scend of the first line of surf as I desperately wound on the starting cord and tugged. The Seagull fired; we surged out with the undertow, away from the coral shoulder off which white water streamed as the breaker receded. Slowly the bow swung away from the danger, hesitated, then climbed the next roller. A minute more and the swells had become lazy, innocent undulations and the reef astern no more than a frothing white line; the crash of the bursting waves but an angry grumbling.

No sooner were we clear than the south-east trade wind came in again, though it remained gentle and fitful all that afternoon.

I looked down at Susie and Vicky squatting on the sunlit cabin sole, unaware that anything untoward had occurred and intent only on their dolls and I tried, though unsuccessfully, to forget the nightmare out of which we had escaped. Often thereafter I would wake at night in a sweat of blank horror, as my imagination, uncontrolled by the conscious discipline of the daytime mind, took charge and pictured what might have happened to the little girls. As the weeks passed these episodes became less frequent until I thought my self-confidence wholly restored. But months later in the Indian Ocean when we sailed out from the shelter of the last coral reef we should encounter in the voyage, I experienced a sensation of an oppression being lifted from my mind that brought home to me how persistent the anxiety had been.

The day was sultry and our objective Mbenga, floated insubstantial in the heat haze. Soon everyone else on board was sleeping, while I attended to the course and the helm and watched the seabirds circling and diving and the hills ahead gradually assuming substance as clumps of palms separated themselves from their flanks. We took four hours to cover the twenty miles to Cutter Passage through Mbenga reef, and here again the wind misbehaved; it switched round without warning and blew off the land, heading us while we were negotiating the passage. But we *had* wind this time so our motive power was intact. One quick tack, then an alteration to starboard, where we could see from aloft there was ample water, and we were stealing over the lagoon into the deep purple shadows of the high land beyond. We rounded a rocky headland, then hung motionless in its wind shadow at the entrance to Maluma Bay, a flooded valley that cut its way deep into the hills.

Three youths in a canoe paddled over to us. They had been out fishing, they told us in excellent English, but were staying temporarily at this end of the island to clear scrub from their father's plantation. Yes, they were at high school but this was holiday time. Would we not anchor off the beach?—see, by their hut over there under the trees? We willingly accepted their offer and taking them in tow, motored towards the shore, where we anchored at the spot they indicated, close in, but in deep water— eleven fathoms.

Over coffee, the eldest who was called Timoe Tanaga, told us that he and another of his brothers were fire walkers. We had known that Mbenga was the home in the Fijis of this strange cult in which, by still unexplained means, devotees walk uninjured across pits of red hot stones, but we were more than a little astonished. Somehow these very normal and quiet spoken boys, so strongly reminiscent of sixth formers from a good English grammar school, seemed most improbable practitioners for such an exotic art. The secrets of the Mbenga fire walkers are family ones, so for reasons of delicacy we forbore to embarrass our guests with questions of 'why' and 'how'. Unfortunately, there was no ceremony scheduled to take place in the near future.

Vicky became feverish and ill that night and began coughing spasmodically. We could hardly have slept soundly in any case, for from the nearby hillside that towered over us in a succession of rocky bluffs interspersed with gullies choked with a flower-flecked tangle of rain forest, with here and there cultivated clearings where grew sugar cane, yams and coconuts, came a weird chorus of chirrups, shrieks and harsh cries. These were so reminiscent of jungle noises in some improbable film that it was hard to realise that all this cacophany of sound was made by night birds and insects, and that a whole menagerie was not loose behind the draped curtains of lianas. From across the still bay a drum was beating intermittently, while much nearer at hand, where the flare from their cooking fire silhouetted the brothers, came the soft strumming of a guitar. All night long our anchorage remained in deepest shadow but across the lagoon the light of the three-quarter moon, despite a layer of overcast, was sufficient to outline the hills of Viti twenty miles away.

We remained at anchor next day, spending the time quietly on the beach, where the children pattered to and fro looking for shells and flowers and building mysterious objects with them on the sand, all with the greatest concentration. We let them both bathe—the cool sea water seeming to soothe and comfort Vicky who is stoical by nature and was as uncomplaining as usual. Whenever she felt tired she would curl up under the trees and rest a while. Some children arrived over the hill path from the village.

"What is your name?" we asked one ten year old girl.

"Saint Mary," she replied.

"Mary?"

"No, *Saint* Mary," she corrected us firmly.

The adults of our crew swam to the middle of the mile-wide bay with Saint Mary and the boys, who insisted that there were no sharks and if they did come that way they were harmless anyway; I was not altogether convinced or reassured. Later Fiona and I put on masks, snorkels and flippers and went sculling over the fringing reef, gazing down at the vivid sea world and diving to peer into mysterious caverns from which orange feelers waved languorously and shoals of startled little fish erupted.

Susie was given a swimming lesson. Now, as so often before, she could *almost* swim. But each time the intervals between successive opportunities to practise were too long. It is rare for a good anchorage to coincide with a sheltered sandy cove where a child can begin to swim safely. In this respect, for all their nautical surroundings, Susie and Vicky probably had less concentrated opportunity to learn to swim than many a child on a summer seaside holiday.

Vicky spent a much better night, not feverish any more but still coughing; but now Susie, though well enough, had begun to cough too. Was it fair to our new friends to stay longer, we wondered? If we remained another day, every child from the village would probably come to play with our little girls. We had best be gone. We hoped to call at one other island in the Fijis but there we had no friends and could anchor well away from inhabited places.

One of the hardest things on our trip has always been to have to say goodbye to kind and simple people who are unlikely to be able to travel far afield. With European friends matters are rather different since they *may* visit England or New Zealand or wherever we are living later, but islanders unfortunately have as yet so little opportunity to be mobile that we know we may never see such friends again. We had been sorry enough to leave Nomuka and saying goodbye to Timoe, his brothers and Saint Mary was just as bad—and at the time we had no idea, as we have now, that we would ever be revisiting Fiji. The boys accompanied us to the entrance of the bay, then put down their paddles and as their craft lost way, they stood up. Until *Rehu Moana* had passed out of sight beyond the point they remained standing, silent in the dignified stillness of a Fijian farewell.

Four hours later, we had sailed round to the western side of Mbenga, crossed the broad lagoon and gained the open sea by Frigate Pass on the opposite side of the island to Cutter Passage through which we had entered. At one side of the gap in the reef was what we at first took to be a rock but as we passed by we saw that it was the rusty hulk of a steamer no more than ten yards from deep water. A near miss, we reflected, but the aim had not been quite good enough. The trade wind was blowing more strongly now, so as we came out from under the land, the catamaran speeded up—this rapid acceleration is one of the thrills of multi-hull sailing—and our hulls began slicing twin furrows of foam that climbed and dipped over the shoulders of the long swell. Nothing but open sea was visible ahead though Vatu Lele was only seventeen miles away, so the tops of its palms must soon break the horizon at the rate of over seven knots we were averaging.

Given good visibility, the distance an island can be seen depends on its height. The formula is simple and we often made use of it. Take the square root of the height of the land in feet, add the square root of the observer's height, and the sum is the distance in miles that it can be seen above the horizon. To be very exact, the visibility distance is a little more than this.

In this instance, Vatu Lele's raised coral plateau rose to 50 feet and was thickly planted in palms. Coconut palms average 70 feet. Total height 120. Square root of 120 is approximately 11. Our look-out was 10 feet above sea level and the square root of 10 is roughly 3; 11 plus 3 is 14, so the palms on the plateau should be seen 14 or 15 miles away.

I know of one particularly unfortunate case where this system broke down, and though I have already quoted it in *Daughters of the Wind*, it seems worth repeating here. A yacht that had come in sight of the island it was heading for at dusk, was prudently hove to await daylight. The distance off was estimated by the height of the palms at a safe five miles. She was wrecked on the reef in the night, daylight revealing to the castaways that the palms they had assumed to be 70 feet high had been newly planted and were only 10.

We raised Vatu Lele from the rigging at 1.30 that afternoon and sailing on a reach with the force 6 trade wind almost abeam, we brought the island close aboard in little more than an hour. The chart of this part of the archipelago is small scale, so we could make out only the general position of Weather Passage, the opening for which we were making. Nevertheless, the Pacific Islands Pilot described it as being bordered by a conspicuous rocky islet on which grew 'six palms'.

Nothing of the sort could we see, and meanwhile the reef came nearer at an alarming rate. No doubt the most prudent course would have been to come about and stand clear, but many of the Fijian reefs are partly submerged and this was no exception. High water was in an hour; the catamaran draws only three feet. So when I spotted from aloft a place through which the rollers appeared to be surging unbroken into the lagoon, we put up the helm and went flying across the reef down a pale green corridor flanked by brown and orange coral heads. Abruptly these fell away and there was nothing but dark blue beneath us and the only sound save for the wind was the rippling of wavelets. Mindful of the children's coughs, which we now suspected were mild whooping cough modified by the protective inoculations, we turned away from the village and headed north along the shore, passing en route the islet that had been so elusive a landmark. No wonder we had failed to identify it, for it now sprouted not six palms but over a hundred! We let go the anchor at the top of the tide in ten feet of water, which was ample, as all small oceanic islands have a rise and fall that rarely exceeds five feet.

No sooner were we secured than a slight wind shift sent clouds of acrid smoke billowing over us. The reason for the fires ashore soon became apparent when some Fijians boarded us to demand our clearance from the Department of Agriculture in Suva. This was a document certifying that there was no soil adhering to any root vegetables aboard that might harbour the eggs of the coconut beetle. This enormous and destructive insect had only recently been discovered by government inspectors to have spread to the western Fijis. (The islanders had long been aware of the infestation but believing for some odd reason that it was spread by the visits of the officials of the Coconut Pests and Diseases Board themselves, they kept quiet.) It was in an attempt to destroy the pest that the scrub between the rows of coconut palms was being cleared and burnt.

Once our documents had been examined, we were free to land, but were disappointed to find that the first groups of Vatu Lele people we encountered were highly commercial, offering bananas at prices well above Suva and asking several pounds to show us the nearby pool of the sacred shrimps that the inhabitants are reputed to be able to call to the surface at will. Since these red shrimps are *tapu* they must never be eaten lest dire consequences ensue. As evidence of this, it is pointed out that the crew of one yacht ate some and in consequence were wrecked later. Feeling that the fee for a guide was extortionate or perhaps it was the unfriendly manner in which it was demanded, we decided to leave these influential creatures unvisited and confine our activities to rambling along the seashore. This was interesting enough.

Formidable webs had been strung among the branches of the shrubs at the edge of the sand and the children were enthralled when we showed them the giant hairy spiders, with only their eyes living and watchful, that crouched in wait at the centres. Second only to the spiders in interest were huge gaudy butterflies, the most striking we had seen.

In view of the whooping cough diagnosis, we decided to sail the following morning but only after we had bought some *tapa* cloth. Priscilla volunteered to stay with the children while Fiona and I walked along the shore to the village two miles away. The people we met seemed much more friendly and helpful than those we had encountered the previous afternoon. The chief's wife invited us into her spacious hut where she initiated Fiona into the art of making *tapa* or bark cloth. This ancient skill, that antedates weaving in Asia and perhaps other parts of the world, is still practised in some corners of the Pacific, notably Tonga and some of the Fijis, of which Vatu Lele is one. The technique is laborious. Stems of paper mulberry about as thick as a man's index finger are first stripped of their outer bark; then the tough inner layer is turned back and peeled off in a tube, which is slit and opened out, and five or six such strips laid side by side on a polished hardwood log. This is the raw material of *tapa* and virtually the finished article (save for knotting the ends of the strips to a waist band) of grass skirts. The next step in bark cloth making is to moisten the strips of inner bark and then beat them out with sharp echoing taps of a mallet until they coalesce into a single sheet perhaps two or three feet square. Squares may be joined together by exactly the same process. The cloth is then dried in the sun and painted in traditional patterns of reddish browns and blacks with indigenous vegetable dyes. *Tapa* cloth is remarkably durable as well as being decorative.

The lesson proceeded very well, the chief's wife being surprised and pleased at her pupil's proficiency and Fiona no less proud, for this is exactly the type of artistic handiwork for which she has a special flair. We trudged back towards the boat laden with stiff rolls of *tapa* that we had bought from some of the village women, more contented with the island and sorry now that we could not stay longer. However, we had spent the last of our Fiji money on the *tapa*. Many currencies are almost impossible to exchange once one has left the country, so we would try, not always successfully, to estimate the amount we should need in order to have as little as possible left over. Back at the catamaran, the periodic coughing of the girls, who by now felt perfectly well in themselves, was enough to convince us of the impropriety of lingering, so immediately after lunch we stood out to sea, taking an only slightly more conventional route across the reef by the Boat Passage which boasted five feet of water, and laid course for the New Hebrides 550 miles to the westward. By the time we reached there the children would no longer be a danger to others.

Running down wind before steepish seas as we were now doing, *Rehu Moana* had a tendency to veer off course so that a hand at the helm was often necessary. This was because the long keels or skegs that we had fitted beneath the after part of the hulls in Auckland were not quite deep enough to counteract all 'weather helm' or the yacht's tendency to turn into the wind, on this point of sailing. We found she steered best if we reduced the area of sail behind the mast by taking down the mainsail and running our westing under headsails alone. This practice cut down our runs to 100-120 miles a day or so but the slowing down was a small price to pay for freedom from hand steering that allowed one to spend the days sunbathing, eating, reading, playing with the children, writing articles and, at night, being able to sleep and only having to wake up enough to glance at the compass occasionally through half-opened eyes.

Medical Interlude

Our hurried departure from the Fijis to avoid spreading whooping cough might be expected to mark the end of sickness aboard. In fact it did not, for Priscilla came down with what appeared to be gastro enteritis and I developed milder but similar symptoms. Fiona seemed quite well at the moment, though in retrospect it seems fairly certain that the adults had all been infected with the virus of infective hepatitis which was epidemic in Fiji. Only in Fiona's case did the illness develop later and run its full clinical course, marked by prolonged jaundice. For the time being, however, Fiona's illness still lay ahead; we will come to it soon enough. Perhaps this is an opportune moment to pause in the narrative and say something about our medical supplies and our approach to the prevention and treatment of family illness at sea.

The subject of treating illnesses and accidents at sea or in remote places where doctors are not available is obviously a tremendous one that would easily occupy a book in itself. In touching on so vast a field any assertions one makes are apt to sound dogmatic. If these do, I apologise, they are not meant to be so. On the contrary, they are intended as suggestions as to logical and practical ways to approach the subject—nothing more.

Many medical kits that I have seen recommended for sea voyages, mountaineers or explorers suffer from one defect—they would be excellent first aid lists for a suburban home, where only such things as constipation and headaches need be treated since the nearest hospital would cope with real illness. But there are no hospitals at sea or in many lonely places on the earth. Now it seems to me that nature is perfectly well able to look after minor disorders, illnesses and injuries that regulate themselves or are self-limiting or will heal spontaneously anyway. What one must cater for on long yacht voyages are the serious conditions which, in civilised communities, are the subject of skilled medical attention, not first aid at all.

Treatment at sea may have to cover *more than* first aid since it may have to be *continued for weeks*. By this of course I do not mean that a knowledge of conventional first aid would be other than extremely useful; but the question arises, is prolonged treatment of major conditions in the tiny world of a yacht, isolated from the rest of mankind by a thousand miles of ocean, entirely beyond the powers of a layman? I do not think so.

The risk of misuse of a modern antibiotic, for instance, when one of the crew is plainly very ill or badly burnt, or has a compound fracture, is negligible compared to that of the untreated complaint. Moreover, such drugs can be used with comparative safety in a wide range of conditions.

Clearly, any list of medical supplies should be compiled to take account of personal sensitivities and proneness to particular illnesses and will vary according to climate and special health risks of areas to be visited. The yachtsman's own doctor would be the best person to give advice and, in any case, a doctor would need to be consulted to prescribe some important drugs and indicate appropriate doses.

After these introductory remarks, let me describe our own practice.

The children have had the following inoculations:

Against diphtheria, whooping cough and tetanus combined: poliomyelitis (oral): vaccination against smallpox: B.C.G. for tuberculosis: typhoid, paratyphoid inoculation (T.A.B.): yellow fever. The adults did not have diptheria and whooping cough injections, their tetanus being combined with the T.A.B., and I belong to a generation that had ample natural contact with T.B., so B.C.G., important for young adults, could be omitted in my case.

All the party, adults and children alike, took vitamin C (ascorbic acid), in the same dose of one 50 mgm. tablet a day when fresh fruit became exhausted, as a preventative against scurvy. In addition, the children had a fluoride tablet at night to ensure healthy dental development, as some countries have not yet introduced fluoridation of water supplies. It would be logical to ban sweets, as refined carbohydrates are a major element in tooth decay—but who could be so inhuman as to deny the children something they like so much? Fiona, reading this through, says the girls can twist me round their little fingers—well, perhaps they can!

Another preventative—in malarious areas the adults have a whole and the children a half tablet of Daraprim (Pyrimethamine) once a week. I should have said that this is a suppressant, not a preventative. The distinction is important as it should be continued for about six weeks after leaving a malarious area or an attack of the illness may follow the cessation of the drug.

One precaution that we have never taken is to boil or otherwise treat the water we take into our tanks from whatever harbour supply is available. We have suffered no ill thereby and indeed were still drinking West African water for some time after arriving in Plymouth.

To go on now from prevention to treatment:

It may be remarked that malaria—while the subject is fresh in mind—can generally be cured by three days' treatment with chloroquine phosphate, the dose for a child between one and five years old being half a tablet a day and that for an adult two.

A cautionary word should be said here to remind the reader that the name of a medicament may vary in different countries, or indeed in one, so to avoid a list of synonyms I have used the British nomenclature, either the best known name or the official one from the Pharmacopoea. It must be remembered too that new and improved drugs are constantly being produced, so any particular one is advocated mainly as a *representative* of its class.

The Broad Spectrum Antibiotics of the *Tetracycline* class. I think these should take pride of place because of the variety of conditions in which they are effective—sometimes very effective indeed —and their relative freedom from side effects, and safety even in excessive dose. They are used to treat infections, including pneumonia, bronchitis, infected wounds, skin infections like coral cut sores and impetigo, and to forestall infection in severe burns, compound fractures and to prevent pneumonia developing after rib fractures in older people (a very real risk at sea). Then there are certain conditions which they can alleviate and *tide the patient over*, until more adequate treatment, often surgical, is available. One such complaint has been particularly dreaded by isolated people—appendicitis. By using one of these drugs it should be quite possible not only to keep the appendicitis patient alive but to maintain him in good enough health for him to sail his boat to port even if it be a month or more away. Of course he must then have hospital treatment. In the same category of alleviation rather than cure, come ear infections and dental abcess. Later in this book there is an excellent example of what happens when someone (in this case myself) neglects the rule that such an infection, which will have been rendered chronic, should be eliminated on reaching port.

In all the cases we have been discussing, a dose of one 250 mgm. tablet four times a day would be appropriate for an adult, and 50 mgm. for a young child. If in doubt, it would be better to err on the side of high dosage.

Sulphonamides for intestinal infections, such as *sulphadimidine* are invaluable in diarrhoea, especially when blood and mucus are present. The dose might be two tablets four times a day. This complaint is one of the few where, because of its inconvenience in a small boat, an additional remedy that gives only symptomatic relief is worthwhile—any kaolin mixture would suffice.

Agents for dealing with specific infections may be indicated according to the composition of the party. They might include *urolucosil*, a sulphonamide useful for cystitis, that uncomfortable complaint to which women are specially prone: *Chloramphenicol*, a dangerous drug, but possibly lifesaving for a child with typhoid fever: and to descend to the more commonplace, something like *Antepar* for round worms and threadworms in children. (I forgot this—the girls caught both infestations.)

For *relief of pain* there are remarkably few remedies intermediate between *soluble aspirin* and *morphia*. Since the former drug is very safe and fairly effective, and is useful also to reduce fever, I would be quite happy to make it my only analgaesic. Very young children excrete the drug poorly, so lest it accumulate it is best to give it for not more than four days at a time. The actual dose is less important than the length of the course of treatment. As an additional agent in severe pain *alcohol* has much to recommend it—provided always that the patient can be kept warm and not subjected to cold, damp and exposure.

Now for the thorny problem of *seasickness*. The cynical may say that all one can do is to be comforted by being in the same boat as Nelson (no pun intended) but there are remedies, though they may vary in effectiveness in different people. Antihistamines like *Avomine* and *Dramamine* are widely used. Much more effective in certain cases (including Fiona's) is *Hyoscine Hydrobromide*, one 0.3 mgm. tablet taken four hourly. This is the drug of choice in conditions of very violent motion such as might be experienced in an inflatable life raft in a gale. For this contingency alone it is worth carrying, because it is easy to forget that in situations where water is short, the dehydration produced by the vomiting of seasickness may well turn the scale against survival.

To turn from illnesses to *accidents*.

Major burns are best cleaned with fresh water when the pain has eased a little and then, whenever possible, exposed to the fresh air and allowed to dry, flies and dust being excluded meanwhile. Should circumstances (the position of the burns, climate, etc.) render this impossible, clean wet dressings that are kept moistened are the next best. Everything available to relieve pain should be given, copious fluids must be drunk and an antibiotic such as tetracycline will be needed to hold infection in check.

Minor burns will heal themselves whether they are treated or not.

Fractures need to be immobilised, pain relieved and, if infection is likely as in compound fractures, where there are extensive lacerations or internal organs might seem to be affected, it is wise to use a tetracycline type antibiotic to counter infection.

To immobilise leg fractures long splints can be improvised out of well padded floorboards. A broken arm should be strapped to the side, where it cannot be used automatically to maintain balance when the vessel gives a sudden lurch. A word of warning about strapping up the chest to ease the pain of fractured ribs; the chest movements are restricted and pneumonia may follow. So aspirin, alcohol and antibiotics are best—and no strapping.

Major wounds require cleaning with fresh water, clean dressings, pain relief and again an antibiotic.

So far we have not considered medicaments for *local application*, but for the major injuries we have been describing the following would be useful: a few rolls of *crepe bandage*, rolls of *Elastoplast* (and Elastoplast dressings, preferably waterproof, for minor injuries), an antiseptic solution such as 1% Cetrimide.

Children's skins remain healthier if they can be washed in fresh water. We found this possible except for part of the longest stretches. Three valuable applications were a *cream* containing 1 or 2% *Cetrimide* for septic conditions like sores, coral cuts or impetigo (in the two latter cases the giving of an antibiotic was the main part of the treatment); a soothing *sunburn* cream or lotion of one of the many varieties obtainable from any chemist; an antihistamine ointment or cream like *Benadryl* for insect bites and stings.

The subject of *insect repellents* naturally follows and includes three kinds of agent: *Knock down spray*, e.g. pyrethrum compounds in aerosol containers, or the 'burning incense' type of repellent that is mostly made in Hong Kong or Macao but is widely available throughout the tropics; *residual* insecticides like D.D.T. powder. (Our cockroaches and ants seemed to thrive on it but I know of nothing better); *personal repellents* to be applied to the skin, those containing *dimethylioluamide* being particularly effective.

One other substance completes our list, *cocaine eye drops* 5%. This strength will provide complete temporary anaesthesia for the eye to allow foreign bodies to be removed, or if this is not possible, will give periodic relief to the torment a patient with a bad eye injury must suffer while making for land. A doctor's prescription is required.

The suggestions given above are similar to those in an appendix to *Daughters of the Wind* but I have made some modifications in the light of further experience. I would again recommend two books to the reader. The first is *Child Health in the Tropics* by D. B. Jellife (Edward Arnold, London, 1962). The other is called *Exploration Medicine* (John Wright & Sons, Bristol, 1965). It is edited by Edholm and Bacharach and the chapters contributed by various authors. (I was one of these and since the last cheque for royalties was 14/6d. I have an obvious personal reason for recommending it!)

All this discussion of risks and remedies can easily affect one's sense of proportion; life at sea is healthy and, as far as the tropics are concerned, they are excellent places for children. Some general principles of the effects of heat on young children are, however, worth bearing in mind. When very young they are particularly susceptible to fluid shortage or loss. They are even more vulnerable in this respect when feverish and more so still when there is vomiting and diarrhoea as well. In such conditions no measure is as important as maintaining a good fluid intake with fruit drinks, cordials—anything. Additional salt is not generally necessary but if it is given, ordinary table salt is better absorbed than salt tablets. Under normal circumstances in the tropics, the amount of salt in the average European diet is quite sufficient. An odd point is that children often do not seem to realise that they are thirsty. Until the end of our voyage we were forced to remember this and when Susie or Vicky became tired and irritable, 'top them up' with a glass of orange drink was the remedy and usually worked wonders.

As regards special clothing, I am sure a hat would keep the sun out of one's eyes but in point of fact none of us possessed one. While at sea in the tropics the children seldom wore any clothes at all!

There are of course many hazards—I was thinking particularly of tropical ones—that we never catered for, since a yacht's medical kit can be based only on the likelihood of encountering them and the necessity for an effectiveness of possible remedies. Thus we did not carry a snake bite kit. Antevenom sera are the only specifics and they vary with the type of reptile; rest and reassurance are as important and the avoidance of time-honoured heroic methods of cauterization, burning or sucking the bite, which are always harmful in themselves, as well as inducing panic —and the cause of death after snake bite is believed to be generally fear. Some interesting figures from Malaysia, where particularly venomous species are common, suggest that only 1% of people bitten by venomous snakes die, and the statistical chances of meeting one's end by this cause are approximately equal to the danger of being killed by a falling coconut.

One of the sea's most venomous creatures is a jelly fish, called 'sea wasp', found off northern Australia during the three months' wet season. Its sting has been proved fatal, so it is far worse than the better known Portuguese Man of War. Avoidance of bathing is desirable in the months of risk.

Certain of the cone shells have venomous stings that they shoot out through their apices, so they are better picked up by their wide ends. Fiona, an enthusiastic underwater collector of reef shells, reminded me to mention the cones.

The New Hebrides

Let us return now from the rather macabre world of appendicitis and poisonous sea shells to the wholesome and healthy reality of the Pacific. Out of the lee of Vatu Lele the trade wind was blowing very hard, reaching gale force 8 in periodic squalls that were accompanied by flurries of rain. The wind was from the south east, our course towards the north west, so the seas were coming up from very nearly astern and it was clearly one of the occasions when the mainsail must come in if the catamaran were to self steer. The sky was overcast and the sea grey; rain was scattering on the Perspex; we might have been making a summer cruise in the English Channel but for the temperature— 78°F. This dictated a different technique, as far as clothing was concerned, when sail changing in the rain off Fiji compared to English waters. In the latter you put oilskins *on* before going on deck, in the tropics you take *off* your clothes, or at least most of them, to keep them from getting wet. Once the mainsail had been lowered, *Rehu Moana* virtually looked after herself, and even after halving her sail area, she covered 105 miles in the next 19 hours.

The going was decidedly bumpy, so much so that the adults had difficulty in keeping their feet. The children—perhaps because of their lower centres of gravity—seemed more attuned to the dip and sway and occasional jerk, as the sixteen foot seas (as judged from the lower rigging), passed under us. The cold supper —no one felt like cooking—consisting of cold baked beans, potato crisps, bananas, pawpaw and, for Vicky, her favourite black olives, was eagerly consumed by the two youngsters.

Fiona read them a story—she always chooses one of the Dr.

Seuss books because she likes them herself. She had just reminded me forcibly that I rarely read to the children at all when Susie shamed me by saying most nostalgically, "Do you remember the time Daddy read us *Cat in the Hat*, Vicky?" and I remembered that this had been a good month before! On this particular evening the girls made no demur about going to bed after their story, though they are unpredictable in this respect. They cleaned their teeth, the paste having first been squeezed on to each brush, for they would use unlimited quantities of toothpaste and go on cleaning their teeth for ever if we let them; they washed, then scuttled into their cabin on hands and knees and proceeded to make their beds, which are mattresses placed side by side.

They snuggled down. Then followed thirty minutes or so of those maddening bedtime afterthoughts that children are so adept at thinking up.

"I want a drink, please."

"So do I. That's a little one, I want a big one."

A period of quiet succeeds this. Then an angry wail is heard from Vicky.

"Susie took all my *pareu* and I'm cold."

"It's Vicky, Mummy, her feet are on my bunk. I'm going to smack you Vicky very, very hard!"

"Fiona-Mummy, Susie said she is going to smack me!"

"I will do all the smacking—both girls," threatens Fiona, in so menacing a tone that silence descends again for a while.

"What are you coming out of your cabin for?" Fiona is thoroughly exasperated.

"Forgot to go to the potty. But I *have* to Mummy!"

"And why do *you* think you are coming out?"

"Just to kiss you Mummy, Daddy."—Vicky at her most disarming. Then at long last, with unexpected suddenness, the girls' cabin becomes quiet—they have gone to sleep.

The sky remained unseasonably overcast next day, the wind erratic, varying from near calm to violent squall but everyone, including Priscilla, was feeling better. I had been too lazy to run the portable generator to charge the batteries while we were in harbour where it could be done quite easily, so as this weekly chore was now several days overdue, it had to be tackled despite the choppy seas. The little motor needed lashing securely in a corner of the cockpit and shielding from spray while it was running. However, it went perfectly and I kept it going for a satisfactory 45 minutes.

The results of another piece of neglect on my part came to light at this time. I had forgotten to grease the Hoffman bearing that carried the steering shaft, so that it had begun to wheeze and creak and the steering wheel to move jerkily. The whole thing had to be dismantled and greased and some shamefully rusted ball bearings removed.

But there was one duty that could not be left with much impunity—checking the rigging to make sure that sheets, sails and lashings were not chafing. It is true that the Polythene tubing (ex garden hose) that sheathed our wire shrouds did away with the main source of damage through friction but it is surprising how a rope can wear itself through, see-sawing against a rail or the mast or another rope, in only one night at sea. In the course of my round that day I came upon a large defunct flying fish partly hidden by the Avon rubber boat. Unfortunately, *Rehu Moana*'s decks—they are curved laterally for strength and to shed boarding seas—shed flying fish that come aboard in the night just as promptly. That is to say the larger ones generally have the agility to escape, though we find several small ones each morning that have been trapped. This morning's find, which was big enough to cook for the children's lunch, was only their second flying fish meal since we had left New Zealand.

Though it was far too bumpy for comfort, Fiona unselfishly took the children on deck, where they could work off surplus energy for half an hour. Without being told, they picked up their harnesses from the deck beside the hatch and slipped into them, turning round for Fiona to fasten them behind. There is an absolute rule that they must always wear their leads on deck and never go up there unless accompanied by an adult. The harnesses are modified pram ones, each having six feet of line attached which is tied to the base of the mast, thus allowing the girls to roam the deck to the rail at each side and from the safety net between the bows to the main hatchways. In a vertical plane they can climb the mast far enough to stand on the halyard winches and the boom goose neck and can scramble up the lower one or two ratlines, from which they love to swing, hanging upside down like bats. Another favourite pastime is to lie on deck peering down through the Courlene safety netting at the water rushing past between the hulls, as often as not trailing their skipping ropes in the water in the forlorn hope of catching a only (I must concede in all honesty that my own efforts have been fish. a little more successful!)

In the early part of the trip the children used to become entangled in each other's lines, which progressively cocooned them until helpless wails of frustration eventually announced that all movement had become impossible. But by now they could handle their 'umbilical cords' with unconscious ease, picking up a coil or two and stepping across each other's leads with the practised grace of an elegant lady lifting her train.

Keeping Safe

Whenever we are asked about our life at sea, the question of danger comes up sooner or later; sometimes the implication of an expressive lift of the eyebrows is that we are criminal lunatics whose doings are not subject to logical examination; but generally people realise that an appreciation of potential dangers leading to intelligent steps to avoid or circumvent them, is the foundation of a successful ocean passage. The little girls' safety harness routine is the precaution that preoccupies us most. What other measures do we consider important to ensure security? The whole thing is rather like learning the highway code in driving, except that the vagaries of wind and wave, storm and shoal, are far less predictable than the behaviour of even the most erratic driver, so that sea rules have to be more in the nature of general principles that each ocean voyager applies for himself.

Safety begins with the ship; its hull must be water-tight and no vulnerable points exist in cabin top, portholes or hatches. Then comes the security of mast and rigging, and of the rudder and its fastenings. Given good design and construction in the first place and meticulous attention to maintenance of ship and gear thereafter, the basis of safe cruising has already been laid— a boat that will float in the worst weather, with a stick on which to hang canvas and a rudder to steer with. High among other items that have to be beyond reproach are anchors and ground tackle. The Admiralty pattern, incidentally, is better among coral or boulders than the patent anchors that show such marked superiority in mud and sand. We carried one of each.

I suppose next in importance come routines designed to keep the crew on board the ship. We have discussed one of these, the children's harness, already, but there are times when the adults need to wear them too. For example, we have a rule that anyone on watch alone at night in rough weather should not go forward unless wearing a safety belt, nor without waking another member of the crew. This precaution is specially necessary with vane steering, for if someone should go over the side, the yacht would sail on through the night with nobody any the wiser. All this obviously does not do away with the need for adequate guard rails. One of the great advantages of sailing alone is that you have no responsibility for others. At night sometimes the weight of this responsibility would strike me and a horrible panorama of possible accidents would parade through my mind. Then I would get up and read to fix my thoughts elsewhere, for I could not sleep. Gradually, the fantasies of fear would recede in face of the cold logic of the fact that every precaution and safeguard I could think of were in operation and had reduced risks to a minimum; for life can never be wholly secure; one can only take all practicable steps and in the knowledge that one has done so, face life unafraid.

It has always been a matter for regret to me that shipwrights and garages are not to be found at sea because in times of difficulty I tend to rely on others to do things for me. However, when necessity forces you to be self-sufficient, it is surprising how well you can manage and how much self confidence this knowledge brings. There must be adequate tools and spares aboard to cope with damage to the yacht or her gear. This assertion is of course a mere cliché and next door to meaningless for how do you decide just *which* spares or *how many* tools? The answer depends so much on the type of yacht, the part the engine plays, the rig and so on, that everyone has to work this out for himself.

Our own tool kit was rather sparse but proved adequate in dealing with broken keels and rudders on the first half of the voyage. It consisted of: two shifting spanners, a mole wrench, three screwdrivers, a drill and bits, a gimlet, a hammer, a saw, a hacksaw with spare blades, a machete (bush knife or panga), a file, a portable vice and a sharpening stone. We had our own knives and marlin spikes.

Then there were engine spares and tools and the sail repair kit.

Fire hazard must always loom large at sea but two factors operate to reduce it on *Rehu Moana*: the paraffin we use for cooking is a good deal safer than Propane or Calor gas, which demands the highest standards of installation, ventilation and tap discipline; the other great risk, petrol, is minimised because the outboard motor is outside the accommodation and the charging motor is portable and used in the open air, while our petrol supply is carried—not in built-in tanks but in plastic and metal cans which can quickly be jettisoned in an emergency from their place behind the steering seat or on the after deck. Two large Walter Kidde C.O. extinguishers are in reserve.

Of specific safety devices, by far the main one is a Beaufort six man inflatable covered raft. It is the cover that is the vital factor in survivial conditions, for it was found in the last War that most casualties in rafts and boats were from exposure—even in the tropics. But if a person is completely enclosed by the inflatable and its canopy, no matter how wet he is, nor how cold the weather, heat loss from his soaked clothing will be more than balanced by the heat produced by the body and in the life saving fuggy atmosphere this heat cannot be dissipated into the outside air.

We put several plastic cans of fresh water in the cockpit attached to the life-raft by lines, so that they can be thrown overboard in an emergency (fresh water being lighter than salt, they will float) and retrieved and pulled aboard the raft at leisure. Ready to hand near the raft, are stowed a solar still, flares and some emergency food—Horlicks, rum fudge, sweets and glucose tablets.

It may not be out of place to say a word here about survival food and water. It will be seen from the above that our ration consists entirely of carbohydrate (sugars or starches). This is because only carbohydrates should be eaten when water is very

73

short. The reason—while a little of the carbohydrate is actually converted into water in the body, both protein and fat use up a proportion of the tissue's existing fluid store in their metabolism and excretion. The two points I want to make about water discipline are, first of all, to drink no fluid at all for the first 24 hours after taking to the raft. This is to allow a certain concentration of the blood to take place that acts as a signal to the kidneys to reduce their output to a minimum and bring other physiological fluid retention mechanisms into play. The other suggestion is that the water ration should if possible be two pints a day or over, as this is about the minimum to maintain the average adult (in resting conditions) in something like fluid balance.

A circular covered raft is of course a static appliance designed to keep the occupants alive until someone rescues them and is thus not altogether adapted to a yachtsman's needs, which are for a mobile craft in which he can sail himself to safety from the middle of an ocean where disaster may have overtaken him and nobody be any the wiser. Such a raft-boat would not be too hard to design—catamaran or boat shaped with some skeletal woodwork to take the thrust of mast, rudder and leeboards, it could be assembled in the water after launching; a deflatable canopy that could be erected again quickly in the event of bad weather. However, the market would be small and the cost of production high, so for the present the conventional inflatable remains the most satisfactory appliance. Our own plan for our next voyage is again to carry a circular six man inflatable Beaufort with canopy, at least one inflatable boat and a small fibreglass dinghy. If the wind were favourable, all that would be necessary would be to tie off the life raft's sea anchors and it and the rest of the 'convoy' would blow along quite happily. When manoeuvrability was required, as in a calm or when nearing land, it could be partially deflated and towed by the boats, to be re-inflated in time of need, rather like erecting a kind of seaborne igloo in which to rest secure during bad weather.

One measure will materially offset the relatively static disadvantages of the raft (only partially overcome by the measures suggested above). This is to carry a portable emergency radio transmitter-receiver designed for survival craft. We will have such a set next time—ours is from Clifford and Shell, London, and is completely waterproof and capable of transmitting automatic distress signals on three channels—one of high frequency that in one test was picked up from 2000 miles away under survival conditions. The set is worked by a hand generator and besides being waterproof it will float.

This brings us to the consideration of radio transmitters in general. Those unacquainted with yachts in bad weather are apt to exaggerate their value, whereas cruising yachtsmen who have often had reason to distrust their reliability, probably underrate their usefulness in an emergency. Provided the batteries do not become the first casualties or the wiring is damaged by damp, a distress message may get through to a ship or a shore station, the problem here being one of range. Nevertheless, the crew of a New Zealand yacht that sank in heavy weather during the 1966 Auckland-Suva race, owe their lives to their transmitter—and even one successful rescue makes a piece of equipment well worth considering. But it should have much lower priority, in my opinion, than making sure one is self reliant, that the condition of ship and gear is such as to render trouble unlikely, and that, if it comes, the equipment is to hand to enable one to get out of it by one's own efforts. For we who sail lonely seas, or climb, or explore the waste places, should not expect others to spend time and money and perhaps even risk their lives to rescue us from situations that we have entered into of our own free choice.

Two other pieces of life saving equipment deserve mention. A fishing float type spar buoy whose pole projects well up into the air, can be picked out among normal offshore seas when a conventional lifebuoy would be a needle in a haystack. Lastly, life jackets should be available to wear in the dinghy in particularly choppy anchorages—I would not be surprised if fewer English yachtsmen have been lost at sea than between the shore and their home moorings.

As *Rehu Moana* swooped and dipped and thumped her way towards Efate in the New Hebrides group, she was a tight and secure enough ship, though her motion was not very comfortable, for the weather remained much the same. The barometric reading was high—1018 mb. against an expected figure for the place and time of year according to the Pacific Island's Pilot, of 1014, suggesting that the strong winds might be connected with the high pressure of an anticyclone. The rough sea did not prevent us from doing justice to the savoury rice that Fiona gallantly cooked on the third evening, although the operation had not been accomplished without an occasional crash followed by a muffled curse from the galley. These mishaps were really a tribute to Fiona's determination that her kitchen table and shelves should remain in the same place for more than a moment or two—and her steadfast refusal to make concessions to the fact that they did not.

As the sun sank towards the horizon next day, our fourth from Vatu Lele, we estimated that there were about a hundred miles still to go. As if in confirmation a snow white tropic bird flapped over us and stayed a while circling the mast head. We knew that the range of these tropic or bosun birds was 100 to 150 miles from land (though we once observed some as much as 300 miles out). Thinking it was as well to try to obtain an accurate fix, we took sights of the first stars to become visible after sunset. We found however that it was impossible in the twilight to be sure we were looking at the true horizon through the sextant telescope and not at intervening swells. This complication of star sights (it hardly arises in full daylight that is a necessary accompaniment of sun observations), is no problem to navigators who are looking out from a ship's bridge perhaps forty feet above the waves, but I am sure it is a major source of navigational error in yachts where the observer's height of eye is often well below the level of even average waves. So it proved on this occasion, when in spite of Priscilla's care—and she is much better at star sights than I am— position lines for three stars were not in agreement. In this instance we were well offshore so there was no need to worry. Moreover the moon was but two days old and since the full moon rises at sunset and sinks at dawn, we could expect brilliant moonlight from about two hours after sunset for the rest of the night. The sky had cleared and the islands we were approaching were steep to and high.

The nearer our landfall came, the more carefully we studied

the charts of the archipelago and of Efate Island with its port of Vila, the capital of the group, in particular, and as usual the process assumed added urgency on our last night at sea. Apart from the ordinary Admiralty charts, there was the Pilot book with its detailed directions, and the Pilot charts that showed monthly or quarterly winds and currents, though these were more important for the actual passage than for making land.

At the risk of another digression; we found that charts of any particular ocean were usually obtainable at any large sea port in the area but, when one was bound far afield as we were, it was not always possible to obtain charts of our destination. This happened to us when we were forced to leave Australia without the large scale chart of the part of the African coast we needed, although we had given three months' notice to the Sydney chart agents of our requirements. Thanks to Messrs. Kelvin Hughes, who generously gave us most of our charts, we were seldom in need. When we had been preparing to leave England, however, it had seemed an arrogant tempting of providence to count on getting any farther than New Zealand, so when we *did* get there safely, we had to send an S.O.S. to Kelvin Hughes for more charts. These they supplied but, being ignorant of our exact proposed route, left certain gaps. These could have been filled more easily had I consulted the chart agents in Auckland in good time instead of at the last minute before sailing—a thoughtless error that I hope not to repeat.

Efate Island seemed to be free from off-lying dangers. We remembered to put our clocks back an hour to conform to New Hebrides time (standard times for all countries are given in the Nautical Almanac), and continued all night under moderate sail. As always when approaching land, we were more watchful than usual, which made the night seem weary and long but at last the sun's rim broke the horizon astern, bathing the lines of whitecaps in a brief splendour of red and gold and flooding the cabin with warm light. The tired watchkeeper stirred, yawned, then swung up through the main hatchway and stumbled forward along the lurching deck to grasp the shrouds and peer ahead. Only cloud! No, what was that pale pyramid to port? And ahead too the faint blue line that slanted diagonally up across the forestay to merge into a layer of smudgy stratus? No cloud ever boasted so straight and hard an outline. Flying high, a tropic bird crossed our stern, appearing transparent as the early morning sun shone through its feathers.

The children emerged from their low decked cabin on hands and knees, sat in turn on their pot, and instead of returning to their cabin with armfuls of toys as we had firmly trained them to do, they trotted aft to look up at the bird. The feeling of excitement that pervades *Rehu Moana* when approaching each new land had evidently communicated itself to them. How richly satisfying it was to venture across the seas in such company thought the watchkeeper, who was myself in this instance, watching their faces, still soft with sleep, yet eager and alert and interested. How much deeper were the experiences we shared and the triumphs we sometimes knew, *because* they were those of a family community! Vicky pointed as her sharp eyes picked out two boobies that followed in the wake of the tropic bird. These began diligently inspecting our mast-head anemometer, then dived away in sudden agitation as a large black bird with sharply angled wings soared abruptly over them. But the foolish boobies had nothing to fear as yet; the predatory frigate bird would hold a watching brief until they forgot him and got on with their fishing. *Then* he would swoop and swerve and 'buzz' them unmercifully until his frantic quarry would regurgitate their breakfasts for the frigate bird to retrieve. But it was still very early in the morning, too early for the children to wait up in hopes of seeing the chase, which in any case they had witnessed before, so I firmly ushered them off to their bunks again and sitting down at the chart table, wrote in the log, '0700. Eromanga sighted bearing 180°T. Efate 290°T.'.

The wind that had held so true since Fiji began to moderate now that we wished to reach Port Vila, on the opposite side of Efate and still over fifty miles away, by nightfall. We hoisted the big red and blue spinnaker and at once the catamaran came to life again, running as if she were on rails and sailing level with a complete absence of the rhythmic rolling that makes single hulled yachts so uncomfortable down wind. The wind became still lighter, so we hoisted the reefed mainsail, lighter yet, and we

78

shook out the reef. After this it held steady, reinforced by the growing strong breeze.

By early afternoon we were in soundings and a lop had replaced the long swells. Shoals of flying fish were breaking out of the faces of the waves like streaks of silver and banking away in long glides, while above them hysterical seabirds were wheeling and diving everywhere. The hills of Efate rose out of white surf a mile away to starboard and climbed in gentle undulations to the distant ridge line. We raced along past mile after mile of red rock bluffs and sandy inlets. At increasingly frequent intervals the palms and bright green foliage of a plantation or village gardens would relieve the gloom of the lowering rain forest.

Beyond the south-east point of the island the coastline began to trend north of west, so that to continue to follow it required us to gybe. With a double ended spinnaker pole this was not too difficult an operation on the level platform of the catamaran's deck. We simply detached the pole first from the sail, then the mast and reversed it so that the end that was formerly clipped to the mast was now attached to the clew of the sail on the lee side of the forestay. Then the mainsail was gybed and guyed out, the spinnaker sheet and guy adjusted, and we were goosewinged again on our new course but with the sails on opposite sides.

This was a glorious spinnaker run, made memorable for us by the proximity and interest of the land, so we were sorry when we rounded the last headland at four o'clock and opened the town at the head of a deep bay, The big running sail (the spinnaker) had to come in then and the jib and staysail be hoisted in its place so that we could turn to windward and tack towards Vila against the fickle winds that filtered down to us through the palms that fringed the coral cliffs around the bay.

An hour later we ghosted through the reef pass on a dying breeze and soon afterwards started the motor. A man in a speedboat, hailed in our best French to ask for directions, replied in perfect English, and following his advice, we came to anchor off the town in the twilight, on 5th July, three fathoms above an underwater garden. Green seagrass waved above a sandy bottom, out of which coral masses rose abruptly in bollards, dull red fan sheets and branching stag horn. Bright fish were flickering in and out of the crevices and the clumps were gashed here and there by the serrated purple lips of giant clam shells.

We were not able to go ashore at once next day, however, for I had first to report our presence and clear the ship. Now the Anglo-French Condominium that governs the New Hebrides must be the envy of all true bureaucrats because it shows just how elaborate a structure *can* be evolved to adminster a population of only 66,000. There is a French National Adminstration complete with *douane* and police, a duplicate British one and the joint or Condominium Administration. The official languages are French, English and Pidgin and the currency New Hebrides francs and Australian dollars. Nowhere in this elaborate edifice is a voice given to the 62,000 indigenous islanders who, even after recent reforms, have virtually no say in governing their own country. How this state of affairs arose becomes more understandable when it is realised that the historical role of the Condominium (known familiarly throughout the Pacific as the 'Pandemonium') was to reconcile rival claims to the native land of French and English planters. The part the missions played in this sorry scramble varied at different times from siding with their own nationalities to the extent of fomenting native wars, to acting as spokesmen for their island congregations and generally trying to mitigate the worst European excesses. Happily they incline firmly towards this latter course of action today.

It was necessary for us to clear the ship first with the Condominium administration. After the formalities had been completed, they kindly put an official jeep at my disposal with a smartly turned out police driver (khaki shorts and shirt, red cummerbund and green beret with a red pom pom) to take me up the hill behind the town, past green lawns and Norfolk pines as elongated as poplars, to the British National offices. An immaculate officer received me with the utmost courtesy, which masked I suspected a certain dismay for, despite his good breeding, he was unable to hide entirely his evident relief when I assured him that we needed no assistance and our untimely interruption of the even tenor would be brief as we were stopping for no more than a few days. We parted with expressions of mutual esteem and I rejoined the waiting jeep. Since the morning was now far spent, I decided to omit a visit to the French building and go back to the catamaran to inform the prisoners on board that as far as I knew they were at liberty to land.

They were waiting patiently, so we rowed ashore at once past the lovely former Cook Island schooner *Tiare Taporo*, now somewhat squat and shortened after a reef stranding, and after spending an hour or two shopping in the modern town, strolled along the road by the shore of the bay. The friendly New Hebrideans waved and called greetings, often in good English, and made a special fuss of the children. One young mother ran out of her house with the local version of the population explosion clinging to her skirts and pressed a bunch of bananas on the little girls, while her own youngsters gazed at them in shy fascination out of great brown eyes.

Returning aboard that evening, we were laden with our purchases, the bananas and the shells, corals and canoe shaped seed pods that the girls had gathered. There was work to do while we were lying at rest in harbour. First the generator needed dismantling and its fuel line and carburettor had to be cleaned. Afterwards we were forced to desecrate the still, tropic night for a time with its clatter. Then we restowed the bigger anchor in the cockpit to trim us more by the stern for, since our next passage 1400 miles across the Coral Sea to Port Moresby in Papua-New Guinea would be almost entirely a down wind one, we wanted the catamaran to steer herself as much as possible. This re-arrangement necessitated gathering up piles of coral and the beautiful and bizarre shells that Fiona had been collecting on the reefs since we stopped at our first coral island, and heaping them in some sort of order in a remote corner of the cockpit.

We were now in a latitude and time of year when the trade winds never fail. It will therefore come as no surprise to the reader to learn that the inevitable and ubiquitous south-east trade had been replaced by a westerly breeze. We decided to try to obtain a forecast of how long this unusual weather was due to last before deciding when to sail. In any event we would spend the following morning swimming from the beaches and fringing reef of an island called Fila or Vila that lay about a mile away across the lagoon from Vila port.

This little island of Fila is about half a square mile in area and is thickly populated, acting as a kind of dormitory suburb from which people commute into Vila by canoe. A remarkable fact, especially to those fresh from the Polynesian islands where you can sail east or west for a fifth of the earth's circumference and find virtually the same language being spoken, is that the inhabitants of this suburban island of Fila speak their own language —not dialect—that is incomprehensible everywhere else on Efate. The incredible diversity of Melanesian tongues is believed to have developed during the vast time span, possibly as long as 20,000 years in some western islands, that mankind has inhabited the region. For, despite the population mixtures and movements that must have occurred (in the New Hebrides can be found besides the Melanesian majority, Polynesian tribes and Negrito-like semi pygmies), the Melanesians were still relatively isolated and in such conditions separate languages take form in direct relation to the time available.

In default of any common means of intercourse, the use of Pidgin English in the New Hebrides, Solomons and Papua is not a plot by the colonial powers to supplant the indigenous languages but a genuine attempt to establish a means of communication. The grammatical structure of Pidgin is Melanesian and its vocabulary based on English—though one might fail to recognise *bull-a-ma-cow* for instance, as a synonym for corned beef. The language can also be pungently expressive as I learnt to my embarrassment.

A group of youths in outriggers were paddling slowly round *Rehu Moana* inspecting her company with critical interest and commenting in Pidgin.

"Not like schooner, him no want hard biscuit."

Though I did not at the time understand this libellous reference to the alleged practices of the all male crews of trading vessels, the appraising glance from me to the adult members of the catamaran's crew that accompanied the next remark, left no doubt as to the meaning of another phrase—"old feller, plenty sweet biscuit belong him!"

Apart from the uniqueness of its language, Fila Island had another claim to our notice. The picture that will always remain in our minds—unfortunately it was only to be seen too early in the morning to record it by camera—was of the Fila ladies on their way to work.

The canoes of Melanesia are the slimmest and most delicate works of art imaginable; French designed dresses are elegant and urban, while the Fila young women tend to be, to say the least, robust. The plump and graceful ladies dressed in skin-tight frocks, would paddle rather mincingly by, seated on, rather than in, slender *pirogues* that their massive curves quite dwarfed. On reaching the shore, they would pick up their light craft, carry them daintily up the beach, and stack them against the sea wall in a row like bicycles. Then putting on their shoes they would undulate to work in shops and offices.

The following morning, however, dawned overcast and so rainy that the commuter ladies paddled by, shapeless beneath their P.V.C. coverings. The wind was still inexplicably in the west. How lazy we had become! This was a head wind for Papua but instead of setting sail to windward, as we would have done without a second thought in England or New Zealand, we debated how soon the weather might change and where we could obtain a forecast. We were saved from this dilemma by the coming aboard of a French customs officer who was not at all put out that I had neglected to visit his office the day before. In fact he seemed much more interested in seeing over the catamaran and playing with the children. Upon our explaining our problem, he immediately whisked me off at alarming speed in a rattling two seater car to visit his friend at the Meteorological office in the hills above Vila. Here we found another alert and lively personality, an Australian this time, who assured me, after duly consulting his isobars, that the trade wind would return by evening. After thanking him I was conveyed down to the town again at an even more breakneck pace and, almost before I knew it, found myself waving to a rapidly receding cloud of dust, while Fiona, Priscilla and the children clutching ice creams, materialised on a shop verandah.

Regardless of the inclement weather—the rain seemed to have set in in real earnest—and in pursuance of our decision and promise to the girls to go swimming at Fila Island, we pumped up the Avon rubber boat until it was hard and easy to row. This was the first occasion we had added any air to it at all since leaving Auckland two months before, during all of which time it had been carried inflated and uncovered on deck. We rowed across the lagoon, feeling chilly in our wet bathing suits in spite of the latitude 17° 45′S and glad when our turn to row came round. We picnicked rather miserably beneath the trees in a cove below coral cliffs, from time to time extracting thorns from our anatomies. Then we swam among the rocks and out over the fringing reef while the children splashed in the shallows. We rowed back, still in streaming rain and were not at all sorry to be back on board again, towelling ourselves vigorously before changing into dry clothes. Somehow it had been one of our less successful outings!

Chapter 3

THE CORAL SEA

AFTER disentangling our anchor chain from round a coral head, a process that would have presented no difficulty had we not been too craven to enter the uninviting water again, we motored out of Vila on 7th July an hour before dusk under a leaden sky. On two occasions we were startled to see great patches of water beyond the reef being whipped white by frenzied fish swarms. As the brief twilight faded we headed out to sea to give a wide berth to a dangerous tide rip off a salient point of the darkening land. The wind was variable, sometimes dying out entirely, at others blowing so hard that we had to reef the mainsail; it came from different directions but always, in spite of the forecast, from some westerly quarter for the next two days. We made good progress despite these gusty head winds, on the second day covering 115 miles. Although *Rehu Moana* was often threshing to windward against a force 5 head breeze she sailed so upright that, very different from the state of affairs on a conventional yacht, cups of coffee could be left with impunity unattended on the chart table. Nevertheless, we were very glad when the wind backed southeast at last, and her eternal lift, swoop and check over succeeding lines of rollers, gave way to the effortless undulating glide of a broad reach. For the twenty four hours that followed we did not have to lay hand on the self steering gear adjustment or the helm itself nor yet trim a sheet.

Lest we should descend (or rise) to the level of lotus eaters, however, there were daily routines like navigation and cooking as well as sundry odd jobs that needed attention with various degrees of urgency.

The navigational routine in the open sea, apart from when the sun was virtually overhead—I will return to the problems that arise when describing our crossing the equator—was to take two sights in a day. The first was in the morning at a time when the sun bore most nearly east and was high enough above the horizon. The resulting position line was nearly parallel to a line of longitude. The other was at noon when the sun was at its highest point and produced an exact latitude line.

Such a noon, or Meridian Altitude sight, is the only one that does not require an accurate knowledge of the time. For the navigator simply begins taking sextant readings shortly before noon. The figures increase as the sun climbs, then at its zenith where it seems to hang suspended for a minute or two before beginning to sink, the readings become steady and then start to fall. The highest figure is the sun's noon altitude.

The other peculiarity of this sight is that it can be worked out very simply with the Nautical Almanac alone without recourse to other tables.

To obtain the noon *position*, rather than the noon latitude only, it was necessary to adjust the morning position line to allow for the estimated distance sailed between the two sights; the point where the lines now crossed being the position. Priscilla would nearly always take the morning sight and often the other as well, or if she was off watch or asleep by then, I would take the second one and plot our daily position.

It must be obvious to what extent a navigator is necessarily preoccupied with knowing the time accurately. We wound our second hand Naval deck clock at the same time each evening, kept it in a Polystyrene box when not in use and handled it gently when sights were being taken. In spite of these precautions its rate varied rather erratically, so we tried to obtain daily radio time signals as a check on its vagaries. Fortunately, transistor radios render this easy; our Japanese Sony can receive frequencies ranging from 5 to 17 M.C., between which limits we were always able to obtain either the B.B.C. overseas news with its hourly pips, or one of the special time signal stations in Australia, South Africa or the U.S.A. At the time of which we are speaking we were receiving signals from the U.S. Bureau of Standards station, W.W.V. (H) in Hawaii on 5 M.C., and continued to do so until past Darwin in the Indian Ocean. Then, quite suddenly, W.W.V. (H) became inaudible, being replaced by Z.U.O., South Africa, on the same wave length. We must have been in rather a radio blank area then, because Z.U.O. also faded in a few days, though fortunately about the same time the B.B.C. began to come in strongly on 6 megacycles.

Our basic navigational routine, that has taken so long to describe, occupied no more than an hour a day as a rule but I see by the log that on the 11th July Priscilla must have spent a good deal of time testing the sextant for errors, for she noted that she finally managed to screw the index glass down properly so that there could be no more incidents like the mistake in our position when we were skirting Tonga.

That day must have been fairly prolific in assorted jobs because the log notes that Fiona mended the port fresh water pump, adapting an Aladdin lamp washer to fit it and improvising a replacement for a broken spring out of a length of stainless steel wire. It all worked too. We had been conscious of the ship not self steering very well but had put this down to the shortness of the seas, until we noticed rather belatedly that the line round one of the wind vane drums had come adrift. Fiona mended this also as she tended to specialise in this particular department.

For some time we had been made increasingly aware of an unpleasant smell that emanated from somewhere deep in the port hull under the galley and near Fiona's and my double bunk, which it was rapidly rendering untenable. Since I usually slept in the passage berth at sea I suffered much less than Fiona and had been ungallant enough to put off the unpleasant task of locating the cause as long as I could. But Fiona had hardly slept at all the night before, so I was very properly shamed into tackling it. The hull ventilation is poor at the best of times in the tropics and now, as I moved tins and boxes around the bilge, with the yacht bucking over the swells, the stench became nauseating. At length I found and retrieved the offending article, a packet of bacon that had slipped to the bottom of the cupboard in the centre board case and lain there unnoticed since New Zealand waters, a short head before my stomach revolted. Clambering hastily into the cockpit, I heaved the bacon over and immediately followed it with my own contribution.

I gazed round, taking deep breaths of the fresh air. We were quartering along bumpily at around six knots. A noddy flew past and a white tern, having evidently spotted a fish, hovered a moment before closing its wings and plummeting down. A jet black crooked cross against the blue was a frigate bird patrolling high above a pair of brown boobies. All these birds, I thought, must be from the extensive New Caledonian reef complex 150 miles to the southward. Then I glanced astern to see that the line we were trailing was taut and straining.

The fish proved to be a big dorado, all profile with body flattened from side to side and scales shimmering in green and gold as it flapped in the cockpit. I struck with the machete and, apart from the welling dark blood, all colour faded from that glowing integument as it died. Priscilla photographed the proud fisherman who did his best to appear nonchalant as if catching a fish were an every day event. Then the dorado was scaled, cleaned and dismembered to a chorus of bloodthirsty question and comment from the children who were watching intrigued from the hatchway.

The barometer had fallen a little during the unexpected westerlies but it had begun to rise as the trade wind resumed its sway and now, as the breeze became stronger yet, it rose above the seasonal normal. In spite of having reduced sail very substantially to ease the steering, we covered 130 miles in the twenty four hours to noon on the 12th. Towards the evening of that day the Trade was blowing at times at gale force 8, sending ranks of whitecaps surging across the ocean and driving lines of small cumulus clouds close overhead. In the night we changed down to our small boomed staysail and a tiny spinnaker we had made out of a parachute given to us in Valparaiso. This did not require a pole, being set merely from bow to bow, and was an invaluable little sail until it eventually came to a sad end when it dropped into the sea in front of the stems, where it was chewed to ribbons against the chain bobstays.

By the 14th July, when the wind had moderated to a steady breeze, we were a week out of Vila, now 680 miles astern, and two months had passed since we had left New Zealand. We were entering the Coral Sea proper, keeping well to the north-east of the jumble of reefs and atolls outside the Great Barrier Reef of Queensland, and gradually closing the island cluster that streams east from New Guinea like the tail of a comet. Once south of the New Guinea mainland proper, we aimed to sail about fifty miles offshore parallel to the coast until we were far enough to change course sharply and head in to Port Moresby. Traversing this part of the Coral Sea was relaxing because there were no reefs or shoals to fear. Most of our spare time was spent on deck in an even temperature of about 78°F. under the dappled light and shade of the evenly spaced cotton wool clouds that passed endlessly overhead, as *Rehu Moana* steered herself accurately enough. Priscilla haunted the foredeck in the bikini that was her usual attire, sunbathing on an enormous black and white towel and daily assuming a more mahogany tint. Fiona's favourite spot was farther aft, where she would prop a pillow against the Perspex dome and lie reading, dressed in a *pareu* or bikini and wearing sun glasses. The disadvantage of bikinis only came to light when either was frying in the galley and hot fat spattered painfully against bare midriffs. A large towel round the waist therefore became an essential item in a cook's attire.

One of the children's favourite occupations, painting, was not well adapted for the open air as wind eddies made it hard to keep paper on board. Not that the girls minded particularly if the sheets did blow away, for they could always paint the hatchcovers, or a furled sail, or preferably themselves. Needless to say such initiative was not encouraged, in fact a day when Vicky painted herself a bright red was the last straw and the paintboxes were confiscated for the time being. As an acceptable alternative, they baled water diligently out of a bucket with minute doll's cups and teapots in serious intent games.

One day when they had been 'helping' Fiona make scones in the galley, in a moment of inspiration she presented them each with rolls of dough to play with. There never was such a success. They borrowed Fiona's biscuit cutters and with patience and care managed to produce quite respectable looking scones; then they made dough animals, boats and people, and both girls cried when they had to leave their dough at supper time. No craze can continue unabated at such a tempo as this but enthusiasm waned only slowly, so that when we were interviewed by New Guinea radio, Susie and Vicky's answer to every question about their life at sea was "We played with dough!"

But other amusements were not completely neglected even while we were still on the Coral Sea. The doings of birds were always a source of interest and these days they were nearly always around us. Once three brown boobies tried to land in turn on the steeply sloping backstay, sliding down the wire with much ungainly flapping and alarmed squawking. Tiny storm petrels visited us again for the first time since before Tonga, fluttering busily in our wake with a totally deceptive air of helplessness. Then there were afternoons devoted to washing dolls' clothes (the children wore none of their own). They were most conscientious. Equipped with a bucket of cold sea water containing liquid detergent and a nail brush apiece, they would go to work diligently scrubbing the tiny garments spotless, rinsing them repeatedly and finally pegging them out on the ratlines or rail. Vicky at this time had somehow acquired a very special treasure of her own. This was a dead cockroach that she kept in a matchbox. No one else was allowed to touch it, and she handled it with great care, gazing at it admiringly and keeping it (in its box) under her pillow at night.

I took advantage of the unusual peace and quiet in the cabin to finish typing a yachting magazine article. Priscilla was writing one of her own in the intervals between sunbathing and all the other responsibilities she had taken on.

I am dwelling rather a lot on this passage of the Coral Sea because it was such a happy one. It exemplified very well the full life of our 'ship's family', so complete and self contained in itself in spite of, or perhaps because of being so far out and alone on the friendly tropical ocean. Moreover, although this was only mid-July and our way now led through some of the most fascinating cruising grounds in the world, this was to be the last carefree sail we would all share until the New Year.

Susie, who was now four and a half years old, and Vicky who was three, began their first reading lessons on the Coral Sea. Fiona held the classes daily and at first both little girls were fascinated with the new game. But very soon Vicky became bored and lost interest, though Susie persisted. It was all the more galling that her lazy little sister, who must have been listening with half an ear to what was going on while she played her own games, made almost as much progress. Unfortunately, circumstances decided that the lessons would not be resumed systematically until we had crossed another ocean.

Being read to was always popular though sometimes the girls' unusual experiences made them interpret things oddly. In *Three Little Pigs* I remember, to the question "And what do you think the silly pig made his house from?" Susie answered, instead of the expected 'straw'—"Expanded Polystyrene!"

The trade wind became progressively lighter and by 17th July had fallen to a gentle breeze so that we had recourse to the big spinnaker once more. The sea was calm, ruffled by patches of wind ripple, and incredibly blue. I would like to give a complete picture of our life at sea during this period and having already said a good deal about our other activities, will now come to those recurring occasions that loom so large in a very small world like ours—mealtimes. Of course there is really no such thing as a typical day or week on the ocean, because the sea's personality changes so completely over short periods that it is hard to believe you are sailing on the same element. So perhaps the day's happenings of 17th July, with special reference to food, will be as good an example as any other.

We were still working much the same watches as when we left New Zealand, with Fiona carrying on right through the day and taking on the brunt of the children and cooking, and Priscilla and I dividing most of the night watches and the bulk of working ship between us.

I had come off watch shortly before dawn and quickly fell asleep once Priscilla had taken over. She dozed on a passage berth for a while, then as the light rapidly strengthened she extinguished the hurricane lamp in the cabin. A little later she filled both the lamps and the Primus stoves with paraffin, a routine chore that she had unofficially taken on herself (as the only way to ensure it was done regularly I suspect; and because she did it so conscientiously no one offered to relieve her of the unfair burden).

When the chatter and giggling from the children's cabin could no longer be restrained to a reasonable level and further sleep was

91

obviously out of the question, she obtained another half hour's respite by letting the girls take a selection of toys into their cabin. Soon it was time for breakfast, usually cereals, bread or Ryvita and butter and fruit if available. The milk was powdered and not all varieties dissolve evenly in cold water; ours was full of lumps. This was a source of friction between the children, though not quite in the way that might have been anticipated, for one or the other would wail in protest, "It's not fair, she's got bigger lumps than me!"

These disputes failed to disturb me for I had long ago developed the father's protective reflex of selective inattention. I was awakened much later by the pleasant sound of the pinging of popcorn against the lid of Fiona's pan as she agitated it over the Primus flame and the exploding corn jumped like grass-hoppers. Fiona breakfasts or not according to her feelings and her current opinion about her figure. I have no influence with her whatever on this subject, any attempt to urge a sense of proportion being swept aside with some unanswerable feminine rejoinder.

Now that I was fully awake and fed, Priscilla went off watch. Asking to be woken for lunch, she retired to her cabin where she fell asleep almost at once, for she has this very happy knack, or rather has cultivated the habit, of going to sleep almost at will.

We lunched on avocado pears spread on bread like butter, cold baked beans, potato crisps and fresh carrots. The children and Fiona drank well diluted fruit squash; Priscilla, who is always spartan about liquids, had plain water, while I drank cold coffee.

On longer passages, Fiona would slice up the bread towards the end of the first week and dry it in the sun, after which it kept almost indefinitely. There would also be Ryvita and the like, with tinned margarine when we could get it, cheese, Marmite, peanut butter or jam; and of course fruits and salads when pos-sible. When the weather was not quite so hot we often lunched on corned beef rissoles, pancakes, jam rolls or scones. (No wonder my waist-line tended to become a casualty!) Unfortun-ately for the children, jellies would not set in the tropics without a fridge.

Supper was the main meal of the day. Among our favourites

were savoury rice, fried ham or luncheon meat with rice or sweet potatoes, cabbage salad or tinned vegetables. Far too often we found that the more satisfying the dinner, especially when we were relaxed and sleepy after a bottle of wine, the more violent would be the squall that arose and required an immediate change to smaller headsails. This was another application of the 'law of maximum cussedness' but this philosophical reflection was small enough comfort. There was no hardship in being showered with warm spray but the cold rain stung the skin like needles, quite spoiling the contented post prandial mood. Fortunately we were spared such disturbance on the 17th despite the fact that Fiona had produced a delicious Chicken Maryland from tinned chicken bought in Suva. (This was voted the best tinned product we ever had, with the possible exception of the Chinese duck we also purchased in Fiji.)

No mention of meals is complete without the regrettable sequel of washing up. On special occasions we used cold salt water and liquid detergent but, as a general rule, each of us would wipe clean his own plate, cups and utensils, with kitchen paper.

Priscilla had recently had the idea of regular morning and afternoon snacks for the children at fixed times so that they could look forward to them; in the middle of the morning and on getting up from the afternoon sleep (or rest). These became eagerly awaited occasions, the girls choosing with great deliberation and showing marked preference for particular sorts of biscuits, raisins, dried fruit, nuts or 'going on watch' sweets of a certain colour. Consuming these delicacies, one raisin or nut at a time, would occupy Susie and Vicky for a good half hour.

Another innovation for which Priscilla was responsible, was to thrust a glass of fruit squash into the girls' hands and urge them forcibly to drink the moment they began to become fretful, unduly quarrelsome or otherwise unbearable. Within minutes their spirits would be miraculously restored. I am to blame for not having made the obvious deduction myself from the facts I well knew, that a physiological need for water does *not necessarily* give rise to *a sensation of thirst*, so that children in the tropics may need to have fluids pressed upon them at the first indication of heat exhaustion.

A question we are often asked that is of special importance to yachtsmen, is how much water did we carry on long stretches and what was our daily consumption. The problem did not arise on the relatively short crossing of the Coral Sea, but on each of our passages of six or seven weeks in the tropics during which water was kept strictly for drinking and cooking only, the total consumption of the ship's company came each time to a shade under two gallons a day, It must be remembered that we used a great deal of canned food, especially so on such long stretches as these, and most of these contain a good proportion of water. Then sometimes salt water could be used in cooking. For instance, macaroni and potatoes were boiled in sea water, pumpkins in equal parts, and soups in one part of salt water to two of fresh.

Our built-in tanks hold a hundred gallons of water and 14-18 more could be stored in plastic cans, making about 118 in all. Apart from this drinking water, we would fill any spare plastic bottles we happened to have with fresh water before leaving port, and reserve this for washing the children until such time as we could catch rain water. The figure I have given for the water we used under this strict regime probably errs on the high side because as the voyage passed the half-way mark and approached its conclusion, we found in practice that we progressively relaxed the rules.

Since all our cooking and lighting as well was by paraffin, it may be of interest that our requirements were $1\frac{1}{2}$ gallons a week.

No squalls disturbed our after dinner peace it is true, but by ten o'clock in the evening the breeze had become so faint that it seemed unbelievable that we should be moving through the water at all. Periodically the big nylon spinnaker would collapse, folding itself over the forestay with a soft 'whoosh'. These days of light airs had reduced our runs from the hundreds to the eighties, now it seemed that our progress must soon cease altogether. But on this score our fears were unjustified, because we kept slipping silently through a jet black sea beneath an overcast sky all night and part of the next morning. Then about 10 a.m. the face of the ocean puckered and darkened as a steady breeze began from the south-west. This was from forward of the beam but not an un-favourable wind because we could still hold our west-north-westerly course. We lowered the spinnaker and after stuffing it into its bag, took in the spinnaker boom and unrove the sheet and guy. Then we hoisted the mainsail and the large light jib that we call the 'ghoster.'

The sun was now blazing down out of a clear sky and with the thermometer standing at 80°F. in the shade, the light head breeze made sunbathing on deck a real sensuous pleasure again. Susie and Vicky modelled dough busily but every now and then one of them would break off and curl up close to one of the adults for a time as if needing the comfort and reassurance of physical contact. They did this often and it has led me to wonder whether young children do not need to be in closer touch (in the literal sense of the phrase) with their parents than is usual in Western households. The physically close knit family life in an African *kraal* or a Polynesian *fare* is often associated with contagious illness but there is no essential causal relationship between the two, no reason why the rather crowded household should not be retained when the disease has been eliminated. What is certain is that homes such as these produce children who are relatively free from neurosis and insecurity. May this not be due, in part at least, to the reassurance of touch that Western children so largely lack?

As we sailed on through the warm breezy afternoon we noticed that we had acquired an escort of three bonito who had taken station on our port quarter and swam in perfect formation alongside until darkness hid them from view. Several times we saw shoals of other fish jumping and splashing but our bonito never altered their even progress. Not so the birds that kept leaving us and swooping away at every hint of a possible bonanza. There were more of them than ever now, masked faced boobies as well as the brown variety, tropic birds with long trailing tail feathers, storm petrels, terns, with an occasional frigate bird either soaring aloof or else performing spectacular aerobatics in pursuit. Harold Gatty in the *Raft Book* was careful to point out that one or two birds of any species in isolation mean very little at sea, but that such a spectrum of avian life as this would suggest the presence of land within 100 miles. (Our distance from the coast that day was in fact about 90.) Furthermore, if we had watched our visitors carefully towards evening to note the direction in which they finally flew away, they would have provided a near infallible guide to the direction in which the land lay. This is because several of these species prefer to spend the night on shore, the frigate birds always, because their feathers quickly become water-logged if they land in the sea; boobies and tropic birds usually exhibit the same preference though their range or endurance appears a good deal greater, and that of the terns greater still, while the home of the storm petrels is the open ocean itself.

Towards nightfall, when all but the petrels had deserted us, we took in the delicate ghoster lest it tear in the strengthening wind, and set the jib in its place. The glass, that had fallen with the near calm and the onset of the westerly wind, was rising again, so it was no surprise to us when soon after midnight the south-east trade wind again took over. It held true, blowing gently but steadily, and traitorously lulled me into an unjustified confidence in its intentions. For when I dozed off for a minute in the early hours of the following morning ('fell sound asleep' someone was uncharitable enough to say), I awoke about 5 a.m. relieved to find we were sailing still steadily, though much faster, through the last dying splutter of a rain squall. Then I looked more closely at the compass and sat up hastily. The wind and *Rehu Moana* had turned completely round, so that she was gaily heading back the way she had come!

Before long the trade wind re-established its influence over the limited disturbance due to the squall. We hoisted the spin-naker once again and carried it until late afternoon, when a rapidly hardening breeze suggested it had better be taken in without delay. This was easier said than done; the ballooning sail developing a malignant will of its own, threshed away wildly to leeward, ultimately coming to rest like a drag net in the water alongside.

We were south of the New Guinea mainland and slowly closing it by this time, so star sights were once more called for. The altitudes of Rigel Kent, Regulus, Antares and Arcturus were taken, this time with no big swell to confuse the horizon. Inde-pendent observations by Priscilla and myself agreed to within two miles. Though by no means an excellent result, this was quite good enough to give us a sufficiently accurate position for our purpose.

The clocks were put back another hour to New Guinea time which is only ten hours fast of Greenwich compared with New Zealand's twelve. This meant in effect that we had come two hours or 30° of longitude on our way westward, good progress perhaps, but there were still 150° to go before reaching Greenwich Meridian on the other side of the world.

There was another precaution that both custom and simple common sense dictated we should take. When approaching a coast obliquely, as we were in fact doing, it is advisable to plot not only your intended course but also a *danger course* beyond which the land may be met with much too soon. Neglect of this elementary measure once nearly cost me my life on the fog-bound Nova Scotian coast—that was in *Cardinal Vertue* during the first single-handed transatlantic race in 1960. I was determined therefore not to be guilty of such an omission again. *Rehu Moana* was steering 280° Magnetic and the danger course was anything north of 289°. We maintained our heading carefully through a night of sail changes that culminated at dawn in our re-hoisting our spinnaker.

The morning was a disappointment. Low cloud obscured the sky on this grey misty day, when even a sudden drop in temperature to 76°F. conspired to maintain the illusion that we had strayed and that the land we might see at any moment would be Dover's white cliffs rather than the mountains of Papua. In the poor visibility we saw neither. The log had been streamed at the last star fix, thus giving us a measure of the distance run through the water but, unfortunately, no indication of how fast or in exactly what direction the generally west going current might be setting us. So at nightfall on the 20th July, which we expected would be the last before Port Moresby, we reduced sail, both to avoid the danger of overshooting our destination and in deference to the very stiff breeze that had arisen.

We would rather overshoot the port however, and have to beat back against wind and current, than risk encountering the barrier reef in the darkness, so we also altered course a few degrees away from the land and kept strict watch all through the dark hours. Shortly before dawn a steamer passed a few miles to land-ward of us on a reciprocal course—heartening evidence that we were about right. Daylight grudgingly revealed a jumble of dark buttresses quite indistinguishable as landmarks, rising abruptly into livid clouds about ten miles away to the northward. We headed in obliquely until around 8.30, when we were able to equate the contours ashore with a sketch in the Pilot book. Recognising a black pyramidal hill behind which lay Port Moresby, we altered course across lines of steep seas between which we rolled violently. After a period of this uncomfortable rapid see-sawing we sailed over a sunken portion of the barrier reef into the sudden tranquillity of the lagoon, turned to port, and ran down the coast sheltered from the ocean swell.

The appearance of the country was a surprise to us; the hills to starboard were arid and rocky, scantily clothed in thorny scrub. We learned later that this corner of New Guinea is a detached piece of Australia so far as climate and vegetation are concerned. While we were hoisting our blue ensign astern and the yellow quarantine jack to port, we passed a village built out over the water on piles. The girls gazed at the village with interest and then fell to discussing the new island. Incidentally, it is quite a large one as islands go, the eastern or Australian half of New Guinea alone being twice the size of Great Britain.

"Susie, what is this island called?"

"New Guinea."

"Why, Susie?"

"Because it's where the guinea pigs come from, Vicky."

We thought this deduction, even if erroneous, was far too logical for us to have the heart to contradict it.

By rights, we should have been flying the Australian colours at our starboard yard arm. We were not, because when I had gone into a yacht chandler's in England to ask for courtesy flags of nations right round the world, the request had seemed so ridiculous in face of the assistant's supercilious expression, that my nerve failed and I compromised, as with the charts, by purchasing the flags we needed only as far as Tonga. Not until we had left New Zealand did I remember our lack of further flags. We did not acquire an Australian one until much later, when a friend in

Thursday Island made us the very personal gift of the little silk flag that had flown from his rucksack when he was cycling abroad. Soon after midday the wharves of Port Moresby opened out. A forty foot double canoe, powered by an outboard, crossed our bows; a few moments afterwards we saw that a dozen or more similar craft were drawn up ashore, most of them with motors but some still boasting mast and furled lateen sail. *Rehu Moana* had in truth come home to her own country at last, for here the catamaran was the *normal* type of vessel and no longer an exception. We let go our anchor among a group of yachts that comprised three schooners, a trimaran from Queensland, a gaff rigged Vertue from New Zealand, a Harrison Butler five tonner and a Yachting World Seahorse, that lay to their moorings streaming in parallel rows before the steady trade wind. This was 21st July and the fourteenth day since we had cleared from Vila on the other side of the Coral Sea 1400 miles to the eastward.

Our first reaction was to congratulate ourselves on such a snug haven. How wrong we were was to become apparent that night, when at dusk the strong trade was overcome by an equally powerful land breeze from exactly the opposite quarter. The two winds proceeded to do battle all through the night, while the yachts, in parallel rows no longer, swung this way and that, each seeming to have its own individual breeze, so that even when moored at seemingly irreproachable distances, they would grate unexpectedly together. This performance continued all night long until daylight brought back the trade wind and peace to the anchorage. It was repeated throughout our stay.

NEW GUINEA

But it was some hours before we had any inkling of what this unquiet anchorage held in store for us, that we put over the Avon inflatable tender, clambered down into it as it bobbed alongside, and made for the nearest likely looking landing place, a patch of sand by a wharf under construction. Dust clouds were billowing off the scoops of clanking bulldozers, and were borne by the hot wind to lie in drifts against window ledges and mute the vivid pink and red of flowering shrubs with a powdering of grey. The noisy waterfront crowds were our first intimation of the variety of peoples inhabiting this strange land—unique perhaps because where else can contemporary anthropologists pose such questions as 'given no social changes or alterations in the design of implements save the replacement of stone by steel, to what extent will the labour of a Highland farmer be eased?' And the answer, as produced by a direct time and motion study of the transition from the stone age to our own, is that while last year's Neolithic cultivator spent 70% of his working time growing crops for subsistence, a whole historical epoch later the steel blades of his adze, axe and spade, enable him to reduce the proportion to 50%.

As we made our way towards the Customs buildings, men with the enormous hooked noses of the Fly River people stood out from among much darker tribesmen with pierced ears and nasal scepts. Then there were the Motu who, together with related groups, form the bulk of the coastal population in the east and were most notable seafarers in former times. The word *motu* means 'atoll' in Maori and, in fact, the Motu are largely Polynesian in physique and language so that many could pass for Tongans, from whom no doubt they are descended, for they seem to have become established about 700 years ago at the time when the fierce sea roving Tongans were the Vikings of the Pacific. We were intrigued to see that not only the older women but also the smartly dressed Motu office girls in Port Moresby were tattooed up the arms from wrist to shoulder and, as we saw later on when visiting their villages, over the breasts as well.

"It's very becoming," I commented to Fiona, adding hopefully, "wouldn't you like to start an intriguing new fashion of topless tattooed?" She quelled me with a look.

The men of the tribe seemed to be uninfluenced by the bustling activity around them. They undulated along languorously in ankle length scarlet *lap laps*, irresistibly reminiscent of ball dresses —an impression that was enhanced by the rather effeminate way they kept patting their mop of hair from which projected the handles of nit scratching combs and mirrors and a stick from which dangled in front of the nose a kind of mobile made of paradise feathers.

Port Moresby produced a general impression of a lively forward looking community, an impression that was not destroyed even by that endemic characteristic of Australian and New Zealand island administrations, proliferation of officials and forms. This was nowhere more in evidence than in the Customs and port administration. Perhaps some obscure reaction against the free spirit of the pioneer settlers has impelled Australia to devise such complex formalities to comply with at *every* port of call. I want to make clear that I am not criticising the officials themselves who, in every case, treated us with the utmost consideration and did their best to mitigate the rigours of the regulations, but I do query the value of the vast bureaucratic ramifications involved. For instance, Australia—which allegedly wants immigrants with initiative—virtually excludes any who arrive by yacht by exacting a 50% duty on the boat—while Jaguars or Cadillacs enter tax free.

Our first move after that day's quota of formalities was to 'phone Ron and Marjorie Crocombe at the New Guinea Research Unit of the Australian National University. My connection with them is rather an odd one. When I was eight or nine years old we returned to New Zealand from Rarotonga, where I had spent part of my schooldays, and shortly afterwards two Rarotongan girls, the daughters of Bill Hosking, a great friend of my father's, came to live with us, becoming in effect my adopted elder sisters. (We stayed with one of them while we were in New Zealand.) A younger sister who was born after we left the island, Marjorie Tuainekore Hosking, became a schoolteacher and amateur historian and later married the New Zealand anthropologist Ron Crocombe. Oddly enough, I was acquainted with her children's history booklets and with a paper she had written, in collaboration with Professor Harry Maude of Canberra, about the 1814 visit of a trading schooner to her island as recalled from local tradition, before I realised who she was and our adoptive relationship.

While I was telephoning, Fiona and Priscilla, who had taken the children into a milk bar for ice cream, got into conversation with two young Australians. One of them had referred to his medical work. "Are you a doctor as well?" Priscilla inquired of his friend. "No, as a matter of fact," he said, revealing his profession rather shyly, "I am a crocodile hunter." We were still questioning him about this exotic way of life when the Crocombes arrived in two Mini Jeeps and a cloud of dust, accompanied by an assortment of neighbours' children and their own. From then on they took charge of us and did everything to make our stay in New Guinea a rewarding experience, and this despite the fact that they are two of the busiest people I know. They drove us inland next day, up over the edge of the first escarpment to where the rain forest began and the rubber plantations and where a stone monument marks the farthest penetration the Japanese made towards Australia in the last War. Shortly beyond this point the road ends, only foot tracks continuing up and down razor back ridges—or else one travels by air.

"Papua," explained Ron, "is the name of this southern half of Australian administered New Guinea. The other part, the north, was German up to 1914 and that is New Guinea proper. But the whole of the Australian part is officially New Guinea. Never mind the names though—the thing is in a state of flux anyway—the Assembly has been debating what to call the country for a year now."

Ron went on to talk about the Pacific in general.

"The same people live in the Islands that always did, don't they?" he queried, almost aggressively. "They aren't charming picturesque survivals whose changes you must deplore, but dynamic developing societies that *must* keep changing. That is why it is so important that their old traditions are not lost in the process—especially in Melanesia where not many people appreciate the dignity of the traditions."

In fact both Ron and Marjorie were actively engaged in all manner of new developments as well as recording the older culture. The Administrative College at which Marjorie lectures—it has since been merged in the University that was on the point of opening at the time of our visit—was holding an open air party and barbecue that evening to which we were all looking forward. As the afternoon advanced, however, Fiona became increasingly lethargic. She had done a painting of a reservoir beside which we had halted at midday but soon after this she ceased to take an interest in jungle or spectacular waterfalls and retired to her bunk immediately we were back on board. She was evidently far from well because she had lost interest in the party and insisted that Priscilla and I go on alone. This was out of character, as Fiona retains something of a child's eagerness about going to parties and this promised to be a very good one indeed, so I was anxious about the invalid and more worried still to find her no better on our return.

All uncertainty as to the cause of the trouble was ended in the morning when the children paused, startled, in the act of climbing on to their mother's bunk and exclaimed in awed admiration, "Mummy, you are all yellow!"

Fiona had clearly contracted infectious hepatitis, probably in Fiji where it had been epidemic. The causative virus of this disease attacks the liver, producing jaundice. The treatment consists essentially of rest and avoidance of alcohol, other dietary restrictions being now considered unnecessary. (I was behind the times about this thereby inflicting needless deprivation on Fiona until more up to date doctors corrected me.) So as the sun blazed down out of a clear sky—Port Moresby is less than 600 miles south of the Equator—and even the cooling breeze could not prevent our heat reflecting pale blue deck from becoming too hot for even the toughened soles of our feet to stand, Fiona had to lie in the stifling heat of an airless cabin. She is an active person whose temper would normally blaze at any enforced limitation of movement, so I was amazed and more than a little humbled at how stoically and uncomplainingly then and in the weeks ahead she accepted prolonged invalidism in conditions of almost intolerable discomfort. The progress of a case of jaundice may be assessed by comparing the colour of daily samples of urine; if they become successively lighter the condition is improving and vice versa. Fiona's little row of test tubes intrigued the children, who never failed to draw the attention of any visitors to 'Mummy's wee-wee bottles'. Unfortunately no clearing of colour occurred and blood tests at the hospital confirmed that her case was of at least moderate severity.

As if there were not difficulties enough, our rubber boat (it was reconditioned, not new), which was fortunately drawn up on shore at the time took the opportunity to burst. A seam that had apparently perished in the sun, suddenly tore apart. Friends came to our aid. Clarissa de Derka, who is a blonde vivacious Hungarian Ph.D., so much the sophisticated Continental as to seem a most improbable inhabitant of Papua (and an object of envy and mortification to colonial wives, I suspect), loaded the rubber boat and myself into her car and set off to see if any garage could make the repair. Her driving fully reflects her vivacity. I remember thinking as the tyres screamed round one bend, 'if this wasn't a one-way road I would be terrified'. A moment later a lorry hurtled by, swerving, from the opposite direction—it was not a one-way road at all! We did manage to remain intact during our round of garages but none could help us. Peter Lalor, the Public Solicitor, who like Ron is busier than most, then took over the quest and was ultimately successful when he arranged for the Marine Base of the Department of Civil Aviation to do what they could. After a lot of work, for which they refused to charge us anything, they succeeded in making the dinghy usable once more, though it required frequent inflation when in use.

Thanks largely to the Crocombes, we were drawn into academic circles in Port Moresby, though 'academic' is a misleading term to apply to the atmosphere of intellectual vitality that surrounded the launching of the new University. It could hardly be otherwise, given the forceful personality of Dr. Gunter as Vice Chancellor. He was so distressed at Fiona having missed the Administrative College party that he organised another especially for her. Fiona, who was a not unbecoming shade of yellow and should of course have been in bed, thoroughly enjoyed the evening in spite of her malaise.

"Do you know where we are?" she whispered to me under the cover of general conversation, "We are deep in the Somerset Maugham country." And indeed the lives of more than one of our fellow guests could have come straight from that great story-teller's pages. There was Cecil Abel, for example, who at the age of 65 was preparing to embark on his third career.

He looks vaguely piratical, though this is one profession he has never followed. He was, in fact, for thirty years a missionary. He then fell in love with and married his charming wife Semi, a Suau girl (a people related to the Motu), from Milne Bay and surprising as it seems today was discharged from the mission in consequence. Undismayed, he settled down at Milne Bay to teach boatbuilding to his wife's tribe, a venture in which he was so successful as to transform the whole economy of the region. Now the traditional arts of New Guinea are recorded in most impermanent materials; magnificently carved and painted decorations on war canoes and ceremonial meeting houses and tattoo designs on human skin—the former liable to be consumed by white ants in a matter of months and the existence of the latter even more fleeting after the demise of the owner, since if he is no longer consumed as in the day of *long pig*, he has to be buried at once in that climate. Moreover, as civilisation advances so that tribal wars, kinship structures, initiation rituals and ceremonials come to be replaced by football matches, transistorised teenager subculture and the Women's Institute, this artistic heritage is in danger of being lost for ever as the activities of which it was an expression decline and disappear. So Abel began recording designs and motifs by silk screen printing, photographs and other means, until at length he had become such an authority and his work of such national importance that he had been appointed a university lecturer and researcher and, together with Semi and their daughter Fiona, had moved to Port Moresby. He was entering on this new life with all the vitality and enthusiasm of a man in his twenties.

Mixed marriages are no longer the rarity that they were in the territory but a very attractive Australian girl at the party, another Administrative College lecturer, had rather broken new ground. She had greatly startled the more conservative section of the community a few years earlier by divorcing her European husband and marrying a Tolai student from New Britain.

While on the subject of new or changed lives, I would like to digress for a moment from this particular gathering to describe one of our most interesting encounters in three years' voyaging. Among my patients in London had been a conscientious mother who devoted herself to her children to such an extent that their growing up left her life void, the emptiness of her existence giving rise to intractable symptoms of ill-health. Shortly after I sailed, her husband retired and, recalling an old wartime friend, wrote to him. The letter eventually reached its recipient where he was now living—in New Guinea. The friend urged the retired couple to join him and acting quickly before their nerve should fail, this is exactly what they did. When they arrived they had been living in Port Moresby for two years, where they were running a flourishing business between them. They came to see us, smiling and bursting with health; obviously there was no place for illness in their busy life. A bonus, I felt, that their own courage and initiative had fully earned.

To return to Dr. Gunter's party.

"We really are getting on with training the people here to run things themselves," a District Officer told me. "You must have noticed how just about everywhere a Papuan assistant goes round with each expatriate?"

"Yes," I agreed, "I've seen them at the bank and at the radio station."

"Well and it's working out too. Where else, tell me, have Europeans been selected to open seats in an assembly like they have here?" A flicker of movement at the edge of vision caught my attention. A gecko scuttling up the wall had reached a fanlight where he was silhouetted against the verandah light; so was his intestinal tract—in somewhat clinical still life. He paused a moment as if in contemplation, then in X-ray relief, the bulge of a swallowed fly passed through his body in a peristaltic wave.

"The people here *want* to learn," the District Officer was saying, and I turned back to him guiltily. "Take my houseboy, came down from the Sepik with his boy of eight——"

"You sent the kid to school in Australia, didn't you?" someone asked.

"Well, yes, and when he was home last Christmas he got a bit cheeky. You should have heard his dad go crook at him! 'Do you think I like this work?' he said to him. 'I do it so you can learn their knowledge. I am no houseboy but an outboard mechanic and crocodile hunter. I do this work for you!'"

"What attitude do you take?" I asked Sir Alan Mann, who was tall, dark-haired without trace of grey, spoke with gentle courtesy and was Chief Justice of the Territory, "when one tribesman who knows virtually nothing of our laws, knocks another off?"

"Oh, I am very severe in those cases." His expression hardened until he did look harsh, so that I feared that his department must be an exception in a generally enlightened administration. Then he added even more ferociously, "I will go on for hours if I have to. I give him such an awful jawing that he will *never* do it again!"

Drums of the Heri

Seven months before we came to Papua, we had crossed two thousand miles of ocean by using methods that we had laboriously reconstructed from fragmentary accounts preserved in explorers' journals, missionary societies' reports and ships' logs. Kupe, Toi, Whatonga, who—tradition tells us—had sailed the star path from Tahiti to New Zealand, were figures dimmed by the dusty centuries. Our experiment was an attempt to shed a little light upon an era of pre-history that was as epic as the Trojan War— and as completed and long ended. Later we had met Kaloni in Tonga and realised that a portion of the learning and observation of the old navigator chiefs was still alive, in detail accurate enough to be of use to a modern seaman. Here in New Guinea, what we still were thinking of as the long buried and forgotten past began to break surface as it were in the persons of Loheia Loa and Frank Rei who in their youth had been pilots of the great *lakatoi* canoes in their trade cycle of the Motu people, the *Heri*.

The *Heri* voyages were still being made from Hanuabada where both Loheia and Frank lived, into the late 1930's and from farther up the coast until beyond mid-century.

The *lakatoi* were multiple canoes 70 or 80 feet long that carried 30-40 people and some 3000 bundles of sago as cargo. They sailed in September, gaining a good offing by making use of the out-going tide and the early morning land breeze before running north-westward with the south-east trades. They followed the land the first day, anchoring that night in the shelter of Yule Island in Hall Sound at the mouth of the Angabunga River sixty miles along the coast. Next morning they headed out across the Gulf of Papua, 150 miles of open sea to Daru Island among the treacherous tidal shoals and reefs of the Fly Estuary. There the trade fair got under way with uninhibited revelry (this was the reason why prudish Thursday Island Authority banned similar traditional visits from the Torres Strait Islanders), but the serious business was the exchange of sago for pottery, betel nut and timber. In December or January when the Northwest Monsoon had set in, they returned home to Hanuabada.

I owe the introduction to the *Heri* pilots entirely to Peter Lalor's persistence, for it had needed several days first to locate them and then to arrange for a headman of his acquaintance to make the approach. I was already despairing of a meeting when Peter met me at the water's edge one morning as I stepped ashore from a rubber dinghy that hissed gently from its patched seam.

"Can you make it this afternoon? You can use my car and the driver will go with you to translate—he comes from Hanuabada himself and knows everyone there."

The village was big, extending along the shore for several miles with its landward boundary a dusty expanse, at once un-paved street and vacant lot, that was littered with dismantled trucks, derelict canoes and miniature markets, where women squatted beside little piles of bananas, betel nuts, heaps of lime, crabs and coconuts and wooden trestles from which hung the pathetic corpses of wallabies. The planked streets and the houses that bordered them extended out over the water on piles. Women in grass skirts stood around the stalls shopping and gossiping. Their arms and breasts were usually heavily tattooed and they varied in physical type from frizzy haired, broad nosed Melanesian to pure Polynesian.

"They don't mind our visiting their village?" I asked the driver.

"Not us, we were invited, but they don't like tourists who drive up without asking and stare and shout 'just dig those tits old man!', behaving like, like——" he paused, hunting for the word. "Yes, like savages, that's what those ones are, savages!"

By now we had reached our destination and feeling a little subdued, I followed my guide down one of the planked streets to meet the two old seamen—though 'middle aged' might be a more accurate term, since their wrinkled faces, tanned like old leather by sun and wind, gave little clue to their ages. They had observed *Rehu Moana* with interest as she lay at anchor. She was

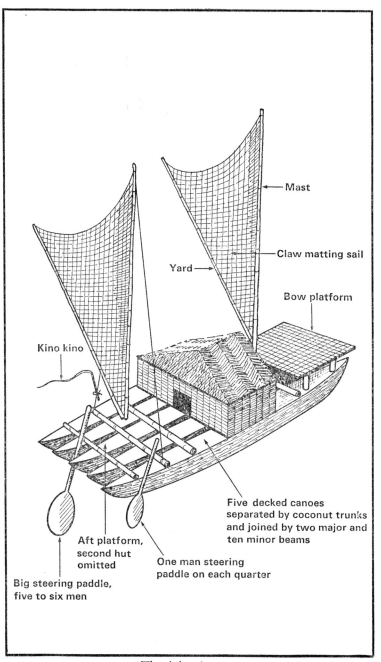

Mast

Claw matting sail

Yard

Bow platform

Kino kino

Five decked canoes
separated by coconut trunks
and joined by two major and
ten minor beams

Aft platform,
second hut
omitted

One man steering
paddle on each quarter

Big steering paddle,
five to six men

The *lakatoi* canoe

a *pau pau*, or double canoe they told me, and they were full of
eager questions concerning her performance. No one had ever
asked them before how the *Heri lakatoi* were navigated, they said.
Yes, they would tell me all about it and gladly.

Everyone aboard the *lakatoi* had his own task. Once the light
airs off the mountains that had blown them out from Yule Island
had given place to the brisk trade wind, five or six men were
needed to handle the big steering paddle at the stern, and one
for the smaller paddles at each quarter. The senior navigator
laid course at an angle to the sun, while noting the run of the
swells and appointed an experienced man to observe the *kino kino*,
a staff with a coconut fibre pennant that was lashed in the rigging.
The watcher's task was to align the *kino kino* on the sun, or a
particular star at night, and note the angle between stick and
pennant, so that if the sky clouded, course could be maintained
at the same angle to the wind. The seas that the navigator used
were not the wind waves, my informant stressed, but the more
persistent and longer swells, that from the south being the most
important. At dusk the *kino kino* was set in the port rigging and
sighted first on Venus until the planet sank towards the horizon,
when the next star to follow it down into the west was used.

"Everyone stayed up, no watches like you have," recalled
Frank. "All the time we beat the sea drums and danced and sang
the old sea songs that told us the course. Everybody was happy."

A mental image took the form of the *lakatoi* wallowing along
under the stars, the groaning of its timbers working in the seaway,
an undertone to the ancient navigating chants and the thudding
of the drums, the watcher's eyes glued to the streaming pennant of
the *kino kino*; and an account I had once read came irresistibly to
mind.

'They have their pennants of feathers and palmetto bark, to
watch its (the wind's) changes by and trim the sail, always taking
their cue for a knowledge of the course from the indications the
sea affords them.' This was not written about the Gulf of Papua
but by Andia y Varela in 1775 and described the practice of the
Tahitians.

The unwieldly *lakatoi* would not sail to windward at all and
only slowly with the wind abeam, so when it became contrary or

calm fell, they must needs drift until the prevailing trades returned to enable them to resume their journey. But usually the breeze did not fail them, so that the second day found them negotiating the Fly River bar. The return journey was made by similar methods.

"Remember," said Frank Rei to me at parting, "in old times navigation had to be exact, far more than now." I must have looked puzzled, for he elaborated, "in my time and yours too, the worst that can happen is to be wrecked; in my father's, make a mistake and come ashore in another tribe's country, and you ended in the earth oven!"

Shortly after these visits to Hanuabada I had to give a talk to the students at the Administrative College about our voyage. All the nationalities of Papua-New Guinea and the off-lying islands seemed to be represented but since the territory boasts some five hundred separate languages they perforce spoke English. They were keenly intelligent, more mature than the usual university intake, having been patrol or district officers or even magistrates, though this did not damp their lively humour; altogether as fine a group of young men as I have ever met. Hopes that I had entertained that they would be particularly interested in their peoples' past were disappointed however.

"Yes, the old arts must not be forgotten but let other people record them, we haven't the time when there is so much that we have to change," said one, expressing the general attitude of the group.

The one notable exception was Joseph Tonnaku, who came from the big island of Bourgainville just north of the Solomons.

"Long ago my people came up from the south (of the Solomons) to settle in Rendova Island," he said. "They saw that 'pigeons' flew out from Rendova to the west-north-west in the morning and returned next day, so they knew that land must lie there. At length they put to sea in their canoes, following the pigeons' direction by day and, at night, sailing at right angles to a certain small star that passes over Bourgainville. There is a swell from the north and another from the south that meet to form a sea corridor that leads for 130 miles to Treasury Island where the pigeons went. My people lived there a long time and then some of them followed the star that passed over Bourgainville and made their homes there but they still kept contact with the islands of their ancestors. Oh, yes," he replied to a question, he himself had sailed down part of the swell corridor in a canoe but only about 70 miles from Bourgainville to Choiseul Island. Then, covered in confusion at having spoken so long, he sat down.

One more encounter was needed to convince me that a mosaic of fragments of a former Pacific-wide system of navigational learning was scattered among the islands only waiting to be picked up and put together; but unless this was done soon they would be lost forever. It was the French botanist Jacques Barrau, then passing through Port Moresby, who told me that trading canoe voyages were still being made without instruments in the Caroline group. I *must* return some day to the Pacific to take up this search in real earnest, I decided—but how would anything of the sort be possible? I was talking about it to Ron Crocombe, not so much seeking suggestions as bemoaning the fate that rendered any such project impracticable, when he promptly cut through my self pity.

"Apply for a research grant from the Australian National University, why don't you?" he suggested.

At first I was dubious. If by some chance an application did succeed, Fiona would be faced with the prospect of further voyaging and I was quite sure she would be heartily sick of life at sea by the time we reached England. It says a lot for my selfishness that I asked her at all and for her tenacious loyalty that she agreed, ill as she was, to my making the application. Ron's advice enabled me to put it into acceptable academic form and before we left Port Moresby it was in the post. Neither he nor I gave it much chance of success.

The cabin aboard *Rehu Moana* was now becoming so stifling in the afternoons that Fiona preferred to break her rest and have me row her ashore to the cool yacht club verandah, while Priscilla nobly walked off some of the children's energy in the burning sunlight up the hilly Port Moresby streets.

Racing sailing dinghies is a fairly general sport but a pair of yacht club members in Port Moresby had achieved local press

Hanuabada, New Guinea

Eua, in Tonga

Sailing in the *Lakatoi*

Frank

headlines in an Enterprise, even though they lost the race. The reason for their failure was an unsporting octopus that slithered enough of its arms aboard to embrace the gunwale, immobilise the tiller and seriously embarrass the helmsman and crew for several minutes before they managed to prise it free. Eye-witnesses told us how the released Enterprise, showing no further interest in the race, made a bee line for the club ramp, on to which it planed with a splintering of centre-board and rudder, and two glassy-eyed men stepped out and marched up the steps of the Clubhouse, saying never a word until they had downed three pints apiece.

I was enabled through the introduction of an assistant at the Radio Station to take part in a sailing race at a village ten miles from Port Moresby, though not in a dinghy but in a 30 foot racing outrigger canoe—and there appeared no octopus to excuse any of our shortcomings. The canoes were of the classical western Pacific type though the last mat claw sail had been replaced with a canvas one in 1959. Most other vessels in the world are symmetrical from side to side while the bow and stern are shaped differently, or at any rate the ends are not interchangeable. But the Micronesian *proas* and the Fijian, Western Polynesian and Papuan outriggers *do* sail either end foremost but always with the outrigger on the same side—to windward. This system allows a vessel to be close winded and very fast on all points of sailing —Gilbertese lagoon canoes having been credited with twenty knots but somewhat deficient in stability. Since the wind must always be kept on the outrigger side, such canoes cannot tack but reverse, changing ends so that the former bow becomes the stern instead.

Five canoes were racing that Saturday over a ten mile course round islets in the lagoon, which was being whipped into white-caps by the stiff breeze. Like all seagoing canoes, ours were completely decked in, a most necessary precaution because their hulls hissed into the seas sending up drenching bursts of spray. The weight of the crew had to be distributed in a constantly changing pattern so as to trim the canoe with its outrigger just skimming, an exercise that required considerable agility even from my clumsy self. The five man crew who had unselfishly invited me were long suffering, for although I learned soon enough to respond to commands in Motu while we were moving at speed, when it came to the skilled co-ordination of changing ends, I merely did my best to keep out of the way. The end-changing manoeuvre was accomplished by turning into the wind and releasing the sheet, when the canoe would stop abruptly and her outrigger dip alarmingly beneath the surface. While one man was passing the sheet through an eye at what had now become the stern and dragging the sail round, others hauled on tackles to rake the mast towards the bow and to windward and one helmsman flung the two steering paddles to the new stern, where they were caught and slid down between the outrigger booms by the second helmsman. Within seconds we were accelerating away in the new direction, hurling ourselves bodily out onto the outrigger as it tried to climb into the air. The race was close and excitement mounted, for we were neck and neck in the lead with another boat; the sharp brightly painted prow sliced the waves like a knife; the crew howled defiance at their rivals; they might have been some fierce warriors in hot pursuit of old Captain Bligh I thought. Then my day dreaming was abruptly ended as the wind shifted and the outrigger plummeted. We scrambled hastily on to the main hull dripping and gasping and swung our weight on the mast to right the canoe and finish the race a sorry second.

On the 6th August we too got under way, though as a result of slothfulness on my part it was not until 11 o'clock that we rounded Boera Head to leave Port Moresby Bay. This was unfortunate because the wind was light while our objective, Yule Island, lay sixty miles up the coast and if we were still under way after darkness became complete soon after 6 p.m., finding safe anchorage would, to say the least, be difficult. We made one detour to try to film a double canoe with lateen sail, a venture that very nearly had us aground on the reef while the *peu peu* threshed by along another channel well out of camera range. Thereafter we kept strictly to the course recommended by a schooner captain in Port Moresby who had sketched us a chart as ours was too small in scale. Only late in the afternoon when the wind got up strongly were we able to begin to make up for lost time, so that when we took in the jib at dusk—in the process it fell into the water under the lee bow—we were skirting the frothing coral edge with the hills of Yule Island ahead but the break in the reef was not yet open.

Given full daylight the approach to the anchorage would have presented no problems, for had not the clumsy *lakatoi* of the *Heri* rested here? But 500 odd miles from the Equator the transition to darkness was sudden, so I was rather tense and anxious as I climbed the ratlines to con us in from aloft. At this inopportune moment a large brown booby bird, as foolish as his name, came flapping and squawking round my head, repeatedly extending its silly feet in an attempt to land.

"Look at the birdie being funny with Daddy!" called the girls in high delight and Priscilla left the helm for a moment to grin maliciously up at where I was cursing and waving my arms at the bird.

"It thinks your beard is a bush—perhaps it wants to lay an egg—do be careful you don't fall." I answered, not her but the booby, with a redoubled burst of profanity, at which it reluctantly moved away to a more respectable distance where it continued to circle reproachfully.

We anchored ultimately well after nightfall beneath the inky loom of a cliff surmounted by the silhouette of what appeared to be a mission station, well clear we hoped of some shadowy moored vessels, for the bay was an exposed one.

We left there soon after first light in the morning, slipping gently along under headsails, accompanied for a while by two small grey dolphins and a less welcome triangular black fin, to fetch up in a quiet cove on the landward side of Yule where the muddy waters of the Angabunga emerging from a dark blanket of rain forest flowed into Hall Sound. The bluffs and hilltops of the nearby island were thick with tangled scrubby bush, while the valley slopes were clothed in tall dry grass interspersed with occasional little cultivated patches of rather ragged bananas. Here was somewhere where Fiona could rest for a while undisturbed by people, that is, once the children had been got out of her way.

Priscilla packed the girls' tee shirts and some orange squash in a basket and collected the new camera she had bought in Suva and with which she was already achieving pictures of a respectable standard. Then we rowed ashore dressed in swimming things and toe sandals, leaving Fiona resting on a mattress on deck beneath a sail spread over the boom as a makeshift awning. We bathed rather cautiously, having seen a sting ray jump close in, but it was more in deference to the possible presence of crocodiles in the murky water that the two adults stood guard waist deep to seaward of the children. After a muddy but not otherwise eventful swim, we set off on an exploring expedition with myself leading the way through the long grass, this time out of respect for snakes.

There was much of interest; the girls' first ant hill, a banana leaf hut standing in a miniature plantation and an encounter with a friendly islander who was out shooting birds. To the children's sorrow no snakes materialised but the discovery of a newly shed snake skin all translucent and shiny, that was carefully gathered up and taken back as a 'lovely thing to give Mummy', did much to mitigate their disappointment. It was such a happy day that when the time came to sail, Susie said wistfully "we haven't been at this island *nearly* long enough," but though we agreed with her, we felt that with Fiona ill and the cyclone season coming nearer we must push on toward Torres, the strait that separates Cape York Peninsula at the northern extremity of Australia, from New Guinea and the Coral Sea of the Pacific from the Arafura Sea which is part of the Indian Ocean.

We put to sea towards evening, close reaching into steep seas with breaking crests that burst against us violently causing the catamaran to lurch sickeningly. Weakened by the hepatitis, Fiona became far more seasick than ever before while more ominous in its implications, her jaundice which had begun to clear, now deepened more than ever.

The strain imposed by illness aboard *Rehu Moana* demonstrated how fallacious, or at least only partially true, is the customary view that two adults with their children constitute a completely self contained unit. For speaking of life on shore at the moment though the principle is the same anywhere, unless grandparents or aunts or baby sitters are available to assist a young mother, she will be all day alone in home or flat with her children while her husband is at work, and so be a potential prey to the fearful

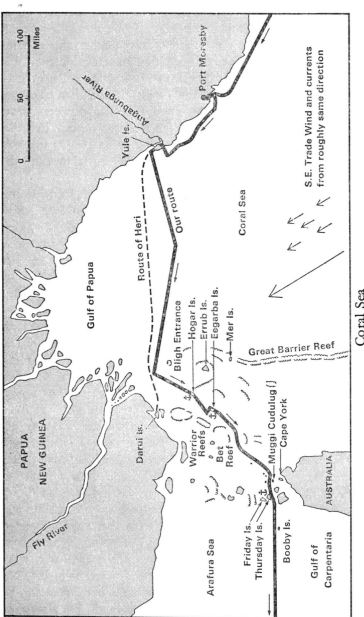

Coral Sea

Miles
0 50 100

Anagabunga River

Yule Is.

Port Moresby

Route of Heri

Our route

Gulf of Papua

PAPUA
NEW GUINEA

Fly River

Darui Is.

Bligh Entrance
Hogar Is.
Errub Is.
Eegarba Is.
Mer Is.

Coral Sea

Great Barrier Reef

Warrior Reefs

Bet Reef

Muggi Cudulug Is.
Cape York

Friday Is.
Thursday Is.

Booby Is.

Arafura Sea

Gulf of
Carpentaria

AUSTRALIA

S.E. Trade Wind and currents
from roughly same direction

loneliness that is so potent a cause of nervous illness. The actual state of affairs in the east of London as demonstrated in a recent kinship survey is that the bond between mother and married daughter is the closest of all family ties, transcending even that between husband and wife. Not that such dependence on an older generation seems really compatible with the confident unity between parents that children rely upon so much. Moreover, fears and prejudices often flow across the mother-daughter link like electricity through wire. But the point I am making is that this does seem to indicate a need to extend the family beyond the parent-child unit.

This train of thought, originated by our dependence on Priscilla and the extra responsibilities she had taken over, led to a realisation of the intensity with which our crowded little group could reflect in its isolation, problems of the outside community. Even before Fiona's illness, Priscilla tended to do more than her fair share of work aboard, a state of affairs to which my natural sloth had contributed; now she assumed a very heavy load indeed.

Not the least of our experiences on the voyage was an exploration into our own characters or less poetically put, a rather salutory process of increased insight but one which on balance did seem to suggest that our fears, joys and struggles were maturing our personalities and making us stronger. Such a crisis as the illness of one of our number inevitably affected us all.

The burden of caring for the children now came to rest mainly on Priscilla's shoulders. Since she was far more accustomed to fifth formers than three year olds, the management of such young children was a challenge that demanded and drew out all her feminine qualities. Parents are apt to lag behind their children's development, failing to notice when a new stage of ability and comprehension has been reached. Priscilla very sensibly treated Susie and Vicky as responsible beings and as might have been anticipated by anyone except the parents, the more that was demanded of them, the better they responded. They were expected to conform more to a routine and seemed to enjoy doing so since it included not only making up their bunks but also more regularity in deck games, snacks and stories before bedtime. The girls did rather well in this latter respect as reading to them was one of the things Fiona was able to do and I was shamed into contributing nearer my share. Then there were long sessions of, "Tell us about when we went to Santiago, Scilla," or the "stone man heads" (Easter Island) or some well remembered outing in Tahiti. Priscilla would patiently repeat the details of one of these episodes and woe betide her if she left anything out for the children knew every word by heart. I am ashamed to recall how little I did to help; how often I took refuge in the excuse of some maritime necessity when in fact Priscilla, in spite of doing so much with the little girls, had given up none of her seagoing responsibilities.

The rising humidity preceding the onset of the monsoon did nothing to mitigate the equatorial heat that intensified as the southern summer approached. Nor did the fact that *Rehu Moana* was behaving rather like a bouncing yo-yo, contribute to comfort aboard. Fiona, lethargic and thoroughly unwell, lay constantly bathed in a pool of sweat and was now doubly vulnerable to the misery of seasickness. She must clearly be drawing on unexpected reservoirs of strength because in the past she had always been impatient and irritable in minor illnesses but now that she was faced with a real calamity she was uncomplaining and incredibly cheerful. The heat was too great for her to bear me sharing the bunk so I moved to the passage berth; in a pathetic attachment to domesticity she seemed to draw more comfort than I could give her from the sewing machine that was securely wedged alongside the berth. I christened it 'my rival'.

The children refused to leave Fiona long in peace and so added to her trials. She had never been over maternal in the sense of sinking her identity in that of her children. I imply no criticism by this remark but the reverse, for in my experience women who *exist* only for their children simply stifle and overwhelm them with a cloying burden of emotion. I recall with amusement the nurse's horrified exclamations when Fiona, after studying one of her newborn offspring with anything but an appreciative eye, exclaimed, "It's bloody ugly, put it back!" As might be expected after such an original beginning, Fiona is a very good mother indeed. Not that she never has recourse to the exasperated woman's outlet of shouting at her children, cause for irritability being increased by the confined space of the yacht; and the constant presence of a husband in the home, while no doubt contributing to the children's sense of continuity, was often an added irritant to their mother.

It is inherent in Fiona's character to set herself an impossibly high standard of accomplishment and then become unreasonably self critical—without ever admitting criticism—when she finds it unattainable in full. She should have realised that the fact that the little girls were able to accept her incapacity philosophically, was the best proof of the security they drew from her and a real indication of successful motherhood. Naturally she did not see it this way at all and was quite unnecessarily mortified to find that the children tended to behave better with Priscilla than herself.

That they should was perfectly natural; children are always more tractable with people with whom they do not share the very deepest of emotional bonds but Fiona was much too unwell to appreciate anything of the sort and felt a failure.

The timing of the illness was doubly unfortunate because for some time past, ever since we had reached the South Seas from New Zealand, Fiona had begun taking more interest in the actual sailing. She had begun to recover a little of the pleasure of participation that had been driven out by the severe hardships of Patagonia the year before. From Tonga onwards she had been finding ever more enjoyment as we sailed from island to island; the crippling of all her activities by illness at this point was therefore a particularly cruel blow.

In the long run, Fiona's character must have been tempered by the fortitude with which she endured her disastrously long drawn out illness, even if for a few months she temporarily and quite unnecessarily lost confidence in herself as a mother; while this confidence came to be restored and even eventually enhanced, any real pleasure from being at sea was lost to her—and that never did return.

Chapter 4

WEEVILS AT BREAKFAST

TORRES STRAIT

Now that we were crossing one hundred and seventy miles of strong variable ocean currents towards the labyrinth of reefs and islets that choke the throat of Torres Strait, navigational accuracy was more at a premium. We reflcted that our route was not far removed from that of the *Heri* and that their landfall in the Fly Estuary would have been even more difficult than ours. Yet they had had only their inherited knowledge and skill, while for all our modern charts and instruments we regarded the passage as no easy one. Bligh Channel which is the usual way into the strait is identified by a sandy islet surmounted by a lighthouse called Bramble Cay. Since the light can be seen farther than the latticed light structure is visible by day, the best method of approach is to raise the light shortly before dawn and enter the strait in daylight. We were expecting to see it about 3 a.m. on the second night out of Yule, having reduced sail the evening before so as not to overshoot. Star sights had not been obtainable because of overcast and the current would be setting us westward at anything between a half and two knots, so the only thing we could really be certain of was the distance sailed through the water which was being recorded by the log.

The sky gradually cleared but three o'clock came, then four o'clock, then five, and still no light appeared. We dared not continue after 5.30 when we hove-to to await daylight and sights, knowing by the log that we must be abreast of Bramble Cay, but whether we had been swept far to the westward by strong currents, or had allowed too much for set in our reckoning and were east of the Cay, we could not tell.

In a hazy dawn with wildly irregular seas making it difficult to determine the true horizon through the sextant, rather unsatisfactory star sights suggested we were too far to the westward. So did the pale green colour and steepness of the waves and to clinch matters, the echo sounder which had consistently been misbehaving, made up for its past misdeeds by recording an unequivocal six fathoms which was only compatible with the mouth of the Fly Estuary. We got under way and shortly afterwards a more satisfactory moon sight confirmed that we were indeed thirteen miles west of Bramble Cay. There being no point in making for it now, we continued southward into the strait down Great North East Channel deciding to stop for the night in the shelter of Hogar Islet.

Around midday the Islet's low silhouette broke the horizon ahead and at almost the same moment, the distant twin hills of Errub became dimly discernible on the port bow. Visual bearings confirmed that we were still being set westward to the tune of nine miles for the last twenty-three we had sailed, but from how on some point of land or other would generally be visible in daylight at any rate, from which to check our drift. There was little to be proud of in our performance over the 170 miles between Yule Island and Bramble however—the old *Heri* pilots would probably have done much better.

Even so, matters had gone better for us than they had for the single-handed Jean Gau in his Tahiti Ketch *Atom* the year before. He had gone ashore on the notorious Warrior Reef that lay in wait stretching for thirty miles to leeward. The falling tide that left *Atom* high and dry, fortunately revealed that there was little damage. Less encouraging perhaps to a man all alone with his boat stranded, was the discovery of a mouldering skeleton among a pile of old wreckage. Jean wrote to a friend, one feels with a modicum of understatement, that he was glad when the tide floated him off.

Once we were well inside the strait, the labyrinth of reefs to the south and east acted as a breakwater giving shelter from the rollers sweeping up the Coral Sea, a relief that was very welcome after the short violent seas characteristic of the shallow head of the Gulf of Papua we had been crossing. Even Fiona recovered sufficiently to be able to sit in the hatchway watching clouds of terns and boobies sweep and wheel above the margins of the reefs. The low coral cliffs of Hogar steadily took on definition as we drew nearer and came to life as separate trees and a little stone chapel by the shore, the whole bursting suddenly into colour. The 200 miles or so of Torres Strait must be one of the world's finest cruising grounds. Islands large and small are scattered throughout its length and there are hundreds more in adjacent waters. It is hardly an exaggeration to say that every one will provide perfectly sheltered anchorage off a beach of dazzling white coral sand. More correctly this is the case for the nine months of the year when the wind remains strong and steady from the south-east and the current from the same direction, while each island is set on the leeward edge of a great plaque of reef. Added to this is the fine weather of the south-east season with a comfortable temperature of 77°-80°F. and the beauty and variety of the islands themselves whether inhabited or deserted.

Having made such a categorical statement, it has at once to be qualified by saying that the beach at Hogar (also called Stephens) Islet is stony and the fringing reef extends some little way to seaward on the lee as well as the weather side.

As we close-reached fast across the edge of the coral shelf in an abrupt transition from dark blue depths to translucent five feet, a ray detached itself from the bottom and slid rapidly away ahead of us. We continued across the shallows to within fifty yards of the boulder strewn Mission Beach, when we rounded into the wind until we lost way with all sails shaking. Once the yacht had begun to blow backwards we lowered the small anchor to the bottom and paid out a suitable length of cable. It took only a few minutes to drop the sails and secure them and put the previously pumped up Avon into the water.

A little knot of islanders in red and green *laba labas* had gathered by the shore. When we stepped out of the dinghy they picked it up and carried it well up the beach.

"We all hoped you would come ashore," said the chairman of this little community. (Hogar is ⅞ths of a mile long and ⅖ths wide), as he welcomed us with quiet dignity in perfect English. They were Eastern Torres Strait Islanders sharing a common language and tribal links with the much larger islands of Mer and Errub farther eastward, and appeared to be of Papuan stock with a strong strain of Australian Aborigine.

"I read a book once by an Australian Ion Idriss called *Drums of Mer*, that was partly about this island," I remarked to the chairman, whose surname like most of the inhabitants was Stephens, as we seated ourselves on a log beneath a great twisted wongai tree. A group of women were chatting with Fiona and Priscilla with increasing vivacity as their natural high spirits overcame their shyness, while the children had promptly appropriated Susie and Vicky and taken them crab hunting in the tidal rock pools.

"I used to have that book myself, only I lent it to someone," Mr. Stephens replied. "A lot of what it said about the old times was true. Do you remember how trees like this," he pointed up at the weirdly gnarled trunk of the wongai above us, "were the sacred trees beneath which were held the great festivals of war and trading?"

"Do you still have any canoes with double outriggers?" I asked. For the Torres Strait Islanders alone among the Pacific peoples used this characteristically Indonesian type of vessel. He shook his head.

"No, we just have planked rowing boats now. That canoe over there drifted over from the Fly River country in Papua." His massive chest shook with a rumble of laughter—I learned soon that these men's apparently splendid physique was really the end result of years of over-inflating their lungs until the microscopic alveolar walls were broken and the chests became fixed in full expansion. For they all had spent the bulk of their working lives on pearling luggers, skin diving without any artificial aids— "Sometimes," he continued, "less welcome things come over from New Guinea like a crocodile or two, and then in the Mango season, swarms of flying foxes fly across."

At this point, a Susie almost incoherent with excitement and clutching a red and green fish she had somehow caught in a rock pool, led a stampede up from the beach. We duly admired the fish and dried her a little, removing some of the sand from her face and hair, before suggesting she might like to go back to the waterside.

"But the bird," she protested, "he made us go away, he wouldn't let us play any more." Sure enough, a large white pelican was swimming close inshore rolling a yellow eye malevolently at the children who had been trespassing on his private fishing preserve. He had been kept as a pet from a chick we were told but when he was still small his wing had been savaged by a dog so that he could not fly though he was an excellent fisherman. Now that he was full grown, no village dog dared approach his snapping beak, while he terrorised the poultry and as we had seen kept the children in their place. We even found him trying to peck through our anchor warp that evening—if he had succeeded this would surely have been the most exotic cause of a stranding!

"Now," said the chairman, rising to his feet, "would you like to see over our island?" The path up the fifty foot high bank was steep so Fiona thought it best to remain beneath the wongai. The rest of us set off up the track, accompanied by most of the inhabitants and much agitated chirruping from the tiny honey suckers that flitted in flashes of primary yellow through the branches overhead.

The red soil of the plateau was evidently rich for it was closely cultivated. The heads of coconut palms waved among tree tops forming an upper layer of foliage that cast a dappled shade over dense clumps of citrus bushes, yam plants, paw paw and the roofs of the wooden houses that were almost enveloped in flowering creepers. Vicky, who has eyes like a hawk, suddenly darted away from the other children to plunge purposefully into the long grass, emerging in a moment with the minute bright corpse of a honey sucker. All the rest of the way Susie followed her, sick with envy, begging, "Only let me touch it, Vicky, just stroke it!"

"Mine," replied her unkind sister smugly, holding her treasure all the closer. The other children picked flowers for Susie, gave her fruit and even a fragment of a hornet's nest but she refused to be comforted until at long last Vicky relented and allowed her to caress the dead bird.

These Hogar children were the most thoughtful of playmates, yet like so many tribal peoples, they had not developed any feeling for animals. So for all their kindness to other boys and girls they plucked the legs off locusts and crabs quite as unconcernedly as they would have pulled petals from flowers. Nevertheless these Torres Islanders will always remain in our memories as a particularly colourful and quietly confident little group, who were among the most pleasant people we met. It was typical of their unobtrusive generosity that when we returned to the Avon we found it to be literally brimming with gifts; paw paw, oranges, bananas, wongai berries and some lovely sea shells. Since these latter were about the only products of Hogar, apart from copra, that could be sold 'down south'—in northern Australia—for cash, we were particularly touched and not a little reluctant to accept them.

We came ashore next day to return these gifts in some measure with corned beef, cigarettes and a yellow plastic lion and a book from the girls, and to bathe at the pelican's discretion. Our departure, which was scheduled to take place immediately after lunch, on 7th August, was delayed because we had grounded at low tide, so we finally got away with barely time to reach the uninhabited islet of Eegarba eighteen miles away, before dark.

Having previously stressed the absolute reliability of the southeast wind, I am forced to admit that it made an exception in our case by veering to S.S.E. and remaining in that quarter for the next two days, so that we had to sail close-hauled all the way to Thursday Island. Of more immediate moment we were forced to tack before we could reach Eegarba, thus wasting a lot of time, so that night had already fallen before we stole cautiously into its lee, rather optimistically alert for coral heads that would be quite invisible in the darkness. The noise of the light surf breaking against the fringing reef was gradually swamped by the din of seabird colonies ashore, which rose to a crescendo of drumming wings as they took off in their thousands and circled over us crying in alarm. Then the anchor splashed down on to a postage stamp of sand that gleamed white among the coral boulders and after a little while the massed squadrons began to break up as the birds gradually calmed down and landed again.

This was our only desert island; even Fiona, who had little enough energy for enthusiasm, felt a thrill when we beached the dinghy after breakfast on sand bare of footprints save our own.

Above the spring tide-mark the islet was thickly grown with ironwood, young coconut palms in rows, wongai trees in whose branches both blue and white herons were nesting, thorn shrubs and a particularly noxious type of prickly creeper whose spiky burrs were almost indistinguishable against the sand. At one end of the islet the white terns had been nesting, though the chicks were now fluffy bundles of agility, who could run briskly or freeze into camouflaged immobility. I caught one with difficulty for the children to stroke and croon over for a minute before we let it scuttle thankfully off into the bushes. With even more difficulty and the expenditure of far more energy, I succeeded in getting up a young coconut palm and wrenching down half a dozen nuts, though when Priscilla arrived with her camera to immortalise the feat, I had neither the breath nor strength to repeat it. Meanwhile Fiona wandered along the shore hunting for sea shells among flotsam and jetsam of planks, barnacled logs from New Guinea, empty plastic bottles and seaweed. She found a perfect pearly nautilus, a helmet shell, some spider conches and a number of attractive fragments of coloured coral.

Coral grows profusely in the Torres Strait region, which is in effect the apex of the Great Barrier Reef that runs for a thousand miles up the east coast of tropical Australia. This is in accordance with the general rule that coral thrives towards the western side of oceans and the eastern margin of continents. And of course we were on the extreme western flank of the Pacific. As other examples of the same rule it may be noted that Equador, Peru, Chile and Mexico are very poor in coral in comparison with the West Indies, and the West African coast is devoid of the growth that almost chokes the coastal seas from Somali to Mozambique.

We took the children bathing in the shallows and afterwards lay on the sand drenched with sun and the salt sea breeze. At length we rowed very reluctantly back to *Rehu Moana* where we piled shells and coral and coconuts into the cockpit—not really to be recommended; you stub your feet on sharp shells at night and go sprawling over slippery coconuts—then hauled the Avon on deck and lashed it down firmly fore and aft. There being no further excuse for lingering, we winched up the mainsail whose kiwi emblem looked decidedly in place off this bird islet. Then it was the turn of the staysail and as the two sails flapped lazily, we brought in the anchor, made it fast to the fore beam, and when the sails were sheeted home and the yacht gathered way Priscilla took the helm and I coiled down the warp and lashed it to the butt of the bowsprit.

The white terns took our going far more philosophically than they had our advent the night before; only a frigate bird—locally, a man-o'-war hawk—patrolling high over Eegarba, seemed to take notice of our departure by executing a series of spectacular aerobatics. We would not be stopping again before Thursday Island 95 miles farther on for although the deepness of Fiona's jaundice fluctuated from day to day so that we were alternately encouraged and cast down, I could not but admit to myself that there was no sign of permanent improvement. The sooner we got to Darwin, the nearest city, the better.

The afternoon sun soon disappeared behind a thickening layer of overcast, leaving the sea slate grey. Stately rain squalls marched across it but always contrived to miss us; nor did they impair visibility for long. There was never a time when three or four islands were not simultaneously visible, even if their presence was revealed by no more than a fuzziness of tree tops breaking the symmetry of the horizon. One sandy cay was left close aboard, less than fifty yards to windward; later we tacked in the green and brown shallows over a reef to avoid another. Always as we threaded our way to windward of the steamer channel, the west-going current set hard across our course, requiring us to remain close-hauled to the freshening south-south-east wind. A rather anxious hour followed sunset before we picked up the Bet Reef Light and were enabled to ease our sheets to run thankfully down Vigilant Channel past the end of Warrior Reef.

Beyond this channel we came on the wind again, this time in more open water where the catamaran threshed through the darkness into steep seas that had swept up from Australia. Every now and again one would burst across the deck in a volley of warm spray. No harm was done until at midnight one bigger than the rest lifted the fore hatch to soak Susie where she lay in her bunk. Priscilla dried her and bundled her on to a passage berth while I steered, as too much vigilance was required in those waters to

Priscilla navigating in the Indian Ocean

The children in the main cabin

trust to the wind vanes. In fact two of us were needed that night, one plotting on the chart and looking out for lights and landmarks, while the other remained at the helm. Fiona, after the brief respite at Hogar and Eegarba, was very ill once more. At 2.30 a.m., with the distant but powerful Cape York Light winking away to the southward from the tip of Australia, we hove-to close off Twin Island. Beyond this point the best sailing boat route to Thursday Island was unlighted, so Priscilla and I could take turns to relax after the tension of the last few hours, while *Rehu Moana* bobbed quietly until daylight. Heaving to is accomplished simply by hauling the main sheet right in and winching in the *weather* headsail sheet. The headsail being a-back across the wind, prevents forward progress and tends to force the bow away from the wind, while the hard sheeted main works in opposition, turning the vessel towards the wind. The end result is that the yacht remains steady and almost stationary and to get under way again it is only necessary to free the sheets.

THURSDAY ISLAND

Feeling sleepy and jaded, we set off at 6.30 as day was breaking, very little pleased to find that unexpected calms and light variable winds had come to plague us. We cheered up a little when we were tacking between Wednesday Island and another farther east on finding that it rejoiced in the name 'Muggi Cudulug'.

"Gaelic as spoken with a cold," suggested Priscilla.

"No, an Irish endearment," was Fiona's contribution.

The breeze freshened as we threaded our way among the Tuesdays, passing between numbers one and four islets into Flinders Pass, down which we squared away with the first of the flood beneath us, slipping rapidly past desiccated hills and bush covered lowlands. An hour and a half later we zig-zagged between anchored pearling luggers to bring up beside a trimaran that was lying off Thursday Island slipway. The crew, whom we soon met when they came over to us in their tender, a canoe with a removable outrigger, were two young Norwegian-Australians who were bound up the Fly River for six months' commercial crocodile hunting. They were anxious to take advantage of the unusual

S.S.E. wind that was still blowing, so they left that afternoon.

Priscilla sent her parents a cable which read—'Arrived Thursday Friday leaving Saturday'.

We were more than ever determined to push on quickly to Darwin when we found that the strong breeze was doing little to mitigate the heat ashore, merely blowing streamers of dust off the stony hills and whirling them in billowing clouds down the streets. Fiona made only the brief visit to the island demanded by the port authorities, afterwards preferring to remain aboard lying in the cabin despite the fact that the anchorage was exposed and rather choppy.

Forty or more pearling luggers lay in the roadstead, all commanded and crewed by Aboriginals and Straits Islanders. Most of these boats had a rather neglected air, a result we were told of the natural pearl shell industry being undermined by twofold competition—the cultured pearl beds the Japanese were establishing off northern Australia, and the development of plastics that was replacing pearl shell. The luggers, which are in fact gaff ketches, were a disappointment, being slab sided and narrow gutted in the tradition of the least successful varieties of English workboats. They were very deep, a fifty footer drawing eleven feet and the smallest thirty-four footer, five; though even the largest did not boast standing headroom anywhere below.

My memories of our fleeting visit to Thursday Island tend to be a shade kaleidoscopic. There was the schoolteacher from Alligator Creek who gave us an Australian courtesy flag that we belatedly hoisted, and a *palga* or clack stick for beating time to dances, that his pupils had made. Then we met another family whose little girl had been brought up afloat, the Forencrofts who fished for trochus in their forty foot topsail cutter. Their daughter Tracey had succeeded in climbing up the ladder of the ratlines at sixteen months old, which so alarmed her parents that they removed the ratlines altogether. Thereupon Tracey, nothing daunted, scrambled up the shrouds themselves by gripping the wire between her toes. Later when she was old enough to attend school and the class were asked to draw a seaside scene, her drawing unlike any of the others showed beach and houses as seen from seaward.

We were privileged to witness the arrival of the Coles' forty foot trimaran, *Galinule*, that came pitching up the channel with the family's 92 year old grandmother, hat set square on her head, ensconced in a firmly lashed deck chair, knitting industriously. *Galinule* had beaten her way clear across the Indian Ocean from East Africa in the teeth of the trade wind, and for much of the time this indomitable old lady had occupied her place on deck. We met the Coles except for the son who was taking his turn at 'granny sitting' and Granny herself, at an impromptu party got up by the crews of the yachts that had called at Thursday Island.

It may well be asked why a number had converged at one time on this small port, poised as it were and ready to take off over the Indian Ocean rather like swallows that had congregated on the eve of their migration. For apart from those already mentioned, there were the New Zealander Tom Corkill in a minute trimaran in which he later reached Durban after an eventful passage through Indonesia; the American Chuck Kenahan, also single-handed, in *Vaquero*, and several Australian yachts. Like ourselves most were bound towards Africa or the Red Sea and hoped to be clear of the Indian Ocean before the start of the cyclone season.

The earliest date when these storms may be anticipated— Hurricanes, Cyclones or Typhoons, are but local names for the unimaginably destructive tropical revolving storms—is never a fixed time; yachtsmen do not suddenly become fair game like grouse on the 12th August, for instance. But the *probability* of encountering such a disturbance increases sharply with the beginning of the season. The best one can do is to study all the data in the British or U.S. Pilot Charts and read the sections in the Pilot Book covering the area. There were naturally as many opinions on how long it was safe to tarry as there were yachtsmen at Thursday Island. Of them all I think I was the most conservative and cautious. I find as much satisfaction as most men in pitting my wit and foresight against the sea in its more violent moods, but to risk encountering conditions where the wind may reach 150 knots is no test of one's seamanship but purely a gamble with luck—the penalty for the loser being destruction.

It may be of interest that we found the most valuable guide, not only for its information on storms and prevailing winds but also for its unique section on recommended sailing ship routes, to be *Ocean Passages for the World* published by the Hydrographic Department of the Admiralty. It was our standby throughout our circumnavigation and the worst conditions we met with, notably round Patagonia and off equatorial West Africa, were on routes that it most emphatically did not recommend.

My other recollection of that evening is of tracing someone's chart of Van Diemen Gulf and hoping that wind and tide conditions would not make it necessary for us to anchor when we sailed through it, since I thoroughly mistrusted my draughtsmanship.

Some Australian friends with a motor boat towed us from among the luggers in the morning, casting us off in Normanby Sound. Almost before we had time to sheet the sails, a fierce five knot ebb tide that had forced one of the channel marker buoys completely under water, gripped us, and in a moment had swept us beyond the point of Thursday Island and then past Friday as well. (I know these island names must by now be suggesting a certain unimaginative sameness—but I am not to blame; these *are* their names but this one was the last we sailed past.) After this we continued at a rather more sedate pace down a channel between sandbanks until we passed Booby Island and debouched from Torres Strait into the part of the Indian Ocean that separates Indonesia from Australia—the Arafura Sea. Like the North Sea it is shallow, so that we only crossed the twenty fathom line at about 11 p.m. on 11th August, when we passed the Carpentaria Light Vessel, whose revolving beams flashed intermittently three miles away to port. There were then about 645 miles to cover (730 from Thursday Island). In round figures, 200 across the mouth of the Gulf of Carpentaria—on which leg we prudently kept ten miles south of the shipping lane; 400 more past, and generally well out of sight of, the indented coast of Arnhem Land, which is a vast Aboriginal Reserve; and finally 100 odd miles through Van Diemen Gulf to Darwin.

The Gulf of Carpentaria was rough, the waves being irregular and lumpy and the water a pale green. By way of compensation for the discomfort, at night it blazed with phosphorescence as if each wave were lit from within. Steamers passed near too often for our comfort; we did our best to avoid their route but with shallows to the north and the promontories of Arnhem Land coming up on the port bow, there was but little scope for manoeuvre. One night we had to alter course sharply to avoid a ship that went by in a glare of lighted portholes with diesels thumping, to leave us tossing wildly in his wake—and he in all probability blissfully unaware of our presence. But apart from the ships and a few storm petrels the waste of green pyramids was deserted and the entrance to Carpentaria seemed a lonely place.

The rough sea moderated magically once we came under the invisible lee of Arnhem Land. Fiona even became well enough to give me a much needed hair cut. (I detest going to the barber's who take so long and insist on talking about racing. Fiona has been cutting my hair since we left England and still does so.) The days were hazy with fine floating dust from the arid Australian continent beyond the horizon; sometimes we thought we could detect the acrid smell of bush fires. Apart from Fiona's condition which failed to take any radical turn for the better—a worrying state of affairs since uncomplicated hepatitis would by then have been improving—this would have been a pleasant enough passage. The children spent hours on deck. Modelling in dough had not lost its attraction; once they were occupied for a whole morning in patiently bailing seawater out of a bucket with tiny screw caps, squatting in the intermittent shade of the furled mainsail dressed only in safety harnesses. For the rest we carried out the routines of trade wind sailing—altering sail as the strength of the wind varied, conscientiously running the generator, renewing some varnish work—and then inevitably being forced to tread on the sticky surface, repairing chafe, sunbathing and reading.

The sky became overcast for a day or so but to our relief it cleared as we closed in towards the strait that separates Arnhem Land from Melville Island, another Aboriginal Reserve and strictly forbidden territory without special permission. We picked up the light at Cape Dan shortly before dawn and soon afterwards, as we corkscrewed through the first of the off-lying tide races, a wave crest fell on deck and splashed into the children's cabin, abruptly and prematurely waking the occupants who were loud in their lamentations. They were pacified however by being given their first look at the approaching land, even though this presented the rather monotonous prospect on either hand of flat bush country unbroken by hills, whose coastline alternated between red sandstone banks too low to be called cliffs and mangrove choked creek mouths.

We tacked through the tidal overfalls of the strait and by ten o'clock in the morning were barely inside Van Diemen Gulf when the spring tide began flowing strongly against us. So we beat to and fro trying to make progress, then as the wind progressively died simply to hold our own until the tide should begin to make again. We lost a good deal of ground until, the force of the ebb being nearly spent, we started the motor and by dint of skirting the shallows off Melville Island began inching forward again. The day was sunny and we were finding the temperature of 86°F. in the windless shade rather too hot for comfort. Then we forgot the heat at the sight of a furry creature that twice poked its head briefly above water while we were negotiating a swirling overfall, regarding us curiously and diving before anyone had time to reach for a camera. We thought it must be either a dugong or a sea otter but not knowing which or indeed if he was either, simply logged it as a 'water wombat', a name which, even if imaginary, did carry a distinct Australian flavour!

The jumping rays however that belly-landed with a crack that was audible above the sound of the motor, were well known sights from our day at Yule Island. Less familiar were great cockatoos both black and white, that fled shrieking among the casuarinas and gums of the monsoon forest close on our starboard hand. By five o'clock the tide was beginning to flood, bearing us westward into a faint stirring of the air that we thought at first to be solely due to our own motion through the atmosphere. But soon there could be no doubt that a true air current was blowing from the north-west—a sea breeze, that allowed us to shut off the motor and glide into the sunset until we came to a minor indentation dignified by the name of Napier Bay, which both the Pilot Book and our hand drawn chart suggested would be the least exposed stopping place. We had no choice in the matter

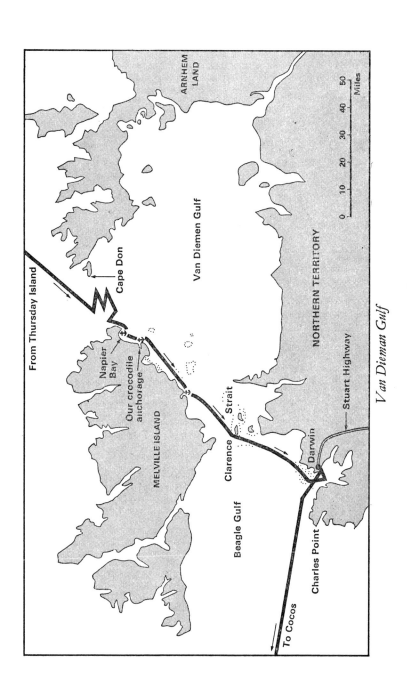

Van Dieman Gulf

although it would provide but poor shelter in the event of a south-easterly blow, for we dare not continue along that unlighted shoal-strewn coast in the darkness. Trusting the night would remain calm we brought up in six feet of water—one fathom. The night was indeed still, for presently even the gentle sea breeze faded away so that the only sounds were the occasional shriek of a cockatoo and the steady drone of mosquitoes. I was restless and ill at ease because of our exposed position, though I gained reassurance with the peaceful passing of the hours. *Rehu Moana* grounded at 3 a.m. and was afloat again two hours later. Half past five, when at last I was ready and aching for sleep, found me instead paddling along the muddy bottom among the pointed mangrove shoots, the beam of my torch transforming lethargic shoals of fish into darting streaks, while I freed the anchor warp which had twisted itself round a rudder.

Then I called quietly to Priscilla so as not to wake the others. It was necessary to take full advantage of the tide that would turn against us earlier now that we were in the Gulf than it had in the strait the day before, so first light saw the catamaran already under way, making alternate long and short tacks into a light south-east land breeze. In due course the children awoke, emerged demanding breakfast and were fed on cereals and bread and butter, much as they might have been on land, except that the patches of green mould decorating the bread might for some reason have rendered it less appetising ashore. Fiona was not hungry, nor did she feel like doing anything more energetic, I suspected, than crawling between cool sheets in some air conditioned room.

The tide began to ebb and the wind to fail almost simultaneously, forcing us to anchor in the nearest mangrove-fringed bay to await the afternoon flood. Inshore was the dark cave mouth of a creek that had wound a tortuous way among the overhanging mangroves. With its air of somewhat sinister mystery it was very attractive, irresistibly inviting exploration, but apart from excited acclamation from the girls, there was no marked enthusiasm for any such project. As the day was already very hot this was understandable. I inflated the Avon, whose air leak had by now grown much worse, and was preparing to launch it when I noticed a brown blur approaching beneath the water. Something big was swimming towards us; it was far too large to be a turtle and much too elongated. I watched fascinated, not daring to call out lest I startle the creature. The Australian Pilot had listed bandicoots among the fauna of Melville Island but here was an even more exotic denizen—a salt water crocodile about eight feet long. It continued to approach, paddling effortlessly with its four leathery feet as if unaware of our presence until it encountered the catamaran's shadow, when it came about with a violent convulsion of its whole supple body and glided rapidly away into obscurity.

The news of this encounter redoubled the children's keenness for the excursion, on which we embarked ten minutes later. They appeared circular in their bulbous life-jackets which had been put on as a precaution against the collapse of the rubber boat. The pump was connected to the main valve in readiness to replace the air that was hissing slowly out of the partially repaired seam that had ruptured at Port Moresby. As pumping proved necessary every few minutes our progress was not spectacular, so slow in fact that it took us nearly an hour to skirt the shore to the creek. But there was so much to enchant the passengers both at the edge of the forest on stilts and up the stream itself when we began to row along it, that the time seemed to flash by. Susie, who is not as a rule the most observant of children, really surpassed herself. In short order she was first to spot a turtle that boxed the compass round us, regarding us curiously from every possible angle with his periscope head and repeating the inspection on our return, a small shark, a swimming crab and rows of fish hanging in the water motionless except for their gently sculling tails.

"If you hear a noise calling out and sounding like a crocodile, what will you do, Daddy?" she asked, with more pertinence than clarity of expression.

"Splash with the oars." I hoped I sounded more confident than I felt. "Look at that lovely white heron, girls!" I had to save my breath for rowing after this because the water in the creek was flowing out fast with the ebb. Eventually what with pumping and the increasing power of the stream, we could make no further

progress. We made fast to the aerial root of a monstrously con-
torted mangrove while I drew great lungfuls of steamy air into
my chest and the sweat trickled down my forehead into my eyes
and gathered into coalescing rivulets that poured down my body.
Little bright green birds flitted through the gloom beneath the
dark olive roof of foliage like tiny balls of St. Elmo's fire. All
around us the drowned forest of the swamp was emptying into
the creek carrying with it its watery inhabitants. A shoal of pipe
fish skipped past along the surface, while close under the scummy
integument we could see through the surprisingly clear water
that the mullet-like fish that had previously been sculling motionless were now streaking down stream.

The time seemed to be ripe for us too to go lest we be stranded,
so after Susie and Vicky had picked some 'lovely flowers for
Mummy'—in sober fact mangrove berries, we pushed off to go
swirling down the winding creek, ducking for overhanging
branches, far faster than we had ascended it. The air was heavy
and still, the thermometer we found when we reached the yacht
was reading 90° in the cabin. As soon as the excited little girls,
chattering non-stop about their expedition, had been hauled
aboard and the dinghy made fast, I dived over the side regardless
of possible crocodiles and swam leisurely to and fro revelling in
what to me was the luxurious coolness of the tepid water.

We got under way in the heat of the afternoon even before
the tide began flooding, motoring away from the land more in
the hope of finding some cooling zephyr than of making much
progress; indeed after a time the Seagull overheated and stopped.
However the air overlying the pencilled line of Australian mainland across the Gulf was now superheated and rising and was
being replaced by cooler sea air from the north beyond Melville
Island. This atmospheric stirring that breathed past us on its way
to the baking continental plain was the first of the sea breeze. Soon
it freshened, depositing us ultimately at dusk a full twenty miles
farther along the coast of the island well beyond the 'watershed'
where the tidal streams reversed, so that we had reached that
part of the Gulf that emptied on the ebb out of its *western* outlet
—whither we were bound—instead of the eastern. Given any
luck at all with the wind on the morrow, from this anchorage we

should be able to carry the tide out through Clarence Strait to win clear of the Gulf at last.

DARWIN

So it turned out next morning. Sail was hoisted at six and escorted for a while by a curious turtle, we made good progress, passing out of the Gulf through Clarence Strait at noon, to set off up the estuary towards Darwin, moving briskly at first then slower and slower as the land breeze declined and ultimately died away. For a time it seemed likely that the sea breeze would fail to replace it but around mid-afternoon it began to make from astern and the water towers and storage tanks of Darwin rapidly took shape. There was one bad moment when I misread the chart— without excuse since we had by then left behind the region covered by the home-made one—and began traversing a danger-ously shallow shoal. Priscilla realised my mistake just in time and promptly put the catamaran about on course towards the main channel, her vigilance probably saving us from an ignominious stranding. We did succeed in reaching Darwin that night but only just, for by the time we got to the port the wharves were no more than etched silhouettes against the incandescent western sky and the outflowing tide was almost too much for the little outboard. We had to win our way inch by inch between the pierheads until darkness was complete, before being able to anchor in the rather dubious shelter of Darwin's small harbour on 17th August, eight days after we had left Thursday Island.

An odd dream-like interlude intervened between dropping anchor that evening and our official disembarkation with its accompanying formalities in the heat and dust of the following morning. We had no right to land at all that night, much less should Fiona have made a moonlight automobile tour of Darwin and vicinity, but that in fact was what happened.

We were going through our invariable routine after anchoring, stowing the mainsail, securing the headsails, coiling up sheets and halyards, refilling the outboard's tank with petrol, and so on, not only to achieve a modicum of order but, more important, a state of readiness for getting under way again. Everything was reasonably shipshape when we saw a figure silhouetted against the harbour lights sculling a dinghy towards us. He hailed.

"Come aboard, there's coffee on," we invited.

A man in his mid-thirties threw us his painter and clambered aboard, introducing himself as, "The only real Australian in Darwin—the rest are all Greeks, Italians, Abos and New Zealanders." I revealed that I came under the latter category, at which he remarked magnanimously, "It's all right, the mayor of Darwin is Chinese." (He is.) Our visitor shared our supper regaling us the while with facts about the town, on which he told us the Japanese had dropped a greater weight of bombs in their first raid than on Pearl Harbour. This was news to me. But nowadays, since the discovery of the incredible mineral wealth of the Northern Territory, it was booming—all kinds of construction was going on at a feverish pace, houses were at a premium. These were mainly bungalows raised to a height of one story above the ground on stilts; all new ones were fitted with solar heaters.

The relative coolness of the evening and proximity of land acted like a tonic for Fiona.

"I wish we could look at the place now," she murmured.

"Why not?" countered our friend. "I have a car right by the landing steps—come on, the night's young!"

"You two go, I'll stay with the children," offered Priscilla "besides I have so many letters to write." Since she was invariably the recipient of an impressive volume of mail, this must be true enough.

We drove around the town, where even at night the scale of new building was apparent, giving the place something of the air of a new frontier.

After a time we left the town along the road towards the south, Stuart Highway.

"What's the next town?" I asked, indicating the ribbon of tarmac that was unrolling in our headlights between flickering rows of shadowy gums.

"The Alice—she's a thousand miles down the line. Nine hundred and ninety eight," he added, impelled by a scrupulous regard for accuracy. Alice Springs is in about the middle of the continent, so that beyond it the land extends a farther thousand miles to meet the sea at the Great Australian Bight. Fiona and I had nothing to say that would not be a banality in the face of the immensity and emptiness of this land.

We returned the way we had come, resuming our guided tour which was enlivened by scandalous comment too often libellous to repeat here. One interesting institution that was pointed out to us, however, was a kind of transit or halfway centre, where Aboriginal families could be taught something of urban ways, before being accommodated in new houses where they would be living alongside European neighbours. By this time we must have been driving for two hours and Fiona was growing very tired, so our friend saw us back on board, promising to take Priscilla to the open air cinema the next evening—if he could get round his fiancée. Plainly he was unsuccessful in this endeavour for we never saw him again.

"Your cat. is not so cool now!" a voice greeted us as we stepped ashore in the blazing sunshine the following morning. The allusion was to the book *Cook on a Cool Cat*, written by Merton Naydler, who had acted as *Rehu Moana's* cook on our 1963 trip to northern Iceland. (He is my lawyer as well as my friend.) We were very pleased to be recognised—though I would naturally have been happier still if it had been my own *Dreamers of the Day* that had been mentioned! The speaker was Arthur Swain, an immigrant from Tasmania we learned later and the owner of a day-sailing catamaran himself.

"Hop in the Holden and I'll take you to the Immigration and Port offices. There isn't much doing at work today—they can spare me an hour or two," he offered. "Where else do you want to go?" We mentioned the hospital. Coming on top of the previous evening's outing, this further demonstration of practical thoughtfulness in a country where we were complete strangers was more than a little moving.

The streets were packed with a cosmopolitan throng that included a good many Southern Europeans, various Asiatics and very many Aborigines. Standing out among the city crowds were a goodly sprinkling of stockmen and drovers from outlying stations, who appeared at first glance to be wearing fancy dress cowboy costumes until we took in the sun-bleached jeans, the worn leather of high heeled boots and three inch belts and the almost equally leathery countenances above gaudy neckerchiefs. Some were White, others Aboriginal; what was abundantly clear was that their picturesque rig was their normal working outfit.

"I'll drop you and Fiona off at the hospital for the blood test, Dave. While you're waiting there the others can come home with me and see our animals."

"Animals!" Two shrill voices sounded as one. "What animals, Arthur, doggies? pussies?"

"Well we have a frilled lizard, an eagle, a kookaburra, a possum—let's see—oh, there's a nine foot python and a baby fresh water crocodile called 'Davy Crockett'! You see," Arthur continued, "my daughter Sanda—she is much bigger than you, she is twenty—looks after sick and hurt animals until they are better and can be set free in the bush again." (Sanda has kept on with her chosen vocation and was working in a wild life park in Kenya when Arthur last wrote.)

"Can we see Davy Crockett?"

"Please can we touch the python?"

Fiona and I turned away from the station wagon, where the children's chatter drowned out Priscilla's rather less enthusiastic comments, and entered the Out Patients' Department.

"You for a blood test darl?" asked a white coated girl technician, whisking Fiona off down a corridor, while I waited in the hall and passed the time reading notices about Sea Wasps. These innocuous looking jelly-fish—apart from their squarish outline they look very like the smaller English varieties—only appear in northern Australian waters in the 'Wet', the season of the North West Monsoon that lasts from December to March. But unlike the familiar spectacular Portuguese Man-o'-War, whose sting only causes very severe pain and temporary illness without lasting effect, that of the sea wasp can be lethal. On its account sea bathing ceases entirely during the 'Wet'.

Fiona rejoined me in due course minus her sample of blood. On retracing our steps to the hospital entrance, we found that Arthur had returned to take us to his home for lunch. Like most Darwin houses this one was raised eight feet above the ground on piles; what was less usual was the assortment of creatures inhabiting the cages and enclosures that occupied all the space under the house and most of the back garden as well, so that the Swains' catamaran had been consigned to the front lawn. We were introduced to the animals by our excited offspring under the watchful supervision of a very pretty, imperturbable redheaded Sanda.

"You really shouldn't touch the snakes," she warned me a shade unnecessarily "it makes them so nervous—but you can stroke the python gently if you like!" It was clear enough in my own mind which was the nervous one but I was ashamed to refuse. I suppose I must have shared the thoughtless assumption that snakes are slimy because I was foolishly surprised to find that the python's beautifully marked skin was warm and dry to the touch and felt like rustling silk as he flowed languidly down from the tree stump around which he had been wound. The rippling flow of his superbly co-ordinated muscles undulated beneath my hand as he slid gracefully if unsociably into a box at the foot of the tree.

The sharp snap of a triggered rat trap drew our attention to a chastened Vicky, who had been poking her finger through the wire netting round Davy Crockett's pool. She had snatched it back out of danger by a hair's breadth and was now regarding the little crocodile—he can have been no more than two feet long—with healthy respect. Clearly he made a lasting impression because many months later in Africa she asked out of the blue one day, "What was the name of the man who lived in Davy Crockett's house?"

Though the small reptile's delicate blade-like teeth and slim snout were capable of gashing and perhaps amputating Vicky's finger, even adult fresh water crocodiles, unlike their salt water cousins, are relatively harmless to man. The difference between the species was demonstrated by Davy's salt water neighbour in the next cage who, though no bigger, was the possessor of powerful jaws whose crooked lip line was overlapped by conical tusk-like teeth.

The following day being Saturday, the Swains collected us in their station wagon for an afternoon drive into the bush; all of us that is except Fiona, who was glad of the opportunity to rest undisturbed. Once clear of the town we began to catch sight of wallabies thumping off through the crackling underbrush. We watched flocks of budgerigars and gallahs congregating on the trees round a water hole in the cool of the late afternoon. Bug eyed amphibian fish were scuttling on their fore fins like miniature seals over the moist clay sides of the water hole itself. At several points we left the road to bump through the untracked bush, zig-zagging between trees, clumps of dry fern and tall termite mounds—the famous 'Magnetic Anthills' of Northern Territory.

The latter stood six feet and more high and were perhaps eighteen long but so flattened side to side as to measure only a foot or two in thickness, appearing like books on edge. But it was the uncanny symmetry of their alignment rather than their shape that contradicted nature, for their edges all pointed true north and south. I cannot do better by way of explanation than quote the Australian navigator Harold Gatty, author of the *Raft Book*. Writing in *Nature is Your Guide*, he says—

'Magnetic anthills (if we may forget that termites are not ants and use the popular expression) owe their straight north-south shape to a technical necessity. These hills are built of mud and the termites can only build them under very wet conditions: yet in order to become secure they must dry most rapidly. If they are built north-south the morning sun can dry the eastern side, the afternoon sun the western side and no part is left in shadow for very long during the day.

A further advantage in the directional shape of this kind of mound is that the termites can move quickly from one side of the hill to the other. This they need to do in order to obtain the most comfortable temperature during the day; for they can withstand neither the heat of midday nor the direct heat of the morning or afternoon sun. In the winter they move in the opposite way, to the east galleries for the morning warmth, to the west side in the afternoon.'

These hills are of course one of the most important bushman's aids to orientation in tropical Australia.

Another notable feature of the bush: no matter how far into the scrub we penetrated we kept coming upon brown heaps that glittered in the sunlight, while the road borders were literally carpeted with these empty beer bottles. Susie came to the root of the matter with all a child's directness.

"This is a very glassy island!" she said.

As we were boarding *Rehu Moana* on our return, a hail came over the water.

"Hallo Kiwi!" Approaching in a dinghy were Gerry Chailet, Mac Nell, and Dave Baxter, three yachtsmen we had last seen in New Zealand when they had been fitting out *Tamuré*. They had tarried a while in Darwin augmenting their funds by working in a brickworks, they told us. They were bound for England to compete in the Fastnet race. We were to meet again in Cocos, Durban and finally Plymouth, and to become very good friends, but on this first occasion they must have thought us very rude indeed. I explained rather cursorily, "My wife's got jaundice, she's pretty crook." Fiona was in fact feeling far too ill to welcome company, so I did not even invite them aboard and soon hurried below with more haste than civility.

Next day I looked up the medical officer most concerned with dealing with infective hepatitis. He proved to be a fellow country-man from the South Island I think, and one of the most stimulat-ing personalities it has been my privilege to meet. The result of Fiona's test not yet being to hand, we sat and chatted over cans of ice-cold beer while awaiting a message from the hospital laboratory. Very soon I realised that he was something of an expert on the Aboriginals and set myself to draw him out.

"Yes," he said, in answer to a question about an aboriginal medical orderly named Phillip, whose biography had recently been published, "I should know him since I trained him. He's up country now or you could have met."

"Why haven't others like him been trained as well?" I asked, "In Papua——"

"They always quote Papua-New Guinea to us," he interrupted, "but do you know why the Australians are so different?" I shook my head.

"Look, people have lived here as long as in New Guinea but newer migrations entered Papua-New Guinea, though not Aus-tralia, and these took the Papuans across the divide."

"The divide?"

"Yes, they taught them agriculture. You see," he continued, leaning forward in his earnestness, "it isn't industrial civilisation or even cities that mark off modern societies from technologically simpler ones, the enormous gulf is the one between hunting, food gathering, often nomadic people on the one hand—and farmers on the other."

His words recalled a conversation with the French botanist Jacques Barrau whom I had met in Port Moresby, the same who had told me about the canoe voyages in the Carolines. He too had spoken about the paramount importance to humanity of the domestication of plants, saying that this revolution had taken place in three separate places, quite independently as far as is known. Cultivation of wheat and barley had begun in the Middle East, rice and millet in South East Asia and maize in Central America. "And I ask you to make note," he had added with a twinkle in his eye, "that none of these three communities that each made the most far reaching of all discoveries, not one I remind you was European!"

My musing was interrupted by the medical officer beginning to speak again.

"Our Australian Aborigines are the best hunters and trackers in the world. They have phenomenal endurance. They *know* their land, the habits of the animals, the character of every plant—and that's half the trouble."

Seeing my puzzled expression, he elaborated. "It's against their deepest religious convictions, don't you see, to tear up plants or desecrate the soil by ploughing. They pray for forgiveness to its 'dream ghost' every time they spear a wallaby, and to the spirit of a gum tree when they cut it down. It is abhorrent to their innermost ideas to become farmers. And added to that they have a compulsive need to be free to wander all over their bush and desert. They stop being complete people when they lose touch with nature—I'm not sure we don't too—but the difference is that they live *with* nature instead of trying to destroy or change it."

"But," I objected, "the Territory is stiff with Aboriginal stockmen and what about the ones that are being settled in houses here in the town?"

"Well, work on the stations is largely with animals, isn't it?—horses and cattle. That's not so big a break. On the other hand the change to the town *is* so big that there is no bridge left with the past. No, the thing they don't take to is cultivation."

He paused to drain his can of beer, then began twirling the empty tin between his fingers. "You know," he continued thoughtfully, "with all these changes they hang on to what they can of their traditions pretty stubbornly. Have you seen their bark paintings, pictures of animals and legends of the Dream Time?" I nodded. "Then you know the dreaming still goes on in ceremonials and myths? Well, the ones you saw will have been done by town Aboriginals, and what do they paint—jokers who were born in a town or schooled there anyway? Motor cars, houses, trains? No, it's the eternal Dream Time they look to. What's more, there is quite a lot that is free and worthwhile in their attitude to life and nature that we are the poorer for having forgotten—and would do well to learn from them before it is too late!"

I have dwelt much on this question since then, and it seems to me that the assimilation of culture between white and black Australian need not be wholly one sided. Nor indeed has it been. There is not a bushman in the outback who has not indirectly acquired some measure of the Aboriginal's nature lore and who does not live more confidently in consequence. There must be much more that the White could learn from the Black, not only techniques but something of the understanding of nature that produces a sense of unity between man and his environment, an understanding that we so conspicuously have lost. Why not for a start a kind of 'outward bound' movement with the aim 'Black-feller show White'? It would also help the Aboriginal regain some of the self respect that must be a casualty in the general eclipse of his own culture. Perhaps something of the sort will be started; it would be well worth while.

The reader must have been thinking that I had quite forgotten Fiona's illness. This was by no means the case for in spite of the interesting conversation it seemed an age before the phone call at last came through from the hospital.

The virus of infectious hepatitis mainly attacks the liver and a battery of tests is needed to assess the severity of infection and the degree of damage. For the sake of simplicity I will refer to only one of these, which rejoices in the name of the Serium Glutamic Oxalo-Acetic Transaminase test (S.G.O.T. for short) and whose upper limit of normal is 20 units.

On the 4th August in Port Moresby, Fiona's had been 68 units.

That day in Darwin three weeks later, when she might be expected to have improved, it was 200!

Through the agency of the medical officer, she was admitted to Darwin hospital immediately.

Fiona took the blow uncomplainingly, though she is not one to relish the restriction and dependence of strict bed rest in a ward. The only compensations were the air conditioning, the kindness of the nurses and the tender buffalo steaks, for the hospital itself like most of the rest of the town was in process of being rebuilt, so was all scaffolding and half completed blocks. For the time being nothing remained for Fiona to do but rest until her next test was due and its result known.

Darwin being such a straggling city, the hospital is a good three miles from the harbour. Taxis were too expensive for twice daily visits, so I was reduced to plodding those endless, straight, dusty roads in the blazing sun. While this was no doubt good for my soul and figure, I found the effort distinctly trying and began to wilt a little. I was rescued from this difficulty by one Carl Atkinson, who had a boat-yard salvage business at a bay called Doctor's Cove that was not far from the hospital. Why not anchor there, he suggested? It would cost nothing. We gratefully accepted, finding an added advantage in that the catamaran was high and dry much of the time on a sandy beach where the children could play to their hearts' content. We could also scrub weed and barnacles off the hulls for the first time since Fiji and apply a fresh coat of anti-fouling paint.

Local children, mainly White with a scattering of Aboriginals among them, frequented the beach all day long, catching large blue crabs in the rock pools at low water and swimming when the tide was high. They befriended Vicky and Susie and I could not help being impressed by the unaffected natural courtesy of these much older boys and girls in the manner in which they took two such very young children under their care.

Two incidents stand out in my recollection of the time of waiting. One was of driving for several miles through acrid smoke that was billowing across the road from blazing scrub and of how my rather awed question about bush fires had been brushed aside with the offhand comment, "That's nothing, just a flare up in the grass."

The other concerns a remark made by an acquaintance. I must have been bemoaning Fiona's illness, for he said, "All the same you are lucky to be happily married—I had a little domestic trouble myself." I changed the subject, not wishing to intrude on delicate ground. A day or so later, someone referring to the same man asked if I had heard about his wife. "Yes," I replied, repeating the phrase he had used. "A *little* domestic trouble!" he exclaimed, "Why she shot him three times through the stomach with a revolver!" I reflected that the English have no monopoly of understatement.

In less than a week the suspense about Fiona's progress was ended. After five days in hospital her S.G.O.T. figure had fallen it is true, but only from 200 to 140, so was still very high indeed. Three months at least must elapse the doctors decided before she could safely embark on an ocean passage by yacht. Precipitant departure would entail grave risk of chronic hepatitis, leaving a permanently damaged cirrhotic liver or alternatively of acute liver failure which would only be amenable to treatment by cortisone. Neither of these dangers would attend air travel however; it would be quite in order for Fiona to fly to South Africa at once.

A wait of three months would in practice have to be extended to more than six to allow for the cyclone season. I could easily have found temporary work as a doctor in Darwin but such a delay in our return to England would have precluded Priscilla from completing the voyage. Fiona's mother in Johannesburg saved us from our dilemma by her kindness. She offered to pay the air fare.

There is only one plane a week between the two countries, which left Sydney on Saturdays stopping at Melbourne, Perth,

Cocos-Keeling Atoll and Mauritius. In order to catch it Fiona would need to fly out of Darwin before dawn on the Friday and stay overnight in Sydney. Time was short. One full day was occupied in trying to obtain a telephone connection with Africa. By seven in the evening I had still been unsuccessful and was sitting writing by Carl's silent wall telephone. The harsh glare of the unshaded bulb threw into relief the medley of coral encrusted ship's binnacles, dusty blocks and shining new Mercury outboards with which I was surrounded. The jangling of the phone that brought this interminable wait to a close heralded no good news. The operator was sorry but interference from electrical storms had caused the closure for the night of the short wave radio link across the Indian Ocean. I should try again in the morning.

Was there no other way, I pleaded. No, not really—but in very special circumstances a roundabout connection was sometimes possible via England. I explained the importance of Fiona getting away and the reason for my reluctance to tarry another week at Darwin with the cyclone season coming ever closer. The operator promised to do her best; she would call me back later at the hospital.

She proved as good as her word. At ten o'clock that night I was crouched over an instrument at the cramped hospital switchboard connected to Johannesburg at last through Singapore and London, the link-up having been specially made by operators in each country who knew the story. They did more, for since neither Fiona's mother nor I could hear each other, the Chinese girl in Singapore and the English one in London had to relay our conversation. This was accomplished with such effect that the last impediments to Fiona's forthcoming flight were quickly ironed out. Neither of us will readily forget these unknown girls; I can still hear the warmth in their faceless voices that was transmitted to us that night over 10,000 miles of wire.

There were, however, lighter sides to hospital life. This was at a time when segregated hospital facilities had just been done away with and an Aboriginal woman on the eve of her confinement found herself facing a row of unfamiliar white faces in

Fiona's ward. She settled into bed with apparent docility until lights out, when she quietly got up, slipped into the night and walked all of ten miles home. Not surprisingly this exertion precipitated labour so that the baby was born on the spot. What *was* remarkable was that this redoubtable mother picked it up and set off back to the hospital where, tired but more at ease, she went back to her bed and exhibited the infant to her admiring wardmates with smiling good humour.

Meanwhile it had been left to Priscilla to tackle the task of provisioning the catamaran—this was normally left to Fiona. After drawing up extensive lists she followed our usual practice of purchasing in bulk from the least expensive shop we could find. In Darwin this was an excellent establishment going by the name of 'Tom the Cheap's'. A yachtsman friend who was working ashore as a milkman, loaded into his van the cartons of tins, packages and plastic containers that filled it to the roof and weighted it down to the springs, and deposited the lot by our landing place in Doctor's Cove whence it could be carried aboard at low tide.

The children, who had naturally been missing their mother since her abrupt disappearance into hospital, spent much of their time inventing games in which one of their dolls was 'Mummy in the hospital' and the rest were nurses or doctors. Priscilla and I had misgivings about breaking the news about Fiona's coming flight but we were even more exercised as to how to bridge the months—a span of time beyond the little girls' conception—that must elapse before they joined her again. The active encouragement of games such as they themselves had initiated seemed one of the best means to this end. Priscilla also proved amazingly inventive about Fiona's flight or what she might be doing, and incredibly patient too, for her stories remained in demand the whole way across the Indian Ocean and of course had always to be repeated word for word.

Reasoning that the more facts Vicky and Susie had to go on to help them visualise their mother's activities the better, we took them to the airport to see 'Mummy's plane'; Fiona's actual departure would be while they were still asleep. They variously identified the aircraft with a Flying Doctor Heron and sundry ancient D.C.3's—but no matter, they understood what was happening.

To the same end the Ward Sister broke all the rules by allowing me to bring them to visit Fiona in hospital. They were overawed sufficiently by the unfamilar surroundings to remain unwontedly but blessedly still, though this inhibition in no way affected their tongues. Questions were endless about the ward, the aeroplane, the country where Mummy had lived as a little girl and about their Granny.

"Will there be lions?"

"Do they bite us?"

"Can we have one to play with?"

"Is Granny a lion?" I choked. I am very fond indeed of my mother-in-law but it is undeniable that like her daughter she can at times be formidable.

"Well, in some ways——"

"David!" said Fiona ominously, quelling me with a furious look.

The hospital office was most co-operative, discharging Fiona in the afternoon to enable her to spend her last night in Darwin aboard *Rehu Moana* to sort out and pack her belongings.

I loathe partings at the best of times and this one was particularly painful. Even now I hate to dwell on those hours, more especially to imagine what Fiona must have been feeling in spite of her gallant attempt to make everything appear normal. Around five in the morning, the 2nd of September, the beams of a taxi's headlights weaving down the road to Doctor's Cove warned us that the time to leave had come. The children had not yet begun to stir when I stowed Fiona's suitcase in the bow of the Avon and helped her down onto a thwart. A few strokes of the oars and we grounded and after hauling the inflatable clear of the water we stumbled through soft sand to the road. A cheerless drive through the darkened outskirts was followed by a no less dreary wait in the Airport Terminal where sleepy ground staff were processing unenthusiastic passengers.

At length a crackling voice through the loudspeaker summoned Fiona out on to the tarmac where the arc lights were already paling and almost at once she merged with a straggling group who were boarding the aircraft. I made my gloomy way to the exit and engaged a taxi to take me back to the anchorage. The sudden tropical dawn was flushing the night from the last of its refuges when Fiona's plane roared overhead drowning the cab's rattling.

TO COCOS

A Customs officer was waiting by the water's edge to give us clearance. By rights he should have required us to sail back to the main harbour but instead he had done us the favour of coming to our cove and at so ungodly an hour. (Our time of departure had been dictated by the tide.) His visit aboard was brief, so that by eight o'clock on 2nd September we were under way, creeping out from the land on a barely perceptible breeze until in the main channel we could drop down the estuary on the ebb towards Beagle Gulf.

We were bound towards Cocos-Keeling Atoll 2000 miles almost due westward but the first 500 miles was across the continental shelf that Indonesia shares with Australia, which at that time of year constituted one vast lake of calms and light airs. We did not plan to call at Christmas Island although it was not far off our route to Cocos, nor after Cocos would we stop again before Durban, another 4000 miles farther. This was less to avoid cyclones—for we calculated that barring accidents we would still have a little time in hand when we came under the lee of Madagascar and escaped from the danger zone—than to rejoin Fiona as quickly as possible. Furthermore it seemed likely that the children would feel closer to their mother during the relative sameness of unbroken months at sea—which appear to contract to days in retrospect—and in surroundings constantly evocative of her, than they would if distracted by ports of call.

Before very long the need to replace a sheared propeller pin on the outboard and preoccupation about lack of wind, direction of tidal streams and our chances of weathering Charles Point and escaping from the estuary before the tide changed, forced my depression into the background. Boobies were plummeting vertically into the pale green water which swirled yellow with suspended sand as the current ran. Vicky spotted a very large crab swimming by, an interesting enough sight if it had not shamed us by making as good a speed as ourselves. Such modest velocity was not wholly to be despised however because we did succeed in reaching Beagle Gulf, where we continued to drift and move by fits and starts, generally having to tack when there was any wind at all.

After a night of bright moonlight but no wind and a morning of the same calibre, the noon position placed us no more than 50 miles from Darwin and still in sight of land. The coast appeared to consist of an endless succession of sandhills, the only indication of a less barren hinterland being the smoke of widely scattered bush fires that rose vertically in columns before mushrooming out to hang in heavy palls in the still air.

The children occupied themselves with games of 'aeroplanes carrying Mummy', using their more elegant dolls, and ingeniously improvising aircraft from pencil cases with swivelling lids. The 'animal house', as they usually referred to Arthur Swain's family, had presented them as a parting gift with two magnificent toy koala bears that they adored. When Priscilla made up the first of her stories on the second day it was entitled 'The koala bear who went to hospital'.

We were now sailing over the western part of the same continental shelf we had been traversing ever since we had reached its eastern margin before Torres Strait, always with the Indonesian chain to the northward and Australia to the south. The sea remained shallow at 30 fathoms or so. The notable difference from the conditions we had experienced farther east lay in the absence of the trade wind, which we could not expect to encounter again until we reached the edge of the shelf and the bottom fell away to the blackness of the ocean floor two miles down. Whether the coincidence of these two phenomena, deep water and the Trades, was in any way causally linked, I do not know.

What wind there was, and for a third of the time there was none whatsoever and absolute calm reigned, mostly headed us during that first week. When wind breaths did darken patches of the sea into a ruffled mat, winding lanes of glassy calm usually separated the pockets of wind which rarely extended as far as the horizon.

Calms and the faintest breezes, these were our lot for three-quarters of the time all through the first ten days from Darwin.

Sailing a yacht in such light and variable winds is weary work, entailing as it does repeated adjustments of sheet and sail. At one moment the headsails must be boomed out to catch a puff from astern, a few minutes later the booms have to come in hastily and the sails be sheeted in hard to a head wind. An aberrant puff catches the staysail aback so that the yacht has to be gybed round. Always there must be an alert readiness to tack on wind changes in order to gain the most favourable slant. Then there is the changing over of sails, from ghoster to spinnaker and back again, and the starting and stopping of the motor.

On one occasion the big ghoster jib went overside beneath the bow, whence we had carefully to disentangle it from around the chain bobstay lest its delicate fabric be torn. The spinnaker, which was even bigger, once collapsed over the port upper spreader, embracing the yard so lovingly that it could only be freed with great expenditure of effort from aloft. Nevertheless this great ballooning running sail, despite hours when it hung in lifeless folds, came into its own during the latter part of our crossing of the calm belt when faint easterly winds had begun to predominate over westerlies, and for three days with but a single break it drew us gently forward. All things considered we did not do badly to pass through the 470 mile stretch of calms in ten days. In the four days of steady winds that followed we covered 511 more!

Anxious as I was for news of Fiona and eager as we all were to rejoin her as quickly as possible, those ten days seemed interminable. But to compensate in some measure for the delay there was a teeming sea life the like of which we had never before encountered.

The bush fire smudges were still hanging over the horizon to port when we saw our first sea snake. About four feet long, banded black and bright yellow, he was coiled down like a rope in the translucent surface water, except for the foot long question mark on which his flattened diamond head was angle-poised. He looked so absurdly like some stylised cobra in a child's picture book that it required a momentary effort of will and the sight of the slow undulation of his coils to break the illusion. We continued to sight them during the week that followed, as many as three at one time, always in the same heraldic attitude except for one much larger and fainter banded reptile. This one was forging along on the surface propelled by its gently threshing tail, while the head on its raised cervical segment quested ceaselessly to and fro. Joshua Slocum described seeing numerous sea snakes in just the same area during his voyage alone round the world—(the first, and with the possible exception of the totally unadvertised circumnavigation via Cape Horn by the quiet Australian Bill Nance in 1964 in the twenty-five foot *Cardinal Vertue*, the greatest cruise in my opinion ever made).

Beautiful 8-inch Pearly Nautilus shells began to appear bobbing on the wavelets—on some days we saw several at one time. They looked so buoyant floating on the surface that it was hard to credit that their actual habitat was the middle depths, where their chambered decompression system would adapt to changes in density and pressure. They only came to the surface when their owner, who surprisingly is a near relation to the octopi, was no longer alive. The sight of them brought back nostalgic memories of Fiona collecting Spirulla shells, a variety of small nautilus about an inch in diameter, in Fiji. She had manufactured the most effective ear-rings by cementing them together in pairs and attaching a clip to one. She had also infuriated me I recalled by snipping away sections of the copper strip that formed the radio earth to make into rings, to which she had cemented clumps of coloured coral. I only wished her aboard to do it now.

We did not even attempt to take a noon sight on 8th September since the horizon was so miraged as to be invisible. The thermometer, in spite of the white sheets that Priscilla had draped from rail to rail as awnings over the Perspex dome and hatches, was reading 92°F. in the cabin. We dipped buckets of water out of the sea and poured them over ourselves. Priscilla and I were less tempted than we might otherwise have been by the tantalising green depths alongside, not only by reason of sea snakes but also because of what Vicky described as 'shark sticking his finger out'. For two black dorsal fins had materialised on 5th September in company with a football jersey striped pilot fish and the number of our shadowers was augmented each day until we were being escorted by five. Admittedly they were small —the biggest 4' 6" in length, too little I thought to be worth tempting with our big shark hook.

But why not try? So I put it over the side and holding the line negligently let it run through my hand as I payed it out in the direction of the nearest lethargic shark. It whipped round instantly, lungeing with unbelievable ferocity; out sang the line, burning deeply into my palm before suddenly going slack as the $\frac{1}{8}$-inch toughened steel shank of the hook was snapped through. Dr. Perry Gilbert of Cornell University has measured

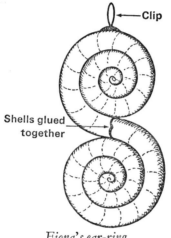

Fiona's ear-ring

the pressure of a shark bite at nine tons per square inch. I could appreciate his findings!

The unrelieved sunlight of the last few months was causing our synthetic sail fabric to deteriorate at an alarming and accelerating rate. This was brought home to us when, despite the lightness of the breeze, the jib tore on lowering and Priscilla had to settle down on the foredeck for the first of the many weary hours she was to spend doing sail repairs on the Indian Ocean. Meanwhile I did my best to render the rubber boat more serviceable, blowing it up, smearing the seams with detergent and water and marking with the girls' crayons the site of any streams of bubbles. When the fabric was quite dry—about three minutes in that sun—it could be smeared with adhesive and a patch applied.

Looking through the log-book I see that we removed the bilge pump outlet pipes which pass through the floor of the centre section above water level. For a little I was puzzled at this entry, not being able to recall any trouble with the pumps at that stage of the voyage. Then I remembered: we had disconnected the pumps in the hope, not altogether unfounded, that the relatively cool air from between the hulls would be sucked into the catamaran's interior.

One of the galley Primuses had become refractory only since our departure from Darwin, but in an accelerating tempo of destruction it soon burnt itself out completely. This did not worry us overmuch at the time since the second Primus was still functioning perfectly and cold meals were rather at a premium in that climate. Another galley complication: although Fiona had once conscientiously labelled all the containers, in the course of time the contents had been re-shuffled, so that the tin marked 'chocolate' might be packed with matchboxes and the white powder in the Tupperware box boldly stencilled 'sugar' could equally well be flour or salt. I found this impossible to cope with and had complained more than once about the perils of foraging for food during the night watches. Priscilla, however, with admirable patience and perhaps a modicum of feminine intuition, succeeded in mastering the intricacies of the galley.

One morning instead of urging the girls to remain in seclusion I called them out of their bunks myself to see a school of dolphins jumping in the dawn. Sunrise on the ocean is the most beautiful of all times when one's spirits rise with the lightening of the sky; whereas by contrast dusk at sea is depressing—to me at any rate. The sight of those dolphins leaping joyously out of swells whose eastern slopes were already gold burnished while their western inclines remained deep indigo, was an experience that had to be shared.

How much there was to be seen on this passage! A giant turtle, sleeping on the surface, only dived when we were almost upon him; we passed a profusion of brown spherical jellyfish bigger than footballs and three foot spiral ones all beaded with jewelled nodes; a swimming squid jetted unconcernedly under our stern; aloft a splendid masked booby circled. For several days we ploughed through fields of plankton, composed we found on drawing up a bucketful, of rafts of needle shaped organisms too small for their nature to be apparent to the naked eye. There was one night of unearthly beauty when the full moon was surrounded by a reddish-orange halo, and the slowly heaving sea was streaked with the reflections of the stars. Then of a sudden the glassy smoothness was shattered by dark shapes breaking surface and a school of small whales called 'Blackfish' curtsied about the ship in a dignified measure.

The children's games began to take on a rather more nautical flavour, perhaps in response to the plethora of sail trimming, hoisting and lowering necessitated by the frequent wind shifts, so that we overheard such resounding if rather odd orders as, "Vicky, you steer and I'll sheet the halyard." An unlooked for source of entertainment that was unquestionably in the true wind-jammer tradition became available at this time. Some flour and several packets of cereals—bought in Fiji not at 'Tom the Cheap's' —were found to be infested with weevils.

"Aren't we lucky to be at sea!" Susie exclaimed. And indeed breakfast time at once acquired enhanced interest and came to be enlivened by such excited comments as, "I saw him wriggle," as the children picked the insects off their plates. Sometimes friction developed.

"It's not fair, Vicky's got three and I've only two," wailed Susie, who is often oppressed by a sense of life's injustice towards herself.

"I did have three," said Vicky smugly, "but I ate one and kept the other two." While soothing Susie's ruffled feelings, I reflected that few children can have first learned to do elementary sub-traction by eating a weevil for breakfast and counting up how many were left!

The aeroplane doll games lost none of their favour in face of this formidable competition, nor did the koalas suffer from neglect.

"What *do* you think you are doing?" I asked, annoyed to see they were poling the points of my dividers into the shoulder of one of their bears.

"We are just vaccinating our koalas to stop them getting sick," explained Susie, effectively reducing me to silence, for the girls had last been injected in New Zealand five months before.

We had been under way a week before we detected the first faint suggestion of a swell from the east that proved to be the harbinger of winds that came increasingly from that quarter, though at first they were no stronger than before. Current lines appeared, their sinuous pathways marked by accumulations of seaweed, and big flocks of white terns and noddies joined us.

The tenth day, 12th September, saw us laying course between Hibernia and Ashmore reefs, two among a crescent of islets and shoals 300 miles long that forms a wall round the western margin of the continental shelf like a parapet along a cliff's edge. The red gaff mainsail of a Broome pearling lugger broke the sea's rim away to windward. The reefs on each side of us were distant enough to be well below the horizon.

It was about one that afternoon when Priscilla gave a startled exclamation and pointed towards the sky to the south eastward. A huge oval expanse on the flat under-surfaces of the cumulus clouds in that quarter was tinted a clearly defined shade of green. Neither of us had seen anything remotely resembling this before. Then, recalling a passage I had once read, I began rummaging in a locker, murmuring, "The *Raft Book*, where did I put it?" Having unearthed it among some paper-back novels instead of with the navigation books, I eagerly thumbed through the pages until I came to the diagram I was seeking. Yes, it did illustrate just such a phenomenon as we were witnessing.

This was the explanation. Ashmore Reef encloses a shallow lagoon 15 miles long by 4 broad. It was 17 miles distant on our quarter but was well below the horizon and invisible beyond 5 or 6 miles, since its highest point rose but nine feet above sea level. The sun which had passed its zenith was on our starboard bow, so that we were between it and the reef and were actually looking at Ashmore Lagoon reflected on to the lower surface of the clouds.

We were being treated incidentally to a demonstration of one

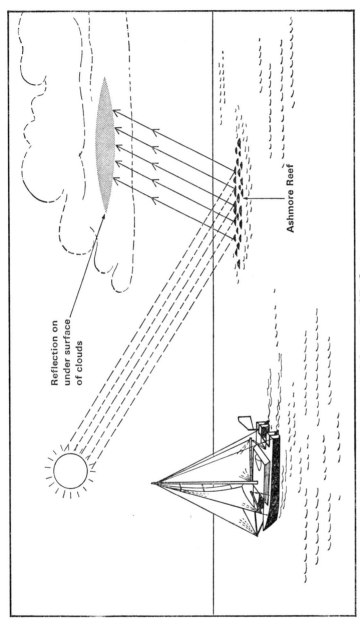

Reflection on
under surface
of clouds

Ashmore Reef

Ashmore Reef Reflection

L

of the classic Polynesian methods of detecting large atolls at a distance.

This was a memorable day in another respect because all morning *Rehu Moana* had at last been accelerating before a real wind that worked round from south to south-east while steadily increasing in power. There was a well defined ocean swell now, 'real waves—the boat has come alive', I wrote excitedly in the log. The little girls sensed the new mood that *Rehu Moana* herself seemed to be communicating to us and swung to and fro from the ratlines in wild abandon.

"Our catamaran *is* tearing along!" cried Susie somewhat breathlessly as she at length ceased her acrobatics and clung to a shroud.

This was no false alarm. The wind did not falter at nightfall and when the sun rose next morning it revealed a wind-swept ocean above which small fluffy cumulus clouds were hurrying. It was hard to realise that this was the same sea that had presented a still polished shield to the previous sunrise.

Now the trade wind hummed in the rigging with a note we had almost forgotten and would soon cease to be noticed at all, though this time through familiarity. The catamaran lurched and dipped, coasting up and over the swells while every now and then a playful wave would thump hard against the centre section, setting mugs and plates on the table vibrating. Gone was the erstwhile comfortable motion—but we were glad!

Towards evening we lowered the mainsail to ease steering, but as if in protest at being superseded the sail gave one sudden flog before there was time to smother its folds, so that a split appeared, more than a foot long. The next mischance was that the remaining Primus began to hiss and flare. We lacked a tool to extract the nipple which we suspected to be at fault, nor in the event could we obtain one at Cocos, so as we progressed towards Africa the flame burned ever more yellow and erratic and its heating power progressively declined until halfway across it flickered out altogether, leaving the Rippingilles wick stove as our sole cooker.

But no minor mishaps could mar our exhilaration as the daily runs, which had varied between 10 and 60 miles, shot up to 120,

151 and 148. Apart from the cooling effect of the breeze the weather had become cooler and reference to the Pilot Chart confirmed that we had left the 80°F. average temperature isotherm for the 75° zone. For the first time for months I had to sleep under a sheet at night for warmth—still wearing only swimming trunks.

Flying fish in greater numbers than we had yet seen sprouted from the face of every wave, their curving flight trajectories weaving a kaleidoscopic pattern of flashing silver. Once a column of dolphins approached at a leisurely pace; then up, up, went the leader twelve feet into the air, to flip over in a half roll and dive vertically. The children cried out with excitement. Up, over and down went the next dolphin and the one after in turn, until the whole line had followed the first. Perhaps they were celebrating a good day's fishing. If so, we soon had reason to do the same, for we hooked a torpedo-shaped bonito that ran deep and did not jump as the dorado does. Its flesh was red and oily, a characteristic of most of the tuna family I believe but tasted very good indeed when cooked at once.

The magnetic compass indicates not the direction of the North Pole but the Magnetic Pole in the Canadian Arctic. Thus in English waters the compass needle points west of true north while off New Zealand on the contrary its Variation is easterly. The actual angle between true and magnetic varies from place to place. As we ran our westing the Pilot Chart's figures for easterly Variation had been steadily decreasing, until on 20th September, when we were about 550 miles from Cocos, the Variation was nil. For that one day only aboard the catamaran the true and the magnetic poles were all in line so that our steering compass *did* point towards the geographical North Pole. But this convenient state of affairs did not last. Next day we had reached a point where the Variation was already 1°W. and by the time we got to Africa the westerly Variation had increased to 20°.

The purely geographical event of September 20th was made memorable by our first sight of a visitant of great beauty. This was one of the lovely golden tropic birds that breed, as far as I know, only on Christmas Island in the Indian Ocean, which was then some 300 miles to the westward. All tropic birds are beautiful. They fly with steadily beating wings, trailing the long tail feather that sailors likened to a bosun's spike—hence their alternative name of bosun bird. They are usually a snowy white but these birds from Christmas with their golden radiance seemed like creatures of the sunshine itself. In the ensuing days we passed only about 60 miles south of their home, when it became no uncommon sight to see two or three together circling the masthead.

In the last paragraph I referred to 'Christmas Island in the *Indian* Ocean'. This was to avoid confusion with its Pacific namesake which under certain circumstances can be unfortunate, as the following anecdote illustrates. The previous year a yachtsman was wrecked on the Pacific Christmas. When he reached land he attributed the disaster to his having used the wrong chart, that of the Indian Ocean island by mistake!

Cocos was not very far away when we saw the last of our golden visitors and now the same problem that Captain Slocum had faced—how much to allow for north-westerly current set across his course—began to exercise our minds. He had had the benefit of neither time signals nor radio beacons and his chronometer had consisted of an old alarm clock, yet he had reckoned so correctly that the atoll duly came up over the horizon at the tip of his bowsprit.

We scorned no modern aids, so were thankful enough to obtain time signals from the B.B.C. Overseas on 6 M.C.'s. to correct our deck watch, for some days earlier, Z.U.O. South Africa had unexpectedly become inaudible.

We altered our cabin clock rather tardily from Darwin to Cocos time. Through continuing to go by the former all this passage we had been achieving a daylight saving of up to $2\frac{1}{2}$ hours. The clocks in Darwin had been $9\frac{1}{2}$ hours fast of Greenwich; those at Cocos were $6\frac{1}{2}$; Durban in South Africa would be only two hours fast of Greenwich Mean Time. These time differences brought home the sheer size of the Indian Ocean which is second in magnitude only to the Pacific because the difference between Darwin and Durban, which should strictly be a little under seven hours, corresponds to about 100° of Longitude or more than $\frac{1}{4}$ of the earth's circumference.

By eight o'clock on the evening of 24th September, a Saturday, about sixty miles remained to go. We now cheated shamefully on Slocum's dead reckoning. I mentioned that the day was Saturday. From our knowledge of Fiona's flight schedule three weeks earlier we were aware that the weekly plane touched down on Cocos around 1.30 a.m. on Sunday mornings. A reasonable deduction therefore would be that the aircraft radio beacon on the atoll would be in operation for a few hours that night, at least until the aircraft landed. After looking up the beacon's frequency and call sign on the Admiralty List of Radio Signals, we tuned our Heron-Homer D.F. radio and switched on. Sure enough Cocos beacon came on the air at 9 p.m. so we had but to head towards the signal in order to fetch the island regardless of the current. At one in the morning a glow of light appeared abruptly on the horizon in front—the landing lights at the airport. They were switched off an hour later but our landfall and position had been amply confirmed.

We lay-to until first light when we let draw our sheets and an hour later passed through the wide entrance to Cocos-Keeling lagoon picturesquely named Port Refuge. Without once looking behind us we headed down wind towards West Island five miles away, one of the segments of the big atoll's rim and the administrative centre, off which we had been told, quite erroneously as it turned out, we must anchor. Had we but glanced over our shoulders we would have seen no less than three yachts lying in the snug shelter of Direction Island. Instead we found dubious anchorage in poor holding ground off the jetty at West Island, where the sweep of the trade wind blowing across the lagoon tossed us unmercifully, and more important, threatened to drive us in towards the land.

But we had at least reached a place where mail at last awaited us. A kindly Australian was soon driving us in his bouncing truck along crushed coral roads between endless rows of coconut palms to seek the postmaster, for this was Sunday and the Post Office was closed. Twenty three days had elapsed since Fiona and I had parted. Though *Rehu Moana* was 2,058 miles nearer Africa, another 4,000 remained to be covered. After our initial crawl of

470 miles in ten days from Darwin, in the subsequent thirteen days we had sailed 1,588.

At length we ran to earth the postmaster who was sunbathing on the beach. He kindly returned to the settlement, opened his office and gave us our letters. There were postcards for the children that bore pictures of Mummy's actual aeroplane, or at any rate one of the same type, which Fiona had posted during her brief stop in Cocos. They were a happy thought on her part and were highly popular.

But how was her health now? I anxiously tore open her letter from Johannesburg. Yes, she had had a further blood test which had been done nine days after her last one at Darwin when her S.O.G.T. had still been 140. The Johannesburg figure was 37! In that short period of time it had fallen to nearly normal.

The relief at learning that Fiona was completely out of danger and must by now be well on the way towards full recovery was literally indescribable.

Chapter 5

CAPE OF STORMS

INDIAN OCEAN

T H E broken rim of crescentic islands that encloses Cocos-Keeling Lagoon is divided between three empires. The whole is under Australian administration centred on West Island, where the civil airport is situated, with a small marine base on Direction Island, but their writ seems barely to run in Home Island, seat of the Clunies Ross dynasty and its model Malay village. The Ross family domain which includes extensive coconut plantations on the other islands, is said to be managed with benign paternalism, though one feels a certain misgiving at their rule that any Malay who leaves Cocos is never allowed to return. But since our letter from Australia requesting permission to visit Home Island was not acknowledged I own that I know nothing of it first hand. The third autonomous entity on Cocos has been the Cable and Wireless Station on Direction Island, though at the time of our visit it had all but closed down.

We had been informed of the existence of the sheltered Direction Island anchorage rather late for we dragged during our night at anchor off West Island, until in the morning but three or four inches of water separated our hulls from the waiting coral heads below. A quick change of location was obviously imperative. Hurriedly hoisting the mainsail and staysail, we began to 'sail out' our anchor by short tacking to the extent of the cable and every time the warp went momentarily slack taking in a few feet —or yards if we were lucky.

To begin with we had done no more damage than to demolish a steel beacon which in any case was a rusty and most unsightly object, when a harbour launch approached with the helpful intention of towing us off into deeper water. From then on the

167

proceedings assumed the character so aptly described by Roger Green in the excellent book of the same name, as *The Art of Coarse Sailing*.

Not appreciating that while tethered to the anchor the catamaran was making sudden little rushes in two directions, the launch incautiously crossed our bows. At my frantic cry, the alert deck hand leapt skywards a fraction of a second before *Rehu Moana*'s metal bowsprit crashed into their coachroof at the spot where his ankles had been.

Under way at last and determined not to be caught down wind again, I kept well to windward unwittingly leaving the main channel and sending the catamaran bowling across the broad lagoon over which the force six trade wind was drumming, at a gratifying pace that had the eight-knot launch rapidly diminishing to a speck astern. All went well until we neared Direction.

"What's that?" cried Priscilla, for once unnerved. 'That' was a coral head actually breaking the surface two yards away.

"You steer, I'll con her!" I sprang for the rigging whence I began waving frantic instructions as each new danger appeared and we zig-zagged among what had suddenly become a maze of brain coral. The inevitable *had* to happen. We hit with a thudding jar that nearly threw me down from aloft but so fast was *Rehu Moana* moving that she scarcely faltered in her stride, even when we struck twice more in quick succession before racing on into deep water.

Our old friend *Tamuré*, and *Renegaat* also from Auckland together with *Safari Too* from Sydney were strung out off a bleached coral sand beach sheltered by rows of wind-tossed palms, and luffing up beside *Tamuré*, we anchored. As the friendly yachtsmen swarmed aboard, I wondered if they had noticed what had happened. Apparently they had not and I was too hypocritical to tell them. Instead of deserved criticism, we were being complimented on the speed and *élan* of our approach. But a man from the Marine Base was among our visitors; he had been bushman, crocodile hunter, mate of a Broome lugger and furthermore he knew the lagoon.

"Rather shallow where you came over," he commented.

"Oh, the catamaran has a very shallow draft—only three feet,"

I replied airily. He regarded me quizzically for a moment, then lowering his voice, he added drily, "You did well not to hit then, seeing that where you were there is only two feet of water!"

It seemed an age before our guests departed and I could sprint down into the port hull half expecting to see water spurting through shattered woodwork somewhere down below. But to my all but incredulous relief, there was only one tiny leak to be found and that was a very old friend, a relic of Patagonia that we had missed during our refit in Auckland. Considerably re-assured but still doubting that we could have got off so lightly, I donned mask, snorkel and fins and dropped overside to make a surreptitious but thorough inspection. Wide swathes of paint had been stripped off but there seemed to be no other damage to the stout bottom that Prouts had moulded so well. However, to be on the safe side lest the Patagonian leak had been aggravated, I followed Fiona's example by stripping off a piece of copper radio earth. Having perforated the margins and backed it with cloth smeared with Bostik I found that nailing this tingle into place under water taxed my breath holding severely and was a heavy drain on our supply of copper tacks, most of which went to the bottom before it was secured in place. Its effectiveness was not particularly apparent but since we would be setting out across 4,000 miles of ocean on the morrow, the precaution seemed worth taking.

That evening the five lonely bachelors from the Marine Base invited us to a wonderful dinner, whose most spectacular in-gredients were the biggest and tenderest steaks I have ever eaten followed by heaps of ice cream. Susie and Vicky did full justice to their share and afterwards taxed the stamina of our good-natured hosts who carried them pick-a-back round and round their mess. It must have been nine o'clock and well past their normal bedtime before the tired girls had been tucked into their bunks under the large open deck hatch. They fell asleep at once. But before midnight Priscilla and I were electrified by the sound of childish voices singing nursery rhymes.

"What *are* you doing?" I called, too astonished to be angry.

"It is *morning time*, we are just singing from our books," they replied defensively.

Sure enough! The two little figures were sitting up in the brilliant light of the tropical full moon with their picture books propped open before them. They knew by heart every word of the rhymes—they could not yet read—but the illustrations did in truth stand out as clearly as they would have done had it really been daylight.

Not unnaturally the girls slept late next morning, 28th September, so it was after we had left the last reef pass of our circumnavigation behind us and had begun to pitch over the bumpy and erratic seas outside the atoll that they crawled grumbling out of their cabin. Perhaps my irresponsible encounter with the coral heads in the lagoon the previous day had revived past memories, but as we cleared the entrance I remembered our narrow escape at Suva all those months before and was profoundly thankful that there would be no more coral mazes for us to face.

Our stop at Cocos had been of too brief a duration to upset the tempo of life at sea for very long, so that before the day was out we had regained the familiar feeling of being at one with the ocean.

Strong blustering winds bearing spatters of light rain speeded our departure and the irregular fourteen foot seas that they built up slapped and pummelled the catamaran. At times they would smack against her beam or without warning come foaming over the quarter, or even more frequently thump hollowly underneath the centre section. These conditions gave way after a day or so to a slow heaving sea that was ruffled only by streaks of wind. The clearness of the atmosphere and the flat brush strokes of dying cumulus cloud painted across the vast sky contributed to an illusion of limitless visibility.

This relative peace was short lived, being replaced by the mere shadow of what far to the south must have been a full-bodied depression. Nevertheless the cold front passed by impressively one midnight attended by rank on rank of majestic thunderheads that trailed skirts of blinding rain. The shackle at the tip of the bowsprit chose this inopportune moment to shear and in view of the spar's violent plunges I cravenly put off the repair for some days. In contrast to the adults, both of whom were affected by the erratic motion and were thoroughly bruised, the girls remained offensively lively, trotting about the cabin in perfect balance. Their pursuits included the ubiquitous aeroplane games, dressing dolls and brushing their hair, cooking make-believe meals, drawing, colouring and so on.

It was now clear that Fiona had been justified in her confidence that the children would feel secure and at ease in the familiar little world of the only home they knew, surrounded by their own toys and belongings and looked after by Priscilla and the one available parent. But if only Fiona could have heard the girls expressing their confident certainty that their mother would be awaiting them by the sea's edge at their next landfall, she might have spared herself an unnecessary worry which I had been too insensitive to anticipate or divine. Though I never realised it, she had been tormented in Darwin by the fear that two months' dependence upon Priscilla would turn the children's affections away from herself, yet she had insisted that the girls remain in their floating home, rather than come to a house in Johannesburg where she herself might not be well enough to look after them. This must have required no mean effort of will.

Priscilla had always been deeply attached to the children and I am sure that she must have become more so during this period of their dependence upon her, so it was to her credit that she was the one to think of most of the ideas for reminding the girls about Fiona. From their eagerness to see their mother again and their conviction that she would be waiting to greet them when we arrived in Africa, it was patently obvious how well Priscilla had succeeded.

There was one small source of worry in the children's attitude. They knew their mother would be waiting for them in the place they variously spoke of as 'Granny's Island' or 'Africa Island,' so they expected to see her the moment we landed. In vain I tried to explain that the distance from Granny's house in Johannesburg to the port of Durban was, as far as I remembered from my last visit, over 400 miles! But they would not be convinced and I was left with a slight sense of foreboding about the effect of the inevitable disillusionment.

The first week from Cocos ended with the catamaran still rolling violently, the strong S.E. Trades just abaft the beam; and they *are* strong in the central part of the Indian Ocean, the pilot chart giving a figure of 56% for force 7 south-east winds (8 is gale force). Daylight on 6th October broke squally with massing thunderclouds, heavy sheets of rain and a force 7 south-east wind —as might have been anticipated from the pilot chart. What *was* unexpected was the nature of the waves; 'hollow eighteen foot seas, estimated from the rigging,' I noted in the log later that day. These were much bigger than the wind could account for.

Breakfast was over and the children were playing in the space near the steering seat. They had left the precious koala bears that Fiona had insisted must be looked after and kept dry in their own cabin. A stunning shock threw us against floor or bulkhead, as our world was momentarily darkened under a cascade of water that crashed roaring over the deck. I was in one of the hulls at the time and for a second gazed horror-struck at the great stream of water pouring down into it, until the realisation came that it must be escaping out of the children's cabin which had evidently filled when the deck hatches were swept off. Mightily relieved, I emerged into the centre section in time to observe two bedraggled figures scuttle into, and at once emerge from, their little cabin doorway, drenched through and howling bitterly, trailing behind them two soaked koalas that resembled nothing more than drowned rats.

"Our koala bears are spoilt, what *will* Mummy say?" they wailed and it was long before they would be comforted or believe that their toys would ever again become dry and fluffy. Not that Priscilla or I could spare much time for them at the moment until we had replaced the hatches, this time securing them firmly, and pumped out the water. Only after this was there an opportunity to rescue the girls' sopping wet belongings and bedding. For the next three days until we had succeeded in drying their sheets and mattresses, they had to sleep on one of the passage berths.

A south east gale of force 8, gusting to 9, blew for the rest of the day, but the freak sea that had swept us so unexpectedly was mercifully not repeated. We often speculated about its origin in subsequent weeks, fruitlessly until we reached Durban, where we heard that the off season cyclone 'Angela' had been raging at that very time and though far to the west of Cocos, could well have been the culprit.

At midnight we took in even the small boomed staysail, the only sail under which we had been running, and continued on our way under bare poles. A sudden banging and clatter on deck, when Priscilla and I had gone below after lowering the sail, startled us until the light of the torch was reflected from the enormous glowing eyes and spasmodically beating iridescent wings of a huge flying fish, just as with a last convulsive heave it flipped back into the sea.

Soon afterwards the moon breaking through the overcast revealed that we were sailing obliquely out from under an east to west shelf of heavy cumulus-nimbus cloud that blotted out sea and sky to the north from whence we had come. From then on the wind began to moderate. When we made sail again the following noon, we found that in the previous twenty-four hours, fourteen of them under bare poles, we had covered 116 miles.

As the weather improved the children were able to resume a pastime that of late had become very popular; scrabbling about the cabin in pursuit of the large cockroaches with which *Rehu Moana* had long been infested. Vicky became the acknowledged champion at this form of hunting, pouncing into corners with astonishing speed and accuracy, so that often enough she would proudly open her grubby hand to exhibit a squashed insect. But if Vicky earned praise as the relentless scourge of the cockroaches, she fell sadly from grace in another respect. The children were wont to take turns at giving out the vitamin C ration until an evening when Vicky was observed to be surreptitiously consuming extra tablets. She was sternly rebuked and the privilege of handing round the tablets was taken away.

How often damage to one's gear seems to occur at the very outset of a spell of rough weather! It was the 11th October before Priscilla could set about mending in some degree of comfort the jib that had been torn when the shackle at the end of the bowsprit had parted on the 3rd, or that I could bring myself to replace the shackle itself. But despite the small sail area we were carrying for greater comfort and in default of a usable bowsprit, we continued to cover the ground logging 1,540 miles in the first fortnight; only once did our daily run drop below the hundred mark and that was on a day of calms.

The children now began to need clothes at night (tee shirts only), for the thermometer had come to read as little as 73°F. as we continued south westward. Another sign of colder latitudes were the little valella or 'sally man' sailing jelly fish that had begun to replace the large purple Portuguese man of war.

In fact the only disquieting factor in our situation was what I described in the log as 'the skipper's contrary humours.' In this phrase I was referring not to any instability of temperament but using the somewhat archaic expression to imply that I was ill. The nature of the complaint was not obvious but the fact remained that for some days Priscilla had been having to do nearly all the work while I had lain about feverish and lethargic, only knowing the relief of coolness when I was dunked into a wave from the end of the bowsprit on one of my rare forrays on deck. Fifteen days out from Cocos the mystery was solved by the discovery that I had broken out in the unmistakable eruption of Herpes Zoster or Shingles. Since the causative virus is the same as that responsible for that homely malady chicken pox, the deduction was not hard to make as to how I had caught it when I recalled that the doctor's small son on Cocos had been recovering from an attack. Shingles is a self limiting illness but one that causes a surprising degree of debility and not a little pain, so it was several weeks before my usual energy or spirits returned, all of which put an additional unfair load on Priscilla's already burdened shoulders.

Fortunately the girls continued active and lively in spite of the generally erratic motion of the catamaran, and to our relief did not develop any symptoms of chicken pox. In a moment of inspiration Priscilla cut holes in an empty onion sack so that the girls could wear it as a play dress. Susie especially was delighted at this new acquisition, dressing up at every opportunity and balancing the piece that had been cut out on her head as a hat. As she undulated across the cabin with her nose in the air, carrying herself with all the cool poise of a model and dangling a piece of wood from one hand, I asked her what she was dressed as.

"A lady playing tennis," she answered, and at my puzzled

question amplified condescendingly, "Yes, I *have* seen them, Daddy, they carry a round thing and wear special clothes and walk up and down beside a fishing net." I was left speechless in face of so essentially feminine an attitude towards sport!

Not that the children neglected their own outdoor pursuits. In fact when they opened their chubby and absurdly babyish hands, the palms, mainly as a result of swinging upside down from the ratlines, were as horny and calloused as those of a Cape Horn seaman. Once Vicky fell, striking her head on the deck with a resounding crack. Before anyone could come to her assistance the tough three year old sat up without a tear, merely remarking laconically, "Broke our boat!"

An even more hair-raising but most ingenious game that the children invented, was the result of seeing a picture book about boys and girls skiiing and sledging. The combined activities they termed 'skedging'. (An accurate enough description of my own performance on skis, which is largely carried on in an ignominious sitting posture.) Vicky and Susie's idea was to place each foot on a scrubbing brush to which they clung with prehensile toes, and timing each roll of the ship, go slithering wildly downhill across the cabin.

Every morning a dozen or more minute defunct flying fish were to be found plastered about the deck. These the girls collected each day, often quarrelling violently as to who had the most or the biggest. Vicky being a natural clown, once carefully put one on top of her head and played patiently in the cabin until Susie noticed it, when she pretended astonishment that it was there.

As we continued to roll down the route of the China tea clippers, along which *Cutty Sark* and *Thermophelae* had so often ploughed their wake, the washing of doll's clothes on deck continued diligently, as did modelling with dough (aeroplanes mostly, or Granny's house in Africa), while working ship games became popular again—hoisting the 'kiwi sail' to go to Mummy, steering, coiling down ropes or making elaborate and complex knots. It was brought home to me more and more what tangible expression children's games give to their imagination, allowing them to act out their fancies. The day dreams of adults probably serve the same end though mentally, so that both are analogous activities, equally essential as pre-requisites to the fullest deployment of a person's capabilities.

But a new development put a term to my philosophical speculations. The appearance of a great swell not readily explicable by local winds must always be treated with reserve in an area subject to tropical storms. Such a south west ocean swell did become apparent on the 18th and though it later proved only to be the harbinger of a westerly gale, it was indirectly responsible for bringing several matters to light.

The as yet unexplained swell had suggested the advisability of checking whether Radio Mauritius had issued a cyclone warning. Since the frequency of this station was not obtainable on our transistor radio we had recourse to the big Marconi Kestrel Radio Telephone that was powered from our main batteries. To our dismay the set was 'dead'. Investigation eventually brought to light areas of severe corrosion in the lead covered cables leading to the 12-volt batteries in the hulls—we found out later that the batteries themselves had also suffered damage beyond repair —so our transmitter was out of action and our battery powered navigation lights must be regarded as only doubtfully effective.

The corroded electrical leads explained a phenomenon that had of late been causing us a lot of worry. The steering compass, formerly quite accurate, had started to behave erratically, developing a varying easterly deviation that at the time amounted to 5°. Our need of a reliable compass would be greatest when we began crossing the strong Agulhas current to make landfall on Africa; now at least we had due warning that the instrument was no longer trustworthy.

The 19th October was the day when south of Mauritius with 1,700 miles still to be covered to Durban, we left behind the zone of South-East Trades to enter an area where easterly (favourable) winds would still predominate, though with much less regularity. From now on the mainsail would be increasingly in demand to enable the catamaran to make headway against contrary westerlies. With commendable fidelity to the prediction on the Pilot Chart, that very day saw great inky masses of cumulo-nimbus cloud rearing ahead, puffed up into explosive anvil shapes. The Trade Wind died away, and in its place the ocean was swept white by a succession of westerly gale-force squalls. Afternoon found us crashing and plunging to windward in volleys of spray, well snugged down under double reefed mainsail.

A sudden crack, like a pistol shot, followed by the noise of tearing sailcloth, sent Priscilla and me dashing on deck. The whole mainsail appeared to our first appalled gaze to be entirely in shreds. The truth was a little better. The rear corner, or clew, had ripped clean away and a ten foot zig-zag tear extending across the sail had destroyed the three central panels. A sorry introduction indeed to the further contrary winds we must anticipate from this point on!

Making the best of our situation, we laced some spare slides on to the tiny storm jib, hereafter dubbed the 'trisail', and hoisted it as an absurdly small main. How odd we must look we thought, had anyone save a solitary shearwater been there to observe us, setting a jib and a staysail each more than 200 square feet in area and a jury mainsail of only 80 square feet!

Nevertheless we managed to make progress even in the teeth of the series of westerlies that now beset us and to take advantage of the intervening spells of favourable wind. Priscilla was able to sew back the clew of the damaged sail so that it could again be used double reefed but so fragile was the result that we thought it better to keep it in reserve. I do not know how many yards of 11 oz. sailcloth were stitched because the staysail soon required patching as well, and I carelessly allowed the jib to fall into the sea beneath the stem one night, so that Priscilla was not only wakened to get it aboard again but presented with yet another piece of sewing for the next day.

As the sun was setting on 27th October, the head of the gaff mainsail of a yacht whose hull was well below the horizon stood out starkly against the blood-orange of the western sky. This could only be the splendid old yawl *Sandefjord* on the last leg of her circumnavigation which had started in Durban. We soon lost the silhouette of her sail in the gathering darkness and though we crowded on sail during the night, we were hampered by our lack of a mainsail and did not see her again until Durban where she preceded us by a day or so.

For the first time since we had left New Zealand waters, we

sighted a hump-backed wandering albatross patrolling on tireless wings. This was on the last day of October, which more to the point saw us passing into the shelter of Madagascar 80 miles to the north one day before the official advent of the cyclone season.

Minor mishaps continued to occur, the most troublesome being the parting at once of two bobstay shackles at the water-line. I did not feel equal to repairing this at sea unless absolutely necessary, since the work would have to be done under water at every wave and I was still feverish. So we continued on our way with our effective sail area still further reduced.

As if sensing the approach of land, the little girls set about prising open their money boxes with a pair of scissors one day. When taxed, they explained that they needed 'pennies to buy ice cream in Africa'. How were they to know that while their money boxes contained a variety of coins from escudos to francs, there was not a single South African tickey among them? Since the first of November when we began crossing the Mozambique Channel, we had been using fresh water without restriction and Priscilla now shampooed the girls' hair and her own. In an excess of energy she even varnished the weathered bright work around the hatches and cockpit. I was gazing idly out over the sea when perhaps a mile away a whale broached completely out of the water, throwing up spray like an exploding depth charge when it belly landed. It must have been a good way off because no sound of that colossal impact ever reached us over the water.

The Agulhas, like other major coastwise currents, varies both in rate and the distance it is felt offshore as it sweeps southward down Mozambique Channel. Bearing this in mind as well as the erratic behaviour of the compass whose deviation had now increased to 10°E., we traversed the Agulhas well over a hundred miles 'upstream' of Durban, to raise what at first appeared to be a row of isolated hummocks of land on 8th November. As the afternoon wore on they coalesced into the northern aspect of Cape Saint Lucia which we rounded after dark, not without some moments of anxiety, as this was the part of the African coast for which we had been unable to obtain a chart before leaving Australia. So cautious were we that by the next morning we had lost sight of the land altogether, though the 'choppy tidal' conditions of the powerful current were only too apparent, since they produced in the skipper a most unexpected nausea.

DURBAN

In the afternoon the coastline separated itself out from beneath the jet black cliffs of thunderclouds that stood over the hills of Natal, and with dusk the lights of Durban itself began to twinkle ahead. Though our attempts to buy a chart of the Natal coast had been unsuccessful, we had obtained a large scale one of Durban harbour. This showed a straightforward well lighted entrance and if the inner channel between the breakwaters was a shade narrow, a system of signal lights was in force to ensure one way traffic.

The state of our navigation lights now justified our earlier forebodings, for in a matter of minutes after switching them on their initial brightness had faded to a barely distinguishable glow. Here indeed was a quandary. A hurricane lamp would do well enough as a stern light but how could we improvise the green (starboard) and red (port) lights? Priscilla's ingenuity and a torch wrapped in a green silk scarf lashed in the rigging took care of the starboard side, while our second torch enclosed in a pair of frilly red pants did duty to port.

While this activity had been taking place *Rehu Moana* had been steadily approaching the harbour entrance. Immediately on switching on the torches, we were gratified to see that the harbour lights changed at once to the signal denoting that the inward passage was clear.

We sailed in past the outer breakwater at 1 a.m. and began to traverse the narrow channel that led to the spacious inner harbour half a mile further on. The wind which had been largely cut off by Cape Natal was just sufficient to give us steerage way. We dawdled along feeling well pleased with ourselves, until the increasingly plain thump of a ship's engines astern caused us to look anxiously over our shoulders. The gratifying change in our favour of the harbour signal lights was now explained, since we had obviously not been seen at all. The signal had clearly been intended for the freighter that, previously hidden behind the southern headland, was now bearing down upon us at such an alarming rate. The first unwritten rule of the sea is for small vessels to get out of the way of big ones, so we lost no time in following this prudent course, seeking the edge of the channel as rapidly as the wind permitted.

Our relief and pleasure on finally entering the main harbour unscathed was mitigated by the final dying out of what remained of the breeze, coupled with the discovery that the Seagull's carburettor was choked solid with salt. It had to be dismantled and cleared by the light of the hurricane lantern while we drifted in slow circles among the reflections of the yellow arc lights on the wharves. But before long the incredible little Seagull outboard stuttered into life and at 2.30 a.m. we anchored in the lee of a sandbank off the Yacht Club, too tired to venture further. We had barely enough energy left to switch off the torches and tumble the sails down upon the deck before crawling wearily into our bunks.

But no sooner did I lie back than I found that my mind would not rest and persisted in going over the voyage. The passage from Cocos had been a long one, 3,990 miles according to the sum of our daily runs—what happened to the other ten miles that we must have sailed, we never discovered—in $41\frac{1}{2}$ days. This was an average of 96 miles a day, poor going until I recalled that the last 1700 miles had been without a mainsail. Our water had lasted well, I thought. We confirmed this next day when the tanks were found still to contain 30 gallons. Allowing for about four gallons of rainwater having been caught in squalls, this meant that two adults and two children had lived comfortably for nearly six weeks on $1\frac{1}{4}$ gallons a day. At length the racing of my thoughts slowed and wondering sleepily how the children were going to take the absence of Fiona on the morrow, I finally fell asleep.

It seemed but a minute before I was awakened by eager excited cries.

"Look, look, David, Daddy, come and see the great big birds!"

The cabin was flooded with morning sunshine so I had little excuse not to get up however unwillingly, and look out through the hatchway. Paddling delicately in the shallows by the sandbank no more than half a dozen yards away, were a flock of flamingoes that were alternately bending their graceful necks to probe under water and stretching to full height while extending great pink-lined wings.

Everyone by now being thoroughly awake, we sat down to an early breakfast. The meal was interrupted by the growing clatter of an outboard motor that gave a series of sharp explosions, then coughed into silence as it reached us. A moment later a boat bumped alongside.

The children were as usual first at the hatchway. The expressions that suddenly lit their faces revealed the identity of the visitor even before their wild shout of "Mummy!"

Fiona and her mother with uncanny timing, had driven down from Johannesburg the day before and looking out of her hotel window in the morning, the first object to catch Fiona's eye had been *Rehu Moana* at anchor.

The girls of course, having known very well all the time that their mother would be waiting for them, were no whit surprised. They greeted her with delight and were full of questions and were equally eager to tell her all about their own doings, but they took the reunion for granted as if their mother had been away for a week rather than two months.

For her part Fiona very soon realised that her unspoken but deeply felt anxieties had been groundless, and the doubts intensified by illness and the lonely weeks of separation that had so depressed her, were swept away in face of the patent reality— that in the children's eyes hers alone was the special indefinable magic of a mother. She could not fail to realise now how unassailable by any disastrous fortuitous circumstances was the bond between herself and the little girls.

A motor launch towed us to the Yacht Club landing where we made fast alongside *Sandefjord* and renewed our acquaintance with our old friends on *Tamuré* and *Safari Too*. For the first time I met personally a yachtsman with whom I had been in correspondence. This was Bruce Dalling, who had recently reached Durban in his *Vertue Carina* after sailing single-handed from Hong Kong to Tasmania, north to Singapore, across the Indian Ocean and finally down the Mozambique Channel inside Madagascar. It was on this last leg that the *Vertue* capsized when running before a gale. She righted herself but had sustained a good deal of damage aloft, so Bruce completed his long voyage with his mast supported by jury stays he had rigged at sea. His comment on this terrifying incident was revealing. Rather shamefacedly, he admitted,

"For a few days, David, I thought I would give sailing a miss for a year or two." Such is the calibre of this modest man who has been chosen to represent his country in the 1968 single-handed transatlantic race!

The children had last seen their grandmother in England two years before, so had little conscious memory of the meeting. But so much had they heard about her, that the reunion was a long anticipated red letter day. Nor were they disappointed. To begin with there was Granny's imposing house—in sober truth the Marine Hotel where she was staying. Then, as is the way with grandmothers, Nancy Sunderland spoiled them a little and for their part, while taking advantage of her patience, they did endeavour to be on their best behaviour.

Nancy was delighted at her grandchildren's manners, no doubt relieved that they showed no sign of having acquired unfortunate nautical mannerisms from their father. Fiona and I realised the impression they were making was too good to last. We were right. A greedy mynah bird was chasing a sparrow away from some crumbs in the hotel garden.

"What a naughty bird!" exclaimed Granny.

"Yes it is," agreed Susie politely, "it's very naughty, Granny, it's a *buggery* bird!"

We were met with the utmost helpfulness and hospitality from the Royal Natal and Point Yacht Clubs, not least of whose good deeds was to steer us through the jungle of officialdom that faces the yachtsman in every South African port he visits. In this respect the Republic far outdistanced any other country at which we called.

"We are completely Anglicised here—and very anti-British," remarked a retired Colonel to me in the bar of the Royal Natal. Indeed, while Durban was in many ways reminiscent of an English city, there were other differences than the obvious one of a more equable climate. One could not help noticing the unoccupied park benches marked 'Whites Only' beside which non-

Europeans, for whom no seats were provided, had to sit on the ground. On ascertaining that we were English incidentally, one such group of Indians and Africans expressed themselves with a bitterness that might well have surprised the Europeans of the country, who in all probability would never in their lives have heard the frank opinions of non-Europeans.

Nor in this prosperous city could one easily ignore the Africans and Indians who, when I emptied our rubbish into the dock side bins, thanked me and immediately set about rummaging in the refuse.

All parts of Africa have been plagued by the type of visitor who writes, 'The Dark Continent From Within' after a fortnight, and I have no intention of joining their number. This book is about our circumnavigation, so our experiences ashore remain largely incidental and of less interest than the opinions of the inhabitants themselves. Not that (even if one ignores the four to one African majority) the views of South Africans are particularly uniform.

There is for instance the conviction of the Rev. Dr. Vorster, the Prime Minister's brother, according to which the Republic is indeed uniquely favoured. For, says the Reverend Doctor, "All Prime Ministers of South Africa (with the exception of General Smuts) were appointed by God."

An Afrikaaner lawyer who became a particular friend of mine in Johannesburg—he calls me '*Rooinek*' which I counter with '*Plattelander*', (the Platteland he says, being "anywhere where you can't see the English mine dumps")—brought home to me something of the gulf between the different European communities. For this man, a well known poet in Afrikaans and a prominent newspaper columnist, had never been to a social gathering in an 'English' home before attending a party given by Fiona's mother.

A character that I recall with affection was a burly, good-natured Police Sergeant from German South West whom I encountered in a Magistrate's Court in Durban, where I was giving evidence about a theft from a yacht.

"Och, man, have you not heard of our celebrity?" he asked with shocked disbelief. "Our court interpreter here Tsafendas, he said a tapeworm in his stomach told him to shoot the Prime Minister

Verwoerd. And man, he did shoot him—all because of that tape-worm. Now there's a real celebrity for you! They say you're writing a book, eh? Well don't you forget to put in about our celebrity." I promised and have been as good as my word.

The kindly sergeant had in his own words, 'been roughing up a little' the African accused. The trial itself however was scrupulously fair and when it ended with a three month sentence, an American yachtsman who was also a witness, obtained the Magistrate's permission to speak to the prisoner.

"No hard feelings?" he asked, shaking his hand. "Got any cigarettes, boss?" The African's eyes lit up with such eagerness that both the American and I were very sorry we were non-smokers.

We all remained a week at Durban to make a start at refitting *Rehu Moana*. The sails were taken over by Bill Reynolds of Fast Sails who managed somehow to produce a much smaller main-sail than the original out of the remaining material. This served us so well that, despite the deteriorated sailcloth out of which it was constructed, it took us to England. We also began the re-placing of the lead covered electric cables with plastic sheathed ones. As only one example of people's kindness, an auto dealer named Wolfe Reiche agreed to supply us with a pair of heavy duty lorry batteries at the trade price but when we came to ask for his bill, he would not allow us to pay a penny.

Priscilla plunged at once into Durban yachting activities much as she had done in Auckland after crossing the Pacific. So many friends did she make there that, save for a fleeting visit to Johannesburg when on her way to join Nancy and the rest of the crew in a trip to the game reserve, she remained in Durban until we sailed. Dr. Hamish Campbell, who is a firm friend to all visiting yachtsmen, was more than a little impressed at her prowess at the helm of a 30 square metre. I cannot resist repeating a story about Hamish that really is quite out of charac-ter, for he is the kindest and mildest of men. (But perhaps, as Fiona often points out, it is true that the sea does have a deleteri-ous effect on the male character.) A 30 square metre offshore in heavy weather is not the most amenable of craft and on this stormy night off East London everything had been going wrong, especially for the man on the foredeck. The culminating mishap, was when the reefing handle slipped and struck him on the head, rupturing his temporal artery. This was the last straw for Hamish. Leaping to his feet he yelled, "Stop Bleeding!"

Fiona, the children and I were preparing to set out for Johannesburg when I had occasion to go into a public lavatory labelled as they all seem to be, 'Whites Only'. To my surprise there was an African inside.

"Pardon me, boss," he said and added not without dignity, "but there are no toilets for us in the town. If we pee in the street the Police arrest us. So what can we do?"

Granny's real home was no disappointment to the girls even after the Marine Hotel. There was a big garden with a stream and ponds that contained goldfish and frogs; there were long suffering bantams to be chased, great lurching Rhodesian ridge-back lion hunting dogs, a slide and a pair of tricycles. We took them every day to swimming pools belonging to friends or relations where Susie, with the aid of inflatable arm bands, at last learned to swim. (Vicky could do nearly as well but was usually too lazy to bother.) The African staff spoiled the children shamefully, with the one exception of a very old lady named Lizzie who had been nurse to Fiona's mother and held strong views on children's behaviour. The little girls regarded her with considerable awe and looked up to her as the senior member of the household.

On our visit to the Kruger National Park game reserve we were treated to the spectacle of an elephant uprooting a tree beside the road. He performed the operation by alternately levering with his tusks and pushing with his forehead, for all the world like a dentist loosening a stubborn molar, before wrapping his trunk around it and hauling it out bodily. This accomplished, he delicately sampled a few leaves that he could easily have reached from the ground in the first place, before losing interest and moving away. The reason why elephants indulge in this practice is I believe obscure and the destruction so caused is worrying to those responsible for forest conservation. Apart from this obliging elephant, Vicky and Susie's great favourites were the baboons and vervet monkeys with their lively offspring and the 'nurseries' of baby impala.

Back in Johannesburg, I took advantage of an invitation to fly to the coast in a mining corporation's plane. During the return flight we witnessed an unforgettable scene. Thunderclouds mass over the African High Veldt in summer as far north as the Congo Basin with a grandeur I have never seen elsewhere. Their summits seemed no nearer than when seen from the ground although we were flying 5,000 feet above the red soil of the plateau, itself 6,000 feet above sea level. As the pilot weaved his way between and around the escarpments of boiling vapour, curtains of rain which probably contained hailstones large enough to crack a car's windscreen, hung down around us like pillars in a cathedral nave. At our very wing tips it seemed, streaks of lightning flickered down to the drenched fields of the Transvaal far below.

Soon it was time for us to move on. Since Fiona had not yet fully regained her former energy and as the children were caught up in a hectic social whirl, we decided that Priscilla and I should sail the catamaran as far as Cape Town, where the rest of the crew would assemble.

PASSING ROUND THE CAPE

Immediately after Christmas I flew back to Durban and after several months' supply of tinned food had been stowed in the hulls, we set out on 29th December. Relations aboard were a trifle strained, as in my anxiety to complete our refit I had tactlessly criticised Priscilla's choice of friends, in the person of a young man who had been unwilling to help scrub off barnacles. In retrospect I can see that my criteria were a little narrow and appreciate her annoyance!

Priscilla however did look very nice in a new bikini as we pulled away from the pier under tow by a motor boat, so much so that someone exclaimed admiringly if rather obscurely, "Look at the cook!"

At five that afternoon we cast off our tow outside the breakwater, only to bounce up and down for the next few hours in the full rip of the Agulhas current that bore us along as efficiently as did the negligible breeze. Priscilla checked the compass bearing against the setting sun—the deviation was 10° East as before so there was hope that it would at least remain consistent during the 800 mile coastal passage to Cape Town. Towards moonrise about 9 p.m. a steady nor-nor-easterly (favourable) wind came up, the seas suddenly smoothed beneath the twin slicing hulls and the land silhouette to starboard spangled with the lights of villages and townships, began swiftly unrolling.

Priscilla had prudently boiled a great slab of bacon before sailing, bearing in mind the watches we should be required to keep so near land and the possible bad weather on passage round the 'Cape of Storms' when cooking might not be popular. The bacon together with tomatoes, avocados, bread and butter, did provide the most acceptable of cold meals while they lasted. There was an ample supply of fruit of which my own favourites have always been mangoes despite their stringy composition and my beard, which makes eating one a process reminiscent of a whale sieving plankton through its baleen.

Judging by the weather forecast, we might anticipate fair winds for at least three days but this expectation was not to be realised. The N.N.E. wind continued true and strong only until 4 o'clock the following afternoon, by which time we were about 135 miles down the coast from Durban and some 15 offshore. Then the north wind failed and unmistakable signs appeared that a south-west gale was imminent.

I could almost quote the *Africa Pilot* Vol. III verbatim to describe this gale, so 'textbook' was its course. Before its onset the barometer as the Pilot predicted, had been falling but, also according to precedent, had started to rise again. The sky initially remained clear 'apart from small patches of cirrus', until 'a low bank of cloud appeared on the south-west horizon and soon covered the sky'. Long before this ominous and quickly moving wall of cumulo-nimbus could reach us we had made everything secure and were snugged down to boomed staysail and trisail, bearing in mind that the Pilot also warned that S.W. gales were 'dangerous for they often sweep down suddenly from the high land in the interior with violent squalls.'

The overcast swept over the zenith at six in the evening, while at the same moment everything visible was extinguished under a seemingly solid avalanche of rain. Nothing could be heard above the howl of the wind. Like a spurred horse, the catamaran leapt forward in the darkness.

An hour later with the gusts reaching force 9, we lowered sail and lay to the kedge anchor which we trailed in the water astern, not of course with any idea of anchoring in such deep water but so that its resistance would hold the quarter to the rising seas. This manoeuvre had the two aims of preventing the catamaran from lying broadside on and of restraining her from losing ground too quickly down wind.

Unfortunately *Rehu Moana* lay in the track of shipping and so little could we see through that blinding rain that we determined to take turns at braving the elements every five minutes by the clock to scan the horizon. This was easier said than done. The rain flung in sheets horizontally by the gale, stung our eyes and would have virtually reduced visibility to nothing were it not for the lightning that had now become almost continuous. This trying state of affairs was of mercifully limited duration; soon after midnight the gale began to subside, the sky to clear so that the light on Cape Hermes could be seen winking away to starboard while to seaward the lights of a ship materialised a little too close for comfort.

We took in our anchor but did not make sail again until morning as the sea remained very steep and the wind gusty and from dead ahead; moreover we were not sorry to rest after such anxious watchkeeping. Even with this indulgence the ground lost in the gale had been made good by noon, though after this progress became disappointing as a short lived easterly was quickly replaced by a repetition of calms and head winds. We concluded reluctantly that another S.W. gale must be brewing, a prognostication that was confirmed before midnight, though this time the wind remained relatively steady at force 8 without such violent gusts and with rain showers of but brief duration. On this occasion we hove-to under the trisail. The lights of East London came into view between the rain squalls as we fore-reached very slowly all night and until three next afternoon, through a very irregular sea set up by the opposition of the gale to the Agulhas

Current and by the latter spilling over the hundred fathom line into deeper water.

Resuming our laboured progress to windward—in these difficult conditions Priscilla gallantly fried sausages—we were relieved when in the early hours of the morning, the unseasonable wind relented and for a time became north east—favourable. By noon, it was the fifth day from Durban, we were off Port Elizabeth having covered more than 400 miles despite the gales and head winds—no doubt in large measure thanks to the Agulhas Current.

This satisfactory if not brilliant progress was not destined to continue for very much longer. Off a particularly featureless stretch of cliffs beyond Port Elizabeth we were stopped in our tracks, first by a calm then by a west-nor-westerly wind, at this part of the coast right 'on the nose', that began blowing that evening and continued for the best part of a week. I must admit however, that these conditions would have hampered us far less had I not misguidedly kept far too close inshore.

We were then over the narrow eastern part of the Agulhas Bank which fans out in an extensive shelf with depth less than 100 fathoms off the tip of Southern Africa. I had no doubt been unduly intimidated by the warning in *Ocean Passages for the World* which read . . . 'it should be borne in mind that there is much less sea on the Agulhas Bank in depths of 60 or 70 fathoms or less, than near its edge and southward of it.' Moreover the French single-handed Jean Gau in the Tahiti ketch *Atom*, whom the reader may remember as having gone aground on the skeleton strewn Warrior Reef in the Torres Strait, had been turned over by a gale there a year before (fortunately without losing his vessel) not far from our present position.

With all this in mind I was afraid of venturing too far offshore, and literally hugged the cliffs for several days while we tacked back and forth into the eye of the wind. This section of the coast being devoid alike of lights and radio beacons, we failed to appreciate at first how little progress we were making. With the realisation, we devoted all our energies to sailing efficiently to windward against blustering force 5 and 6 winds and steep seas, noting our position against landmarks ashore. Though it soon became evident that far from being assisted by the Agulhas, we were having to stem a very powerful counter current, I failed to draw the obvious conclusion—that we needed but to go ten or twenty miles to seaward to escape it.

When I belatedly made this move on the fourth day, a further westerly gale was almost upon us. In the whole of those four days we had only made good a shameful 99 miles over the ground, though we must have sailed many hundreds through the water!

A happier feature of that time was the sea life. Innumerable fishing gannets were busy diving near the cliffs while further out the albatrosses were wheeling and great rafts of brown petrels were bobbing among the waves. But the sealions were the outstanding attraction; every day until Cape Town we saw them playing about the ship. One night when the sea was afire with phosphorescence, six of the sinuous animals weaved blazing trails across our bows and in and out between the hulls in a ballet of breathtaking speed. Another afternoon a female sealion that was trying to eat a fish she had caught was continually being pestered by a pair of brown boobies. She stood their persecution for a minute or two, then bit off part of the fish and threw it with a toss of her head far over the water. The birds promptly swooped down upon it, quarrelling between themselves but leaving the intelligent sealion in peace.

On 27th January, the day when I had at last been sensible enough to put 20 miles between us and the coast with its counter current, we began to make real progress despite the unchanging head wind. The generally overcast skies of the past few days had cleared that morning, the clouds rolling back from a hundred mile panorama of the Outeniqua Mountains. But for all its beauty that afternoon's unnatural visibility boded no good and in fact heralded another gale. Sure enough towards sunset the mountains were all of a sudden engulfed in haze, and by nine o'clock steep breaking seas were sweeping out of the night driven by a strong south-west gale of force 9. So pleased had we been with the way *Rehu Moana* had lain to her trailing kedge anchor in the first gale that we resolved to repeat the experiment, with the difference that instead of using the anchor which had been difficult to haul aboard again, we streamed warps attached to motor car tyre fenders over the quarter.

I had often allowed the catamaran to present her 17 foot beam to the seas and lie broadside on to gales in the past. Gales on the Agulhas Current however have an unenviable reputation for abnormally steep seas. In lying by the quarter the catamaran presented 50 feet (the distance from one stern to the opposite bow) that would have to be upended before she could be capsized and waves of that height are so rare as to be practically unknown—certainly in summer storms in temperate climates. Since *Rehu Moana* had been struck unexpectedly by near gale-force squalls under full sail earlier in her career (off Rio for instance) without once lifting a hull from the water, there was reason to believe that only a freak sea could ever upset her. We were confident of having now ruled out even this contingency by our manoeuvre.

Apart from a split tiller bar that was soon lashed together again, this gale caused us no anxieties—with one notable exception. There had been far too many ships for our liking all the way from Durban but we were not seriously embarrassed until we were lying comfortably to our warps on the morning after the onset of the gale, when a particularly large freighter began showing well-meaning concern for our safety. He steamed round us coming nearer and nearer at each circuit, until we began to fear a disastrous collision. We dared not wave him off lest the gesture be misinterpreted as a signal of distress. In vain we sat shivering on the deck with false smiles glued to our faces, pretending to be drinking with huge enjoyment from empty mugs. The ship only came closer still.

The inspiration of course was feminine. Getting a hair brush, Priscilla kneeled on the wildly gyrating deck clutching hold of a stanchion with one hand, while with the other she began negligently to brush her hair that was streaming out horizontally before the gale. At last the captain of the freighter understood; with a blast from his siren he departed.

We got under way again that evening but as the wind for the sixth day in succession remained westerly, we began to discuss seriously how we could let Fiona know we had merely been delayed because we were soon due in Cape Town. I even considered the heartbreaking course of giving up the ground we had gained and running back to Port Elizabeth to report. Fortunately Priscilla dissuaded me from such extreme measures and hit on the alternative of exhibiting a large notice asking a passing ship to report us to Cape Town as all well. We duly painted one on the back of a chart and the very next day were able to have it acknowledged by the M.V. *Barrier* en route to Cape Town.

The same afternoon the wind freed at last giving us a run of 123 miles in the next 24 hours.

The following day, the 11th of January marked an important milestone in our voyage—the rounding of Cape Agulhas, which in 35° South latitude is the southernmost tip of Africa, 60 miles further south than its better known neighbour the Cape of Good Hope, and divides the Indian Ocean from the Atlantic.

The fact that the extremity of the African Continent should have been christened 'The Cape of Storms' by the Portuguese explorers, emphasises the extent to which major headlands become breeding places for gales, interfering with wind and current circulation patterns. As mentioned above, Cape Agulhas lies only in 35°S while by way of comparison the strait that separates Australia from Tasmania or that between the North and South Islands of New Zealand are both in 40°S; the southernmost tip of New Zealand 47°S; while Cape Horn in 56°S is 1,250 miles further south than any point in Africa. Yet no doubt because of the magnitude of the continent of which it forms the apex, the African cape despite its low latitude, enjoys a reputation for bad weather second only to the terrible Cape Horn.

After passing Cape Agulhas we had altered course decisively northward, so that the coastal lights that came into view and ultimately dropped astern were eastward of the ship, the opposite side from when we left Durban. A fair southerly wind that struck cold in spite of the length of its journey from Antarctica did not falter next morning, when the strengthening light revealed Table Mountain ahead.

By 11 a.m. Cape of Good Hope was abeam to starboard and we had begun passing the rocky shores of Cape Peninsula at a good seven knots. There was no reason why this rate of progress should not have continued, as it would have done but for my error in

Cape Town

Walvis Bay: repairing after the accident

Lobito: the bimba boat

closing in too far and coming within the wind shadow of the mountain. All efforts to escape again were in vain, so chafing at this delay so near the goal, we made the best headway we could with the aid of every stitch of canvas that could be mustered, and eventually the motor as well.

Impatiently we watched as seaside suburbs slowly gave way to the city itself. A broken-backed wreck that lay so close to a lighthouse that the helmsman must have been attracted to its light like a moth to a flame, caused us a good deal of concern for at first we took it for an islet not marked on our chart. Dusk was beginning to fall when we came to the breakwater at last, to see Fiona who had been following the catamaran's snail-like progress for the past three hours, waving from the end of the mole.

CAPE TOWN

Thanks to her efforts and the courtesy of the Royal Cape Yacht Club this was the best prepared arrival of the voyage. A club launch even came out to escort us to a mooring alongside the pontoon in front of the clubhouse where Fiona and hospitable yacht club officials were waiting. So many yachtsmen being present, I suppose it was inevitable that I should do something ridiculous. While making fast I imprudently took a turn round one of our sheet winches, which was instantly flicked into the air to describe a brief trajectory before plopping into the dark water with a depressing air of finality. Prophetic impression! Attempts to recover it on the morrow were frustated by the muddy bottom and icy temperature of the water. I was unpleasantly reminded that it was a very cold current indeed that ran up this side of Africa well up into the tropics.

But to return to the previous evening. Just before Table Mountain was lost in darkness, we were treated to the spectacle of its aptly named 'table cloth' of cloud spilling over the summit into nothingness. Nor were we spared its usual concomitant, a 'howling north-easter' that ensured we spent no restful night.

While Priscilla predictably went off sailing in Table Bay, Fiona and I were taken rock climbing on Table Mountain by Joan and Brian Quail from the Mountain Club of South Africa. After five pitches of the climb, called if I remember 'Bottleneck', I was forced by sheer exhaustion to retreat ignominiously along a ledge, while Fiona and the rest of the party completed the ascent. Reflecting ruefully on how mountains become steeper and higher as the years go by, I wended my way among the protea bushes up an easy track to the flat summit. Here my depression was somewhat lightened by coming across a long black snake which I followed but being uncertain whether it was a mole snake or a yellow headed cobra, forbore to attempt its capture.

After this sorry performance I excused myself from Fiona's next expedition with the Quails, which was up the Falcon Face of Table Mountain, joining instead a more leisurely excursion to a hut in the Banhoek range. This was organised for Priscilla and the children by our very good friend, the veteran mountaineer Bob Hinings. As we bumped along a particularly rough cart track in Bob's car, the girls were reminded of a similar ride in a jeep on Easter Island, site of the famous stone images.

"Are there stone men heads here too?" asked Susie. Without a moment's hesitation Bob, who has an apt turn of phrase, pointed to his companions.

"Yes, there are—those two have both got stone heads!"

The long uphill toil after leaving the cars proved almost too much for Vicky who had to be carried at times but Susie resolutely plodded on refusing every offer of assistance. When we got to the hut which was at the mouth of a *kloof* beneath a soaring knife-edge arrete, both girls were as proud of themselves as if they had climbed the Eiger North Wall. A bathe in a frigid mountain stream soon restored them and whetted their appetites for the *braaivleis*—a superlative type of barbecue—that followed.

Once again I must refrain from detailing all the help we were given in putting finishing touches to the refit initiated in Durban, lest the reader's patience be tried too far. Suffice it to say that everyone we encountered in this city—that must rank alongside Rio as the most beautiful in the world—was the soul of kindness.

We were delighted at the arrival of our friend Frik Potgieter and his crew in the 36 foot trimaran *Zulane*. They had left Durban the day after us on the first leg of a round the world voyage, but had prudently taken shelter in East London and Port Elizabeth during the bad weather.

Another welcome encounter in Cape Town was with the American barquentine *Verona* that had last lain alongside us in Tahiti more than a year before and we spent an agreeable evening renewing acquaintance with Chris Sheldon, her skipper. It was with real distress that we heard later that *Verona* had been lost by fire off Sao Tome in the Bight of Biafra, fortunately without loss of life.

When the time came to clear ship we were amused to see that Vicky and Susie had been put on the Crew List labelled 'Deck Hands'. This was less absurd than it would have been a year earlier; they could now practically hoist the 'Kiwi Sail'—the mainsail—unaided, by dint of swinging their combined weight in unison on the halyard. They had also been of somewhat doubtful assistance to the crew of the yacht *Suhaili* in Durban during preparations for a voyage to England. The paper was being removed from cans of food which were then painted with identifying symbols. The girls were delighted when their aid was enlisted. In fact they proved such diligent and enthusiastic strippers off of labels that the painters were left so far behind that all record of the contents of many of the tins was lost!

Fiona, Priscilla and I stayed aboard *Rehu Moana* during our sojourn in Cape Town but the children shared a suite with their grandmother at the well-known Mount Nelson Hotel (where Prime Minister Vorster had but recently crashed the colour barrier by entertaining Chief Lebua Johnson of Lesotho). Fiona and I were a little concerned as to how the girls would react to the return to their tiny cabin and staple diet of cold baked beans and potato crisps after such luxurious surroundings. We need not have worried at all as it turned out, for they settled down as contentedly as ever.

But we were glad the girls would soon be en route to other lands for a different reason best exemplified by letting this newspaper item speak for itself. A Mr. Van Niekerk of the South African Bureau of Racial Affairs announced that an imported nursery school book was 'to be investigated', adding that "objections had been lodged against illustrations showing a little coloured boy sitting with white children admiring a birthday cake at a party . . . this was a blatant way to indoctrinate the mind of the child in integration."

On 25th January 1967, with a full ship's company once more, we put to sea.

The children had bidden a mutually tearful farewell to their grandmother at the quayside and a little later Bob Hinings had waved goodbye from an escorting launch as it turned for home, so there was only a brace of penguins to watch us clear the Outer Breakwater at 4 p.m. northward bound up the coast of Africa but heading directly towards England at last.

Chapter 6

DISASTER ON THE SKELETON COAST

OUR next objective was South West Africa. Its thousand miles of coast washed by the cold and foggy Benguela current comprises a waste of sand dunes, isolated guano islands and stretches of more than a hundred miles of forbidden diamond territory enclosed by barbed wire and searchlights. It was once the old German South West, now held in disputed mandate by South Africa. The fishing port of Walvis Bay lies about midway along the shoreline of the Namib Desert which extends for 300 miles by the sea and 50 inland. The northern fringe of the Namib is known as the Skeleton Coast and is the haunt of hyena-like animals called 'strand wolves' and the scene of such anomalies as lions padding across the sand dunes at night to prey on the seal rookeries.

We could look forward to fair winds and a favourable current on the 780 miles passage to Walvis Bay and in the event did complete the run in eight days despite carrying but little sail for the sake of comfort and ease of steering and making a large enough detour to keep between 50 and 100 miles offshore. But strong following winds do not preclude rough seas so I was concerned lest Fiona so soon after her hepatitis should be more vulnerable to seasickness than ever. Quite the reverse; this affliction that had for so long rendered putting to sea a dread nightmare of utter misery for Fiona, appeared at last to have been mastered.

We have to thank our friend the Johannesburg anaesthetist Dr. Arne Cilliers, for suggesting the successful drug and for providing Fiona with the 0.3 mgm. tablets of Hyoscine Hydrobromide that wrought such a miracle. The logbook records it.

On the first evening at sea a note of cautious optimism is being sounded—'The Hyoscine seems to be helping F. She is sleeping quietly like the rest of the crew.' Next afternoon's entry reads

'Suddenly sick.' This however refers to myself. There is no mention of Fiona. But a veritable paean of triumph is sounded in the third day's note. 'Fiona on deck, Hyoscine brilliant!'

That this happy resolving of Fiona's appalling handicap was no mere coincidence was proved in all subsequent passages, for never again did she experience more than temporary discomfort.

The steep, choppy waves were generally capped with white and the ocean, which was always shrouded in light haze except when this thickened into a clammy mist, looked as cold as indeed it was. The piercing southerly wind struck chill. Up to about 45 miles from the coast the water was alive with a vast concourse of gannets and cormorants but further out bird-life thinned, coming to consist in the main of Cape hens, storm petrels and albatross.

As if their over-stimulated minds were in need of the peace and quiet of the sea after the variety and excitements of Durban, Johannesburg and Cape Town, the little girls slept solidly for thirteen hours the first night, waking at the unwontedly late hour of 8 a.m. After breakfast they contentedly set about modelling Plasticine animals though Vicky, to everyone's surprise and without exhibiting signs of distress, was sick on a couple of occasions in the next day or so. Each time she seemed perfectly herself again within minutes.

There were some new and popular pastimes now, one of them playing cards, especially Snap and Beggar my Neighbour. The children's ability to count and to add up numbers at once began making enormous strides. I can still picture Vicky, her head barely topping the table but wearing an expression of serious concentration as she shuffled her cards with all the finesse of an expert.

A Snakes and Ladders board was another acquisition that aroused intense and often heated competitive spirit, even if this was manifested in an unconventional way. For the attraction of having one's counter land on a snake's head so that it could slither delightfully down to the tail, far outweighed the much duller aim of winning the game; so much so that Vicky was even caught cheating so that she could slide down the snakes more often.

We had anticipated expressions of nostalgia about 'Granny's Island' so recently left behind and so there were at times as in this suggestion from Susie. "I think I will go with Granny in the aeroplane—you can meet us with the boat, David." But it was with real astonishment that we heard her for no apparent reason recalling a forgotten delicacy from a very much earlier time.

"What we would like best of all are the things we had for going to school in New Zealand, long things," Susie remarked with characteristic circumlocution and lack of clarity.

"Garlic stick biscuits, do you mean?"—an intuitive question from Fiona.

"Yes, do they have them in England?"

"No."

"Oh, what a pity! What a pity! I would like to go back to New Zealand to school."

Fortunately the tragedy of this unattainable longing was soon forgotten.

None of the foregoing gives any indication of the extent and manner in which the girls, especially Susie, were beginning to assert their own individuality at this time. Susie was at the start of that infuriating, compulsively negative phase that children apparently have to pass through possibly to demonstrate their independence. At the time of writing just after her sixth birthday, it seems to be ending. But a year ago she was graduating from the relatively standard, "Mummy, you are horrible" stage, to periods when she complained in the most provocative way she knew, that nothing was right—"Why do you always give me nasty things to eat and such ugly clothes, Mummy?"

Vicky has so far avoided the worst of this, though no doubt she will become exasperating enough in her turn. Her reactions so far have tended to be more odd than awkward. Thus while generally stoical, as in contenting herself with remarking of a bleeding big toe, "I've bomped my mummy toe," she also had the ability to make the most extraordinary fuss over trifles. A single drop of spray on her pillow was sufficient to bring forth ear-splitting squawks and howls.

But generally speaking the girls were content enough and rather better behaved than on land and about as calm as such

CHILDREN OF THREE OCEANS

active minds as theirs could possibly allow them to be. They slept
well, played happily—though they could have done with more
exercise on deck than the weather allowed, and ate heartily. The
morning chill made them appreciate hot breakfasts for the first
time since leaving Patagonian waters two years earlier, their
favourite being mabela, a kind of brown porridge made with
Kaffir corn.

The prevailing southerly wind seemed to vary in strength
during the day in accordance with a well defined pattern. It blew
gently in the mornings and early afternoons, after which it
gradually increased to force 6 or 7 during the night. By midnight
it would have begun to die down again until in the morning it
would once more be force 3 or so. Despite the fact that we were
quite a way from the coast—our average offing was 75 miles—
we wondered if this might be a particularly extreme sea breeze
effect.

The wind vanes had great difficulty in keeping the catamaran
heading straight 'downhill', especially at night when the strong
wind that drove low scud across the face of the pallid moon also
herded toppling seas into our sterns, jostling them until the yacht
slewed off course. However in the latter part of the night lighter
winds and correspondingly greater swells would bring welcome
relief after watches that had been so unwontedly occupied by
steering.

An entertainment that enlivened one of the rare sunny mornings was an aquatic somersaulting display given by a large and
deceptively flabby looking seal. All the rest that we passed were
asleep with their whiskered noses barely breaking surface as they
lolled on their backs with angular jointed flippers sticking up in
the air at odd angles.

Our tactics along the West coast of Africa were to remain well
offshore until within striking distance of the port and then to
turn in sharply across the current, generally taking bearings on
one of the radio beacons that are plentifully distributed round
Africa and being careful to make landfall to windward and up
current of the harbour. We altered course obliquely towards the
Namib coast from a point 45 miles from land and the same afternoon a cormorant alighted on deck and after a thorough in-

spection of the available facilities, decided to make itself at home on the partially inflated Avon rubber boat.

Enthusiastic cries of "Cormint, Cormint!" greeted the visitor and with one accord the junior members of the crew began chanting.

> "The common cormint or shag
> Lays eggs inside a paper bag,
> But wandering bears may come with buns
> And steal the bags to hold the crumbs."

But though it failed to oblige with an egg ours more than made up for this omission by squirting the Avon every few seconds with the raw material of guano. We forgave it the mess it was making when it allowed Fiona to stroke it with no more than a token snap of its bill and at nightfall it tucked its head under its wing and went to sleep. The next morning Priscilla who was on watch saw it groom its feathers, waddle unsteadily to the rail and take off.

February 2nd was the day we expected to make a landfall and reach Walvis Bay if the mist that shrouded sea and low lying desert coast would only relent a little. At 2.30 p.m. we crossed a dividing line between currents that was clearly marked by foam as far as the eye could see. Water dipped up in a bucket as we approached and again afterwards, was found to have increased 2°F. in temperature from 65°F. on the seaward to 67°F. on the landward side. A dark line that came in sight about four o'clock proved to be a featureless stony shore against which lines of surf were breaking. An intermittent lifting of the haze allowed us glimpses of high sandhills further inland.

The children appeared to be solving at last the puzzle of all those apparently unrelated places that were yet parts of Africa, for after ascertaining that here was another, Susie said thoughtfully,

"I think Granny's island is a lot of pieces all stuck together."

At length Walvis Peninsula and its termination at Pelican Point came in sight, a low-lying sand spit with nothing of the bold headland about it. This was not unexpected since Admiralty Chart 629 labels as 'prominent' a pair of sandhills only *six feet*

high. In fact the most noticeable feature apart from a lighthouse
was the concourse of big white pelicans stalking solemnly across
the sand.

We rounded the point at dusk, sailing approximately over the
place where in 1951 the Pilot informed me, three small islands
'had appeared suddenly before sunset rising from a bubbling
sea'. After emitting clouds of evil smelling hydrogen sulphide
gas they had disappeared again before morning, leaving the sea
in the area as deep as before. Walvis Bay was evidently a place
where almost anything might happen!

Altering course beyond Pelican Point we came on the wind
and commenced beating against breeze and tide across the five
mile wide bay towards the town. We proceeded with caution,
taking repeated bearings on the lighthouse and the cluster of arc
lights over the wharves, concerned lest by keeping too long on a
tack we might go aground on one or other unlit shore. Ultimately we anchored a little eastward of the town and a prudent
half mile offshore to leeward of what the smell suggested could
only be the pilchard canning factories.

"A very beachy place, David," remarked Susie with evident
approval as she surveyed the desolate waste of sand dunes next
morning. We were debating the next move to make when an
alarmingly large tug came churning alongside and the pilot,
Captain Jens Von der Fecht, jumped aboard us. He offered us a
tow to a berth but since it turned out that he was also the Vice-
Commodore of the Walvis Bay Yacht Club we felt in honour
bound to come alongside the wharf under our own sail. This we
accomplished for once without mishap (and without any presenti-
ment that our voyage would come near a tragic ending at that
spot).

The quayside was soon thronged with curious onlookers, for
the most part dark skinned Ovambo contract dock labourers with
a scattering of tall high cheekboned Hereros, who gazed with
equal disdain upon their compatriots and Europeans alike. Here
and there among the Africans were individuals whose steato-

phagous buttocks pointed to a Busmanoid or Hottentot ancestry. Lively coloureds from Cape Province appeared to hold
the more skilled positions, crane drivers and the like, while the
port officers and agents were Europeans. Being precluded by
South African law from mixing socially with the rest, it was only
these latter we were able to welcome aboard.

Walvis Bay is a fishing port, originally a whaling station. Even
in German times it was an English enclave and today is a bunga-
low town that exhibits none of the German watering place
character of Swakopmund twenty miles away. In common with
the rest of South West Africa, Walvis is trilingual, everything
from street names to newspapers being in Afrikaans, German and
English. As often as not the town is blanketed in sea mist or by
whirling wind-blown sand. Both fog and the temperatures which
are in the 60's (it is hard to realise this is the tropics), can be
blamed on the cold Benguela current for, once away from the
coast not many miles inland, mirages replace mists and the thermometer reaches the hundred mark. The climate is warmer in
winter because then easterly winds blow out from the warm interior. As if belying the damp atmosphere the rainfall amounts
to only $\frac{1}{3}$rd inch a year.

This is the main reason for the town's roads being made of
salt. So hardpacked and blackened by oil and tyre marks was it,
that I refused to believe it was not asphalt until I had surreptitiously broken off an insanitary looking fragment to taste.
Appreciable rain would of course dissolve away such highways
and they are impractical more than ten miles inland because the
salt crumbles in the drier atmosphere but in the coastal region
they are highly successful.

The salt is collected from pans north of Swakopmund where
the visitor can be guaranteed the sight of great flocks of flamingoes. But we have been unlucky (except in Durban) over
flamingoes. On a later occasion a flamingo hunt in Angola produced only mosquitoes; but we fared better in the South West
because we did see a solitary bird standing forlornly in a salt pan.

A description of Walvis Bay town would be incomplete without
mention of the canneries, slipway and wharves along the foreshore, or of the two locations of tiny hygienic utility houses—

one location for Africans, the other for Coloureds—beyond the outskirts among the dunes.

We were made welcome by the Yacht Club whose members included a good proportion of the German, Afrikaans and English communities which mixed in the friendliest atmosphere, something very rare in South Africa proper. Apart from the sailing people, we found an immediate bond of common interest with Thys Moolman (pronounced 'Tais') the bank manager, in his love for the desert. For the magnificent lonely sweeps of its gaunt rock and sand touches exactly the same chord in a man as does the thrilling waste of empty ocean.

Bank managers appear so often in this book's list of acknowledgments that an explanation may not come amiss. The introductions had come by way of Fiona's banker uncle. It was a novel experience for me to be greeted practically on the quayside by members of a profession that like most of us I had always regarded as minor deities. Though we first met Thys in this way, his and his family's friendship soon grew far beyond the bounds of any official duty.

One memorable day Thys packed us into his station wagon together with his wife and four children, a little dog and the cooking utensils, provisions and wood for a *braaivleis*, and leaving a rather bleak and overcast English summer day at the coast, drove thirty miles straight into the blazing heat of the central Namib. We built a *braaivleis* fire of the camel thorn wood we had brought on the dry bed of the Khan river *kloof* beneath a solitary umbrella thorn. The walls of the canyon were wind eroded into fantastic pinnacles and echoing concavities all veined with red, green and yellow, and they threw back the sun's heat in shimmering waves, so that even in the shade of the thorn tree the temperature was over 100°. While Thys toiled in the smoke and added heat of the fire with the fortitude of a salamander and the children panted in what shade they could find, Fiona, Priscilla and I searched for specially attractive fragments of green copper-bearing mineral and silvery lead ores. Susie had accompanied us at the beginning until she burnt her hand on a stone she had incautiously picked up, after which in high dudgeon she had rejoined the other children.

The appetising aroma of barbecued steaks and *boerewors* sausage told us the meal was ready; the prospect of washing it down with cans of beer was doubly attractive. This was the moment when it was discovered that the car had bogged down in the soft sand. Two hours' hard work, made no easier by the fact that the chromework was too hot to touch, were required to free it before we could squat down to a congealed lunch. The thought of the cold Atlantic water that only that morning would have produced shuddering repulsion now took on an aura of paradise. When we reached the coast again the reality of the green breakers did not affect our resolve and all plunged in to luxuriate in the exquisite coolness.

The swim revived the adults sufficiently for them to give way to the pleading of Thys's children that we should climb a large sand hill. The slope up which we slipped and staggered seemed never ending until it abruptly terminated in the crest line and our eyes were jerked up from dazed contemplation of sand grains streaming past our feet to a vista of interweaving sand ridges that swept in faultless curves to the horizon. It seemed an intrusion when our horde of yelling children surged up over the crest and hurled themselves down the steep leeward slope in clouds of sand.

We climbed into our bunks exhausted that evening and fell asleep at once. We were awakened to a night of terror.

Before reluctantly undertaking the task of re-living and writing about those few hours, I must sketch in the framework, especially our position relative to wharves and other vessels. Did I say earlier that *Rehu Moana* was not insured? I forget whether I did or not but in fact insurance had been impossible to arrange; as the devil dreads holy water, so do insurance companies abhor yachts on long passages.

We were lying port side on to the wooden part of the wharf in the position shown in the diagram, at the berth to which the port officials had assigned us. We were assured that strong winds were unknown from the one exposed quarter—the north. Nevertheless as a matter of ordinary prudent seamanship we had laid out two anchors to hold us off the jetty—our own kedge from the bow and a heavy grapnel borrowed from Jens's tug astern.

Confident in official advice and in part in our own precautions, we retired to bed.

A violent impact that set the whole catamaran shuddering brought us to abrupt wakefulness. The time was half an hour after midnight on the morning of 6th February. Another reverberating thump came as we scrambled hurriedly out of the hatchways. A north wind—the very one we had been told was unknown—was blowing and was getting stronger minute by minute. Moreover it was building up steep vicious seas that came driving out of the darkness into the pool of light cast on the water by an electric lamp on the quay. Each wave was lifting *Rehu Moana*'s port hull higher than the wharf and, as the water receded, letting her drop heavily against the massive piling. The crests were white tipped as the waves built up with incredible rapidity, dashing themselves against the ship so that sheets of spray were flung across the deck to mingle with the intermittent jets that spurted up between yacht and quay.

Every time *Rehu Moana* surged back with the undertow we took a desperate turn or two on one of our anchor warps, hoping to haul her clear. At first it seemed we were going to be successful for the force of the impacts began to ease a little but after a short time it became apparent that the anchors could not hold the catamaran against the growing fury of the sea and were dragging. Now the forward flare of the port hull was being lifted several feet above the level of the quay and as the catamaran crashed down again we began to hear the awful splintering of a ship's timbers that seems to a sailor as if his own body were tearing apart.

The children had been moved out of their bunks and were lying on a passage berth in the main cabin, their eyes big with silent questions. There had been time enough only to make them comfortable; neither leisure nor the fore-knowledge to offer them any sensible reassurance.

We did our best to hold *Rehu Moana* off by pushing with boathooks, with oars, and by wedging our behinds against the curve of the deck and fending off with our feet. But no action of ours could do more than delay further damage. Two feet—three—four—the jagged line of split frames and shelf and crushed plywood extended further and further towards the bow. And still the wind continued to blow harder and the sea to dash against us with increasing fury.

It was clear that, devoid of a powerful motor as we were, the only way to save the vessel from more serious damage was to have her towed clear.

I cannot remember having any particular feelings at the time; my emotions seemed numb; but I do recall how wildly my heart was beating and the feeling of constriction in my throat as if I could hardly breathe and was about to choke.

"Do your best to fend off, but for God's sake mind your legs or you'll get them broken," I called to Fiona and Priscilla, having to shout to make my voice audible above the tumult of wind and sea and grinding timbers. "I'll try to get us a tow."

But how? On gaining the upper dock level, the lights on the overhead cranes showed me only rows of deserted sheds and darkened offices and the blowing sand around my feet drifting against tracks of a dock siding. The dock gate; a policeman was stationed there—perhaps there would be a telephone.

"But man, this instrument is for official use only. Is you a dock employee?" The constable was regarding me impassively. With what remained of my breath, for I had been running hard, and summoning the remnant of my self control, I again explained patiently the situation. After due cogitation he relented. The telephone bell seemed to go on ringing for ever before the sleepy voice of the newly awakened Harbour Master came over the line.

"We must have a tow," I urged trying to control the desperation I felt and make clear exactly what was happening. "But get us a launch quickly please," I finished almost shouting now. He promised to do his best.

I ran back towards the yacht, conscious for the first time of the bruises and cuts on my bare feet from sharp stones, rusty coils of wire and assorted bits of ironwork that the darkness had concealed.

It was shortly after one when I got back. Priscilla and Fiona were still braced on deck, holding off with their feet. This was a dangerous proceeding for if a leg should slip and be trapped between the catamaran and the wharf, it would be caught under the full seven tons of the vessel in its plummeting descent. Both had put on jerseys but were wearing only the scantiest of pants, so their thighs and buttocks had been rubbed raw against the sanded non-slip deck. Neither said a word of this at the time.

Three quarters of an hour dragged by without sign of relief and still the seas increased. The forepart of the hull port was sustaining ever-increasing damage. The rubbing strake was gone and ten feet of the deck had loosened. No major damage so far but what was in store? Might not the yacht break up and if we delayed too long how should we get the children ashore? Thus I reasoned in a mood of near hysteria; reflection would have shown that the catamaran would stand a great deal more and that help could not much longer be delayed but I seemed to have lost the capacity for sober thought.

It was no credit of mine that the serious error of judgment I committed then did not bring consequences too awful to contemplate.

"Get those children ashore now," I shouted to Fiona.

I am sure she knew the decision was wrong but she was also aware that in such a situation only one person could give the orders. Tears were streaming down her face as she bundled them in their sleeping bags and refusing aid picked up Vicky and poised herself by the rail. The yacht was being sucked back from the hardwood piles as each wave receded, leaving a yard-wide gap of swirling black water, then it would surge back on the crest of the next breaker to smash against the wharf with fearful violence. No need to speculate on Fiona's fate or the child's if her timing were other than perfect or her nerve should falter. She jumped and landed safely. Then after wedging Vicky securely against some railings to prevent her being washed or blown into the sea, she went back for the heavier Susie. Once again she balanced herself, judged the moment and made that terrifying leap. Susie was tucked in place beside her sister and they lay sobbing side by side.

The exhausting labour of fending off had not long been resumed by all three of us when the Harbour Master arrived. He made an effort to help us hold the catamaran off for a few minutes,

Nearing the Azores

then realising the hopelessness of the endeavour he sensibly went away to hurry the launch crew.

A week later we heard, he said to one of the pilots:

"You know these girls on the catamaran?"

"Yes, they are very attractive, aren't they?"

"Yes, but that was not what I meant," explained the Harbour Master, "it's their toughness—the way they were fending off that night—I tried it for about five minutes and I'm still so stiff I can hardly walk!"

As the towing launch could be expected at any moment the children would have to be got back aboard. With no more than a reproachful glance in my direction, Fiona picked them up one at a time for the no less perilous return, though this time she passed each one over to me as soon as she reached the deck and I handed the wriggling bundle on to Priscilla.

A few minutes more and the Harbour Master was back with the launch crew and soon that heavy steel boat about the same length as *Rehu Moana*, was churning the water with her propeller and the exhaust of her 400 h.p. diesel was audible above the roar of the breakers. It was around 2 a.m. when we buoyed and then cut both anchor warps and slipped the loop of the launch's steel wire towing cable over the catamaran's starboard bow cleat.

Two explanatory points are appropriate here, even at the cost of holding back the action of the story a little.

First, a towing vessel having two stern bollards, must attach the tow rope to the starboard bollard if she wishes to turn in that direction, and vice versa. It will be clear from the diagram that we could only be swung clear *to starboard*.

In the second place, the case history of the launch skipper which I only learned later, is apposite. Due to incompetence he had been demoted step by step to the command of ever smaller craft until he had ended up in charge of the least important of all—the launch. Below this post he could not sink, being a European who however stupid must not take second place to a Coloured man.

After what has been said it will come as no surprise to the reader that this man made fast the warp to his *port* bollard and throughout the subsequent proceedings, though the frantic Harbour Master was shouting clearly audible orders from the

quay in what Fiona assures me was the most pungent and idiomatic Afrikaans, he neither attempted to move the cable to the
starboard side, nor once eased his throttle.

Until *Rehu Moana* was taken in tow she had sustained only
relatively minor damage. As the steel warp tightened I yelled in
protest, hardly believing my eyes, for the launch had turned
sharply to port *towards* the quay and at full speed smashed us into
the jutting angle of the main concrete wharf. The fearful impact
drove us onto a pile of great concrete blocks that tore right
through our planking in no fewer than six places below the
water-line alone.

Relentlessly the tug kept on pulling us still at full throttle, still
in the wrong direction. The already damaged port decking was
torn away and with a splintering of Perspex and snapping of
metal rails and stanchions, we were dragged further into the
obstruction until our wire shrouds hooked round the angle of
the concrete. They taughtened like bowstrings but held. Something must soon give way. Both the crew were near crying and
Fiona was screaming. "This is too much, it's all finished."

"Get below both of you," I shouted. "The mast will go." The
children's own cabin was directly beneath the heel of the mast but
they were well out of harm's way in the main cabin. The mast did
not come down though its butt was driven downwards, splitting
the frames and mast supports and bursting both deck and cabin
sole.

There was a violent jerk as the port bow snapped off bodily
and at last we pulled free. For good measure the launch skipper
who was still gazing over his shoulder with stolid indifference
at the havoc he had wrought and had failed to look where he was
going, cannoned us into the stern of a moored freighter. After
tearing us clear at the cost of further rending of our woodwork, he
began towing us still at full speed, straight out to sea, bound it
seemed for South America. Eventually we persuaded him to turn
back and to cast us off near a group of moored trawlers, where we
anchored.

"Our boat is all broken up, what shall we do now? We have
no cabin left at all." Susie was shivering with strain and exhaustion. There was no answer to give. We could only make the sisters

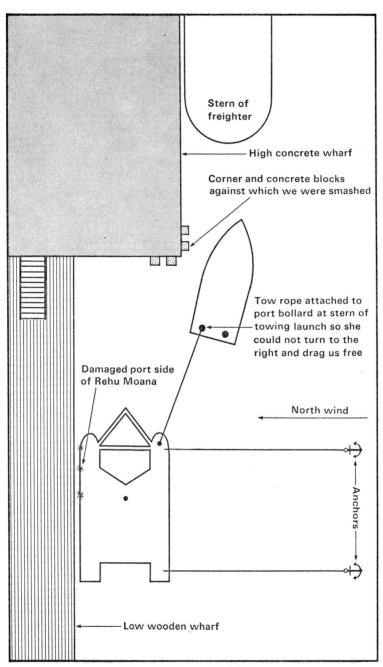

Stern of
freighter

High concrete wharf

Corner and concrete blocks
against which we were smashed

Tow rope attached to
port bollard at stern of
towing launch so she
could not turn to the
right and drag us free

Damaged port side
of Rehu Moana

North wind

Anchors

Low wooden wharf

The Accident at Walvis Bay

as comfortable as possible on the passage berth for what remained of the night. In the darkness it was not possible to assess the full extent of the damage. Water was spurting in through half a dozen places and from behind the sprung collision bulkhead. It could be controlled but only by dint of pumping 600 strokes an hour, so we would have to take turns at the pump until *Rehu Moana* could be beached. The one comfort we had was that if a conventional boat had sustained even half as much damage as the catamaran had that night, she would long since have foundered.

Between spells of pumping we dozed fitfully, jerking spasmodically with nerves as we tried to rest. Depression and hopelessness settled over me while I worked the pump handle and thought bitterly about the launch skipper. Of course it is easier to blame another person or even impersonal chance than oneself (typically men hold the government responsible and women their husbands for any calamity), but in our own disaster there was no doubt who had been the major agent. Still, dwelling on this would help us very little. Susie's question was the only one worth asking—'what were we to do?'.

I was still asking it, even more gloomily after having inspected the damage more thoroughly by daylight next morning, when Jens rowed out to us and took me ashore to find out what could be done. Fiona and Priscilla meanwhile would have to carry on with the pumping. It soon became clear that officially nothing much could be done. Neither government departments nor harbour authorities have any liking for compensating anyone for an employee's action. There were repair facilities but for planked and spiked fishing boats, not glued plywood yachts. The slipway was busy with trawlers and impossibly expensive, £100 being the charge for a single week.

But *unofficially* it was a totally different story.

"Are you able to lie like a gentleman?" The ruddy-faced former sea captain leaned back in his chair, regarding me with twinkling blue eyes. Then he turned back to his desk and picked up the telephone. Jens also did some 'phoning. My memory for names and details is unaccountably blurred for that morning but some incidents do stand out.

"Oh no, you can't go up on the slip." Dave Owen the slipway

manager sounded shocked. "But," he added smiling, "couldn't our steam winch—it can move 200 ton trawlers—haul you up the sand *alongside* the slip, and wouldn't you be as well off? After all the sand is free so it won't cost you a penny."

A conference lubricated by iced canned beer convened aboard the Pilot Boat. The three pilots, Jens, Ian Simpson and John Canner were all master mariners and also active members of the Yacht Club.

"Only one of us at a time is needed here," said John. "We can take it in turns to work on the catamaran."

"We have our own power tools; we built our own racing dinghies," explained Ian.

"No one else can be trusted to work with plywood," Jens clinched the argument. The discussion of ways and means continued. "Ovenstones are bound to let that chap of theirs— what's his name? Yes, Tworek Fagen, do the metal work."

"Wood? We can ask Bill Le Roux."

"Viggo Lund is the chap for electrical work—he can tackle anything really."

To go much further in describing this and similar conversations could lead I fear to breaches of trust. Suffice it to say that in the days that followed materials such as sheets of marine plywood, rolls of glass fibre and cans of resin, topside paint or marine antifouling, would appear mysteriously and when I would ask what there was to pay, the donor would look pained and either answer "Nothing at all," or drop his voice and confide, "it is a gift from the Spanish trawlers (or someone else) but don't tell them!"

I returned aboard in a very different frame of mind from when I had stepped into Jens' dinghy. Half an hour before high water we took in the anchor, started the Seagull, and ran on to the beach beside the slipway, where Dave Owen, his assistant Tom Lund (a Yorkshireman and no relation to Viggo of the same name who is a Dane) and a crowd of grinning Ovambo labourers awaited us and with the aid of the steam winch hauled *Rehu Moana* up the sand to above high water mark.

After seeing the smashed chaos that had once been the children's cabin, Jens went home for a word with his wife Lore and a little later, having re-arranged the sleeping arrangements of their own three children, they returned together to convey Vicky and Susie back to their house to stay. Our little girls made themselves quite at home and even attended kindergarten with their hosts' children. The fact that no English was spoken in the school did not seem to perturb them in the least.

"What do you say to the teacher when you get there?" we asked curiously.

"*Guten Morgen*," replied Vicky looking surprised at such an obvious question. Susie, who has a good natural ear began singing to herself.

"Listen," explained Lore giggling, "that is what they sing when they line up like a train to go and wash their hands."

"Toc, toc, toc. Eisenbahn,
Alle Kinder waschen sich."

Susie was singing in an irreproachable accent.

During the early morning hours of that day we had been consumed with bitterness against one stupid man. The same evening, less than twenty hours after the débâcle, we went to our bunks aching and exhausted (not to mention the crew's skinned behinds) but warmed through and through by the friendship that was being offered in our time of greatest need. Our feelings of renewed hope and gratitude can be imagined—they have to be because I cannot find words to express them.

Three days had gone by since the catamaran was pulled up the beach. Large areas had already been sanded off ready for the plywood patches. Screw holes in hull and patches would be drilled next, then Aerolite glue and hardener applied; lastly the prepared patch would be screwed into place. Once the glue had set the joint would be stronger than the surrounding woodwork but as an added precaution we were sheathing every repair with glass reinforced plastic (fibreglass). The port foredeck had been removed and Ian Simpson, who was spending so much of his time working on the catamaran that his wife complained he was virtually living aboard, was cutting back the damaged woodwork and fitting a new shelf, stringers, decking and rubbing strake. More than once the yacht had the rare privilege of having three master mariners, John, Jens and Ian, all working aboard at the same time.

Viggo Lund had assumed the responsibility for one of the most difficult repairs—making and fitting new supports for the mast. He had already designed and constructed a massive structure of athwartship and fore and aft frames for this purpose and proposed to use one powerful jack to lift the centre section back into position while supporting the weight of the mast itself by another. This whole operation promised to be prolonged and tricky but Viggo was confident of the outcome; since he held a degree in electrical engineering (rather surprisingly, as he owned and ran a large bookshop), this confidence was based on a knowledge of engineering principles and detailed calculation.

As anticipated at our conference aboard the Pilot Boat, Two-rek's employers had given him a free hand and all workshop facilities to deal with our metal work. So the ugly twisted tangle of aluminium rail, bent stanchions and queerly angled rigging screws had now been removed to the engineering shop for straightening or welding.

Some of the Coloured fishermen from the trawlers hauled out on the nearby slipway lent a hand from time to time, though the majority not unnaturally tended to hold themselves aloof. The opinions they expressed were quite as pungent and individual as those of so many other people we met in southern Africa. One for instance—the skipper of a trawler—avowed he would much rather live in South Africa than England. A more common attitude was expressed by the engineer of another fishing boat who gave us a hand with the painting. He told me just as decisively, "We have no rights in this country, they oppress us—things will have to change in this country."

The foregoing paragraphs suggest that *Rehu Moana*'s crew themselves were doing nothing at all to help repair their own vessel. We were not making quite such a poor showing as that. While the skilled guidance undoubtedly emanated from the three pilots and Viggo, we did not spare ourselves either. Among a host of other activities, I can remember Fiona fitting new Perspex decklights; Priscilla grey with choking dust, clinging gallantly to a heavy vibrating sander; myself tossing all night with a violently itching torso, before learning the advisability of wearing a shirt for that particular job.

The empty plastic watercan buoys that we had carefully attached to our anchor cables before cutting them, had been removed by 'persons unknown' by the time we went to recover our anchor and the grapnel we had borrowed. (I suspect our C.Q.R. with its thirty fathoms of $1\frac{1}{2}$ inch nylon warp had gone the way of the buoys.) Tom, the Yorkshire Lund, went down in a diving suit and two Ovambo oarsmen and myself dragged a small grapnel behind a dinghy repeatedly over the site. The borrowed grapnel did come to light but our own anchor must already have been spirited away. Our friends would not allow us to be the losers however, and two small Admiralty pattern anchors off wrecks were presented to us before we left.

One unlooked-for result of the accident was that when all the damaged woodwork had been removed, so much of the actual interior of the vessel's timbers had been laid bare that we were able to inspect them with a thoroughness impossible in the most rigid of surveys. As more and more hidden places were revealed, we had increasing reason to be thankful for the quality of the materials, in particular Bruynzeel's specially manufactured iron-tough plywood and the laminated mahogany frames, and to Prouts for their superb workmanship in the original construction of *Rehu Moana*. After nearly three years' voyaging—four counting northern Iceland—the wood was as good as new—no softening, no dampness, no trace of delamination in the plywood and no sign of attack by teredo.

"Time we had an evening out," said John. "What about having dinner in Swakop, we can get someone to mind the children?" Jens suggested.

This proposition was timely because Fiona had returned from shopping that afternoon with brow black as a thunderstorm over the High Veld and was barely speaking to me. And over dinner at the Kaiserhof in Swakopmund she eventually relaxed sufficiently to tell me what was the trouble. Now Fiona's knowledge of Afrikaans, commonly unsuspected because of her lack of a South African accent, was often a source of entertainment as men frequently made audible comments about her in the street. Since these remarks were generally complimentary even if coarse, she did not mind. In the Walvis Bay shop that day however a woman, speaking in Afrikaans, had asked another:

"Which woman from the English yacht is that?"

"Oh, that is the wife," her companion replied, "the other is the young one." As thirty year old Fiona is two years younger than Priscilla, who through wearing little make-up was often taken to be the junior, it can be imagined why she was in a state of speechless fury. In fulfilment of a husband's role I was the one held to blame!

The lively Kaiserhof evening restored harmony among *Rehu Moana*'s company. When we trooped down the steps to the beer cellar after dinner, the sense of being in Africa, already attenuated by the atmosphere of Swakopmund, was eliminated. The crew off a German ship broke off in mid chorus and crashing their tankards on the table, shouted a gallant welcome to Fiona, Priscilla and the wives of our companions. The notices on the walls, the bottle labels, the lettering on beer mats, all were in German, and the coolness of the air below ground was reminiscent more of Europe than the tropics. It was almost impossible to overcome the illusion that we were sitting round a table in some dockside vault in Hamburg or Bremen.

Repair work continued steadily, so that each day saw the reconstruction advance another step further. Our friends became insistent that we must find time to see something of the country. Some had even gone so far as to make all the arrangements for us to be given hospitality in Windhoek 200 miles inland so that we could be taken on a two day round trip.

"But," we protested, "we can't simply go off, especially on such a long drive as that and leave other people to work on our boat!"

"Why not? You can't be working every minute," they answered and would not be denied.

Their thoughtfulness vouchsafed us vivid glimpses of this strangely beautiful land. There was the brilliance and nearness of the desert stars seen through the clear window of a dry cloudless atmosphere. The stillness at night would seem absolute; then from a dry watercourse would sound the lonely yelp of a jackal.

We saw the Kuiseb River Canyon a hundred miles inland from

Walvis, running deep with mud-reddened water, so that I was swept off my feet when we started to cross and was forced to swim to reach the other bank. Yet on rejoining the same river near its mouth that afternoon, we found the bed to be bone dry—as it had remained dry for years. None of us would have suspected that the river was still flowing seaward—but twenty feet below our feet—nor that a traveller need only dig deeply in any of South West Africa's dry river beds to come across ample water.

Ostriches several times sprinted across the road, sand spurting from under their pounding feet. As a variation from springing off over the stony desert, some would keep on ahead of the car at a steady 30 m.p.h. like rabbits hypnotised by headlights. Once the isolated rocky outcrops that covered the whole of a valley floor came to life, transforming themselves into a great herd of gemsbok that thundered over the skyline ridge in their own swirling dust.

There was the day that it rained towards the desert's inland fringe; such rain that the plain disappeared beneath a six inch deep sheet of water and our two vehicles, a Land-Rover and a Willys Jeep, broke down repeatedly.

Fiona collected specimens of rose quartz, tourmaline, beryl and mica one baking airless afternoon when Thys drove us into the Rossing Mountains in a borrowed Land-Rover. The peaks and gullies of this desiccated range appeared to be as devoid of life as the moon, until we saw how a camouflaged section of rock could detach itself to become an improbably gaudy lizard. An insect that was stone coloured and invisible at rest, took fright at our approach, startling us with the bright scarlet of its underwings. Over a dun coloured waste devoid of vegetation a mottled yellow jackal streaked for the horizon.

I could not help being amused at the Land-Rover belonging to Rudi Allers, our host on the five hundred mile drive that included Windhoek. He has a sense of humour so will not mind my mentioning that in contrast to the thoroughness with which it was equipped with extra fuel capacity, built-in 30 gallon water tanks and supplies of snake bite serum, the tyres had seen better days. Needless to say our only mishap was a puncture.

Hottentots, Batards of Rehoboth Territory, Ovambos, Hereros, even a few Bushmen; the native population of South West Africa is far from homogeneous. It was surprising how little even long resident Europeans seemed aware of this variety. The remnant of the Hereros that survived the Von Trott massacre of around 1909 are still detested by the German population, who speak of them with the utmost dislike.

Knowing of the Hereros' history I had fully expected them to be a broken tribe, especially as they were in trouble again. They were to be shifted from their insanitary, picturesque location on a wooded hill outside Windhoek to a new one which we also saw, a compact grouping of tiny brick houses, surrounded by a high fence and overlooked by a Police Station. But there was nothing demoralised about the Hereros, who had refused to move. In retaliation, the Municipality at the time of our visit had cut off water, electricity and sewage disposal services from the old location. Under these circumstances, it was astonishing to see that the handsome Herero women in the now doubly unhygienic location were still splendidly turned out in colourful ankle-length dresses, while their arrogant men folk showed haughty disdain in their manner towards the Germans.

Near the lip of the mile-high escarpment where the High Veld falls away to the red rock and sand of the Namib, we halted for lunch by a ford across the bed of a *kloof*. Susie had missed this particular drive through having tonsillitis and it was noticeable how Vicky, without her elder sister, was showing unwonted initiative and originality. It was more than we bargained for, however, when she carefully put on her sandals, peered intently for a moment at the summit of a rocky hill, and set off purposefully, a minute sturdy figure that was quickly hidden among the dry reeds and boulders of the river bed.

"Where are you going?" I asked curiously, having hastened to catch up. She never paused in her stride.

"To play with that monkey." She pointed. Following her finger I could just discern a tiny blob on the skyline of a *kopje*, though its nature would have been beyond me to determine.

"That's a baboon sentinel," confirmed the amused Rudi back at the Land-Rover. "Listen!" From but a little way up the *kloof* sounded the coughing grunts of a troop of baboons.

Two and a half weeks after sustaining her injuries, *Rehu Moana*, resplendent in fresh red paint and newly anti-fouled, stood ready for launching, her repairs carried out to such a standard that she was a stronger boat than ever before. All damage that is, that we knew of then. There was one sprung seam that I had failed to spot as it had yet to open and was virtually invisible.

Viggo's mast supports were a considerable improvement on the old which had been constructed in Seydisfjordur hard by the Arctic Circle in 1963. Decking, stanchions, decklights and fittings had either been replaced or rendered as good as new. The girls were back in their fully restored cabin. We still found the achievement difficult to accept; a little more than a fortnight earlier it would have been inconceivable.

If it has been difficult to find space to acknowledge benefactors at other ports, here it would be impossible. I can only hope to have related the story well enough to give an idea of what we owe to the people of Walvis Bay. From the financial angle alone, it has been estimated that had the repairs been carried out professionally the cost would have been between £500 and £1000. They were done for us for nothing!

We did what little we could. *Daughters of the Wind* was published three days after the débâcle. Cabling the publishers in London to send out copies, we left autographed slips with Viggo (including one in his name), and arranged for him to distribute them to our principal helpers. Unfortunately, the books could not arrive until we had left, so all we could say to our friends was, "Whatever you do, don't buy that book!" My own club, the Royal Burnham Yacht Club, air-mailed a burgee to the Walvis Bay Yacht Club and this did come before we sailed.

Further delay was inadvisable once *Rehu Moana* was ready. A wire cable was led from the steam winch round a block at the end of a pier and thence to the catamaran. Back into her element she slid to lie that night off the fish wharf. Next day we put to sea. The date was 25th February—*nineteen days* after the accident.

Crowds saw us off. The yacht had to be warped along the pier to allow us room to sail clear. Willing helpers using a warp belonging to a shore installation, dragged the catamaran to the point of departure. Up went the mainsail and staysail, flapping in the breeze as if anxious for the curb of the sheet. I began casting off the shore-warp.

"Wait," shouted a figure on the pier head, "keep your end fast, I am casting off *this* end." Feigning deafness to my shout, he undid his end of the warp, then abetted by several others quickly knotted two more lengths to it, so our whole fore-deck was covered with its coils when we had hauled it aboard. How typical of Walvis Bay was this farewell! The gesture may well have saved *Rehu Moana* from a future grounding for we were to rely on this 90 fathoms of help to hold us during a West African Tornado.

The question that the reader (like ourselves at that time) must be asking, was how would the children react to a return to sea. Would their ordeal have destroyed their former confidence? They did show concern at any loud bang on deck especially at night and seemed to want explanations of what was happening more often. For a day or two they sometimes asked for reassurance that all was well. But this was all. They evinced no sign of having been fundamentally upset nor did they develop the slightest fear of the sea or its storms.

Viggo had arranged to speak to us over the Yacht Club radio, mainly to find out how the repaired catamaran was doing during the first two evenings of the passage. Two only, because the Club's radio though not ours had a very limited range. Viggo's voice was becoming faint by the second occasion. A most unfortunate occurrence, that may in part have been the sequel to some misunderstanding of this radio schedule, was a rumour that 'radio contact with us had been lost'. Much worse: a newspaper report appeared in South Africa that *Rehu Moana* had been cut down by a steamer off the Skeleton Coast and lost with all hands. The papers concerned had failed to live up to their normal high standards of accurate reporting because when the item was printed, we had already been a week at our destination, Lobito, in Portuguese West Africa or Angola.

It was partly this report that encouraged me to take a liberty with geography in the title of this chapter—strictly speaking, the Skeleton Coast lies northward of the town of Walvis Bay.

Chapter 7

MALARIA ON SUNDAYS

OVERCAST skies, from which curtains of dank mist hung down over a cold bottle green sea; chill southerly winds; conditions remained much the same as those between Capetown and Walvis Bay, with the sole exception that the wind was generally lighter and diminished steadily as we advanced. Our tactics too were unaffected, save that we kept further offshore—over 100 miles—in an effort to escape the land/sea breeze/calm effects exerted so powerfully by the vast superheated continent on our right. Not that Africa had any 'superheat' to spare for us that first week because only on the seventh day out when we were as deep in the tropics as lat. 15°S. did the temperature soar from 69°F. to 87°F. in the course of a single day.

Fiona's initial anxiety lest the dramatic effects of hyoscine on the last passage should prove to have been no more than an exception, was soon relieved. She hardly dared credit the fact that at last a permanent answer to her suffering had been found—yet it was so.

All three of us were alert to every creak and movement of *Rehu Moana* at first. Had anything been forgotten? Had any unsuspected weakness been overlooked? But when repeated inspections failed to reveal anything amiss, even after a series of sharp squalls had tossed the boat about violently, we began to relax, confident in the success of the rebuilding. Whether in any way connected with the repairs and alterations, I do not know, but the catamaran had never steered herself so sweetly down wind.

The day following our departure (a Sunday) we began taking tablets for the prevention of malaria. The drug of choice was Daraprim, the dose, a single weekly one, being one tablet for an adult and a half for a child every seventh day. Daraprim does not destroy the malaria parasite but is a suppressant, so to lessen the danger of an attack coming on after stopping it, we did not discontinue the tablets until eight weeks after leaving Sierra Leone, the last malarious area. The girls regarded their 'malarias' as a new treat to add to the already popular daily vitamin C. and fluoride. For convenience, 'malaria day' became Sunday.

The reader may recall that I had forwarded from Papua an application to the Australian National University at Canberra for a fellowship to continue research into ancient Polynesian navigational methods. Apart from a certain nostalgia when my thoughts wandered in that direction, I had resigned myself to trying to forget the project as probably unattainable. To my surprise and delight, official notification reached us in South Africa that I had been awarded a two year fellowship that was to come into effect when we re-entered the Pacific.

So certain had I been of rejection that I had not seriously considered the problems, notably the effect on Fiona, and only now did it begin to dawn on me how thoughtless I had been. Even so, I was far too ready to accept Fiona's support without realising what it was costing her. Selfishly I failed to appreciate how ardently she had been longing for 'a house that did not rock about and taps with hot water in them'—very modest ambitions after all, to be so cruelly postponed!

Another question to be determined was, what boat to use. Two years that must include library work and writing in Canberra, was little enough for adequate field work among the islands. A motor boat would be required I concluded, fully powered to be able to keep to a plan of island visits in any conditions, and capable of carrying enough fuel for at least 1000 miles. *Rehu Moana* like all multi-hulls is sensitive to heavy loads. With the weight of four or five people and two months' stores aboard, she begins to labour a little. What would be the effect of installing a big motor and taking on so much fuel? Seeing no way round this difficulty, we had decided prior to the Walvis Bay accident to change boats in England before proceeding to the Pacific. But so impressed were we by the catamaran's toughness and the perfect condition of her timbers revealed by the crash, that we promptly changed our minds. This left the weight problem as unsolved as ever,

and subsequent reflection impelled us to re-examine our decision
once again.

The end of the first week, coinciding as it did with such a
dramatic improvement in the weather, in fact marked the transition from the South East Trades proper to the region dominated
at that time of year by the South West Monsoon. The wind declined, the spinnaker was in continuous use for $2\frac{1}{2}$ days before
being replaced by the ghoster and calms became frequent and
prolonged. The 843 miles from Walvis to Lobito took us ten
days. There was complete or virtual absence of wind for nearly a
third of this time, more marked towards the end when the sea
breeze we had expected near the coast failed to materialise—
though the moment we made fast it began to blow and continued
each afternoon thereafter!

Few birds were seen on the passage but dolphins abounded
and once we passed close by a sleeping turtle without disturbing
it. We caught a dorado so large that we had difficulty in getting it
aboard. In general it was an idyllic cruise or would have been
had I not developed violent toothache on the first day of fine
weather. Fearing with some reason, that a dental abscess might
be forming, I took antibiotics in full doses as well as aspirin for
the pain. Within a day or so only a dull ache and glandular en-
largement beneath the angle of my jaw remained. This showed
the value of antibiotics in such a condition at sea—*provided that*
the tooth was extracted in the next port.

LOBITO

The modern residential part of Lobito occupies a sandspit
that shelters the harbour from southerly winds. The docks lie
towards the root of this spit and across the head of the bay is
the crowded native city. We slipped quietly past Restinga Point
at the tip of the peninsula at 2.30 p.m. on 7th March but in the
absence of a sea breeze it was nearly two hours later that we
reached the town quay. Captain Melo Cristino, the Port Captain,
courteously came out to us in his launch en route to arrange for
our reception. We must lie alongside a wharf initially (we were
understandably sensitive about this), but could move later to an

anchorage off Lobito Sports Club, where there were showers, a restaurant and a sandy beach.

"You have come from England but what a long time you have taken to get here!" the Captain exclaimed. We were experiencing increasing difficulty as we got nearer to England again in explaining how circuitous had been our route since we left there. One easy way out was simply to say we were from New Zealand; another was to produce the inflatable globe on which our track was marked.

"Chin chin," said Captain Cristino, raising his glass, "you have come a long way." (How has 'chin chin' come to be regarded so generally as an idiomatic English toast, just as 'Tipperary' is believed to be the national hit tune?)

"That extraordinary boat we passed drawn up on the beach, what was it," I asked.

"Oh, that must have been a *Bimba*. It is a raft really because although it is boat-shaped the water is allowed to run in and out freely between the logs. The wood from which it is made is called 'bimba' also—it is light like balsa. Such raft-boats are known nowhere else in the world except Lobito."

"What are they used for then?"

The fourteen foot craft built of such light and fragile treetrunks had not impressed us as particularly seaworthy.

"Shark fishing—by harpoon!—and ten miles offshore," he answered, grinning at our surprise. We discussed their probable origin. A likely possibility seemed that the Portuguese themselves might have carried the idea across the Atlantic after seeing the Indian *Jangardas* at their then colony of Brazil. For these South American balsa rafts though not boat shaped like the *bimba*, are constructed on the same principle and are still used for fishing— as we had seen ourselves in Brazil. Another suggestion arose out of the *bimba*'s shape, which resembles that of reed boats the world over. Could it be an adaptation, in which ultra light wood had taken the place of reed bundles, of craft such as are found on the Ethiopian Lakes?

The generous Port Captain gave us a *bimba* some days later. We found it rowed very well but we felt uncomfortable to be using so unique and irreplaceable a boat as a humble tender. So we stowed it on deck where despite the extreme softness of the wood it miraculously escaped damage. Having survived the journey to England, it was presented in Captain Cristino's name to the National Maritime Museum at Greenwich.

The Port Doctor was the next to call upon us. Though free with clucking noises of sympathy, he remained inflexible even in face of Priscilla's tears of angry frustration at having mislaid her Yellow Fever Vaccination Certificate. Fiona's certificate was found on inspection to have expired. While they fumed silently, both girls were innoculated again.

"Chin chin!" exclaimed Amandio da Silva, glass in hand. He was a young man who should have known better, having visited England and Ilkley Moor to boot. He had taken us under his wing and piloted us through the maze of Immigration and Political Police documentation that seemed to be required and was always ready to abandon his own work to act as our counsellor and friend.

We very soon took advantage of the hospitality of Lobito's Sports Club and anchored about 100 yards out from their modern and well equipped clubhouse. Here we settled down contentedly to enjoy a lazy tropical holiday, especially welcome after the hard work at Walvis. March and April are the hottest and wettest months in Angola but although thunderclouds built up to spectacular proportions over the mountains inland every afternoon, the weather on the coast remained warm and sunny.

"*WE* want to swim ashore like you do," begged the children after a day or so. "We can wear our armbands." So much had they gained in proficiency since our arrival that we were minded to let them try. On hearing the good news they hurriedly pulled on their inflatable armbands and as Priscilla ran below for the cine camera, they scrambled and slid on their tummies over the stern and plopped confidently into the water. Fiona and I provided the escort. Susie made reasonably consistent progress, though resting and floating at increasingly frequent intervals. But Vicky was too lazy to do much else than bob about contentedly, perfectly at ease and prepared, in spite of dire threats, to remain there all day. When Fiona at last succeeded in shepherding our charges ashore (Vicky under tow), a cheer for the girls went up from the audience that had collected—though the tired parents felt the more deserving of praise.

True to my resolve, I visited a dentist, Amandio's, in company with him, his wife and Priscilla. All of us were patients. By-passing the waiting room we were all ushered together into an exceptionally large and modern surgery. Neither the dentist nor his lady assistant spoke any English but this was not what made the visit so unique for Priscilla and me. For in place of the customary gloom here was an atmosphere of infectious gaiety, in which the smiling dentist would demonstrate his current victim's mouth to those waiting their turn, his racy Portuguese commentary punctuated by the giggles of his attractive assistant. Unfortunately the history of my complaint that would have clearly demonstrated the need for extraction, became lost in translation, so that my tooth was only filled. Undoubtedly I was the one to blame for not forcing the matter (through cowardice). Trouble was bound to follow.

Some interesting and unusual people came our way. One that I remember was a ship's chandler, the son of a Portuguese father and Negro mother, who spoke fluent English.

"I went to school in Lisbon, now I am back here and I have absolutely no complexes about my colour," he averred—I thought protesting too much. I must admit though that he showed no sign of complexes but then he was an extrovert and extroverts seldom do—not on the surface. It is true of course that Portuguese colonists have always been less racially prejudiced than most; though political and economic discrimination is another matter. Our acquaintance had been intrigued to see how eagerly South African crews ashore in Lobito exercised their unwonted freedom to pursue native girls. Having noticed how graceful and vivacious these could be, I reflected with amusement that even white South Africans were the poorer for *apartheid* restrictions.

A bronzed couple who came aboard from a rowing boat one day, turned out to our mild surprise to be missionaries. As they talked I was struck not for the first nor the last time, how odd it was that missionaries in Africa so often seem to be so very much more practical than most Europeans, being clearly aware of what is going on and knowing the people without illusions. This latter quality I find particularly refreshing in contrast to the wishful fantasies so common in southern Africa. As a case in point it is obligatory to pretend in the Portuguese lands that Angola, thirteen times the size of Portugal, is simply a province of the latter. There was also an item of faith that civil war in Angola had ended, an illusion that was to be dispelled at our next port of call.

I was interested to hear our visitors referring casually to the son of a friend of theirs being at school in Congo, Kinshasa, because for some months past men would draw me aside and with meaning glances in the direction of the ship's women folk, utter chilling warnings about the fate in store for them in Black Africa. And here was the boy's going to and from the Kinshasa Boarding School being discussed just as if it had been in Cheltenham!

We did indeed anticipate certain difficulties over our Congolese visit. For one thing we lacked visas, which were unobtainable without parting from our passports, which we could not do. Then for want of a powerful engine, we could not hope to make our way forty miles upstream to Boma, the port of entry, against the flood of the Congo in full spate at the height of the rainy season. The only place we could hope to reach was Banana very near the mouth but this we had been officially informed, was a restricted military port.

Banana was not in fact our next calling place. This was to be Santo Antonio do Zaire on the southern shore of the Congo estuary, which here separates Angola to the south from Congo (Kinshasa) in the north. After endless poring over charts, we had decided to enter the river by skirting the southern bank (we seemed to be reasoning that we might slip past the entrance point when the 'river was not looking').

Of all the unusual people we encountered in Lobito, one was remarkable in that he showed us something we thought did not exist—a further dimension in hospitality. His card proclaimed that his name was Evaristo Ferreira Guedos from the neighbouring town of Catumbela. He had read about us in O *Lobito* and had come to take us for a day's drive into the 'jungle' and for lunch at an inn in the mountains. Now the remarkable fact was that we learnt all the foregoing by Amandio's interpreting—for Evaristo did not speak one word of English!

Nothing daunted by this minor inconvenience, he shepherded us all into his Mini Morris, which settled lower on the road and appeared to bulge a little as we squeezed inside. To our relief we found ourselves able to attain a reasonable degree of mutual comprehension thanks to Evaristo's unselfconscious and expressive gestures (sometimes to the detriment of his control over the car), and a smattering of Spanish that we had in common.

For an hour the road undulated across dry thorn scrub country before beginning to climb into the mountains up valleys suddenly become verdant with lofty liana-hung trees, past groups of circular grass-thatched huts and patches of banana and yam cultivation. Unexpectedly our host braked to a halt beside a small African boy who was offering a bird for sale, which was flying round his head, tethered by one leg. Muttering away angrily to himself, Evaristo bought the bird and then immediately told the boy, whose mouth opened in incredulous amazement, to set it free. Then sliding back behind the wheel, the kindly Portuguese shrugged as if to say, 'what is the point; he will soon catch another one' and drove on.

The inn was a pleasantly rambling building—somewhat the worse for the attentions of termites, white ants and wood-worm —that was also homestead and farm, so that goats, pigs, dogs and chickens were continually enlivening the dining-room with their attempts at gate crashing. It was festooned with flowering creeper and shaded by a kind of palm we did not recognise and bulbous trunked baobab trees. The proprietor, a former baritone who had abandoned Lisbon Opera House for the jungle, provided a magnificent cold lunch. Only after we had done full justice to this did we realise it was merely the *hors d'oeuvre*, to be followed by soups, salads, fried meat and blood sausage, for a further leisurely two hours. He was very taken with Priscilla, to whom he gallantly presented a superior looking carved wooden giraffe. (On noticing how much wood powder it was shedding from innumerable worm holes, she prudently banished it to the cockpit to undergo a fortnight's quarantine soaking in paraffin!) All too soon the time came to compress ourselves into the inexplicably shrunken Mini where, somnolent with wine, I for one dozed back to the coast.

I was pleasantly surprised to find that no difficulties arose over our clearing for Santo Antonio do Zaire, since it is purely a Naval and Military frontier garrison strategically situated inside the mouth of the river the Portuguese call 'Zaire' and others 'Congo'. In retrospect, it may have been that among the array of forms and documents the authorities overlooked the one saying where we were going.

*

On the overcast humid afternoon of 14th March when we left Lobito the thermometer read 82°F. By the afternoon of the 17th the temperature had climbed to 93° and the children were panting in the shade of awnings rigged across the deck, glad to be periodically dowsed with buckets of sea water and content to confine their acrobatics to the early mornings. Drinking water in the hull tanks that was usually cooled by the sea outside, had become unpleasantly warm; my electric razor clogged so frequently with greasy sweat as to be unusable; all our skins were suffering.

Winds remained as favourable as they had been before Lobito but were very much lighter now. Calms, complete and nearly so, took up *two thirds* of this passage. At times spinnaker or boomed out goosewinged headsails were able to give the catamaran steerage way, but for a total of 45 hours the outboard motor was the only means of propulsion. It consumed not only eleven gallons of petrol (which we did not grudge it) but apparently some of its own interior as well, so that an old tooth brush became an essential piece of equipment for brushing away the fragments of fused metal that periodically bridged the spark gap and stopped the engine.

The little girls once again tended to become dehydrated just as they had done in the Coral Sea and north of Australia. Once again they did not feel thirsty but at the first sign of irritability or when tears began to be shed over nothing at all, a dilute fruit drink had an immediate effect.

The intense heat no longer decreased appreciably during the

night, so the thermometer never fell much below the 90°F. mark. Humidity likewise increased and ahead, astern and abeam lightning flickered continuously. For this was high summer in the Congo basin, the hottest month, and the middle of the rainy season. An eight foot shark slid by to port, its fin knifing the surface like a periscope; a fluttering storm petrel was faithfully reflected in the mirror of the sea, whose glassy undulations were broken only by fish jumping. One of these, a bonito, we succeeded in catching.

The temperature itself, and the lightning that played hide and seek through the heat haze, both increased the potential risks of fire. A petrol conflagration being much the worst danger, we stowed every can of fuel in the cockpit under cover of a white sail. (The plastic containers themselves were white.) A large CO_2 fire extinguisher was placed on the steering seat in readiness for any emergency.

We turned in towards the coast on the sixth day, the winds intermittent as ever, the temperature 95°F. Soon after noon the even line of sea horizon away to our right was unexpectedly broken by of all things, a clump of trees. How was this possible, since the land was ten miles away in that direction and the African Pilot referred to the fringing vegetation as 'mangroves'? I opened the book to re-read the passage more carefully, blinking away the sweat that ran into my eyes and brushing ineffectually at the sodden patches that coalesced across the page. Yes, mangroves was correct enough but 'mangroves a *hundred feet* high' was the actual wording. Having never previously seen any taller than about twenty feet, I was astonished. These giants would be easily visible from ten miles.

A bee crossed our bows on course for America, an aromatic scent of wood smoke and tropical flowers was wafted to us over the water—so was a loud alarming *crump*, and as we looked out startled, first one, and seconds later another tall spout of water erupted several miles ahead. The explosions which appeared to be confined to limited areas straddling our route continued as *Rehu Moana* advanced by fits and starts in the feeble breeze. Darkness had long since fallen before we came up with the scene of the disturbance, related it appeared to a cluster of red and white lights, which as we approached resolved themselves into those of a stationary vessel.

BANG! By far the loudest yet and not far off!

"Light the pressure lantern and get it on deck quick," I urged Fiona who was on watch with me.

"Priscilla," I called, stepping down into her cabin and shaking her into wakefulness, "what lights does a vessel carry to show that it is engaged in target practice?" (Priscilla, having studied for her Yachtmaster's Certificate, is a mine of nautical information.) Not unnaturally this sudden question stumped her.

With all three of us now awake and watchful, we anxiously continued running the gauntlet. Three possibilities presented themselves. An oil drilling rig carrying out seismic tests—most likely and least alarming, though how to guarantee that a charge was not scheduled to go off directly beneath us? Then there was the target practice theory. Worst thought of all, was the tenuous peace between Portugal and Kinshasa being shattered by a naval battle? Mercifully, a land breeze sprang up around midnight, which allowed us to slip off rapidly into the friendly darkness leaving the noises to fade out astern.

From midnight on was Priscilla's watch, so it was she who picked up the intermittent flash of Punta do Padrao light some way up the estuary that had abruptly opened to starboard, while at the same moment she became conscious that the catamaran had been gripped by a mighty current that was setting it briskly out to sea. She called me, and we came about onto the other tack to close in towards the dark smudge of tree line that stood out against the stars, until the low growl of the breakers began to sound menacing. Helm hard a-lee then, a moment's pause until the yacht's turn into the wind set the sails shaking and way was lost, then over with the anchor in six fathoms. Over went the torch as well, though inadvertently. Six fathoms! What had the Pilot warned? Once more we consulted it. 'Rollers appear without warning and break in five fathoms'. That was cutting it fine— but we did have that one fathom to spare.

The latitude was 6°S. 360 miles from the Equator. The catamaran was anchored two miles off the lip of the estuary and perhaps five from the southern entrance point to the river proper at

Punta do Padrao. If we could but creep past this headland we could escape out of the current into shallow water overlying extensive mud flats fronting the Angolan shore. Meanwhile the time was 3 a.m. and the tide would begin flooding at seven, by which time we ought to be under way.

Six and a half days for the 400 miles from Lobito had not been bad going considering the absence of wind. Before going below to rest we could not resist testing the water, for after all one did not sail to the Congo every day. Dipping a mug full of water from overside, we tasted it gingerly; it was brackish but fresh.

We were still half asleep as we got under way tardily at eight o'clock to begin moving forward with tantalising slowness, all fore and aft sail set and motor waking the echoes, against current and dying land breeze. The sandy shore close aboard to our right was backed by mangroves that did indeed rise a hundred feet or more, their aerial roots hanging down with the regularity of suspended palisades. There were occasional clumps of palms, a thatched hut or two, some canoes drawn up on the beach. A converted L.C.T. with the latticed superstructure of an oil drilling rig amidships chugged past us bound for the open sea and the previous night's bangs were explained. Not that our fears had been entirely groundless we learned next day, for they had succeeded in blowing up their own forty foot tender!

To our relief the sea breeze began to make from astern about 11.30, after which with headsails boomed out to catch as much wind as possible, the catamaran began to slip along faster. We edged in nearer to the shore, for out in the main channel very close at hand now, the full force of the flood pouring out to sea had at last become apparent. Rafts of greenery, made up in the main of broad leaved semi-aquatic plants and of reeds, rotated slowly on their axes as they drifted by. These were the famous floating islands that the Congo bears out to sea in the rainy season.

The sun was blazing down from a cloudless sky sucking out the colour from vegetation whether on shore or drifting on the river. The children, diligently scrubbing their dolls' clothes in what shade the mainsail offered and then pegging out the tiny garments carefully on the ratlines, were for their own part in Vicky's phrase, "not wearing any clothes, just ourselves." They broke off their activity to gaze with curiosity and interest at the floating islands waltzing past, so different from anything they had ever seen before. The Congolese shore of the estuary had come into view by this time in the form of disembodied trees suspended in mirage, backed by undulating 'Sussex Downs' hills of greater substance.

Padrao Point now only two hundred yards ahead was a steeply shelving sandspit onto which lines of breakers were curling. Would we get past? The tide was due to turn in another hour so there was not much time to spare. I steered a little further out to keep clear of the breakers and scant minutes later Padrao Point could no longer be distinguished against the rest of the rapidly receding shoreline. We hurriedly turned back to angle in towards the land and after some debate about the farther ground that must be lost in the process of changing sail, dropped staysail and ghoster and ran up the spinnaker in their stead. As the big nylon sail ballooned out with the snap of an opening parachute before the strengthening sea breeze, we knew we had acted correctly. The only chance of entering the river that day lay with the spinnaker.

The next hour was spent recovering lost ground to regain the point. This time we had no fear of the breakers knowing only too well the strength of the offshore set, so right in among them we swept, determined at all costs to keep inside the current lines that streamed by to port. The time was 1.30 p.m., the flood nearly spent and this our last chance. We had made good five miles since eight o'clock.

The edge of the sand on our right was but twenty yards off. Then our forward progress ceased—still too far out! We approached even closer, to fifteen yards, ten, when individual shells on the beach became landmarks as the boat surged to and fro, buffeted alternately by surf and backwash but moving forward again though literally by inches. I see on looking back through the log-book that *Rehu Moana* was only wallowing among those breakers for ten minutes. At the time it seemed an age and still does so now in recollection.

At last the headland came abeam. Of a sudden the catamaran jerked forward through a scum of yellow foam and flinging aside floating reeds and banana trash, went tearing along past the point and round a corner to rush by the very backyards of a fishing village. The startled inhabitants leapt to their feet and after momentary hesitation, waved us welcome to the great river Moienzi-Nzadi, the 'Eater up of Waters'—the Congo. There was now time to gaze around. The half naked fishermen still stared after us beside their dugouts drawn up in a row and the chocolate-brown split fish hanging from frames in the smoke of slow fires. Fringing the backwater across which we were speeding and as far as the eye could discern upstream, stretched a wall of giant mangroves. 'Gloomy, mysterious, the heart of Africa'— the successive *clichés* passed through my mind.

"Just like sailing on the Norfolk Broads, isn't it?" remarked Priscilla, and the spell was broken!

SANTO ANTONIO DO ZAIRE

"What is that?"

I turned. A gunboat had emerged from the mouth of the winding creek on whose banks lay Santo Antonio do Zaire, and was heading towards us foam creaming under her forefoot. Exchanging the spinnaker for the staysail to enhance our manoeuvrability, we awaited her with interest. On coming up with us the flat bottomed river gunboat swung about and kept pace with her engines barely turning over as she edged alongside. A British Naval Officer with reddish hair and beard was the first to step aboard. While we remained stupidly staring, he introduced himself in an accent that was clearly the product of Dartmouth or one of the public schools, as "Lieutenant Paulo Marques, Portuguese Navy," and grinned wickedly at my ill disguised surprise. Later we learned that his mother was English and that he had been educated there.

Following in the wake of the little warship we entered the creek and the sea breeze holding, were able to stem the tide without recourse to the motor. At 3 p.m. we brought up under sail alongside a moored P.T. Boat—eight miles from our overnight anchorage—time taken seven hours!

We looked about curiously. Alongside spindly wooden jetties

or lying to buoys in the muddy stream, was an assortment of 'Saunders of the River' gunboats and launches. Soldiers were everywhere, dressed in jungle camouflage battledress, some wearing berets, others steel helmets, but all with automatic weapons slung across their chests. Notices, flags and unit insignia proclaimed that the most substantial buildings along the waterfront had all been converted to Naval or Military use but further back from the creek, the dusty streets were lined with stores and with villas surrounded by high-walled gardens.

No word of our impending arrival, Paulo told us, had come from the authorities in Lobito, an impression that was confirmed when he took me to the Political Police headquarters to make my report.

"Are you not aware that this is an area of active military operations where civilians are not allowed? Where is your permit to enter a closed military zone?" To all of which I had little to say, except that Immigration, Customs, Civil Political Police in Lobito had each been officially notified of our destination, and none had warned us either that it was forbidden or that permits were required. The Police Captain was not impressed.

Paulo at length turned to me.

"Like all good soldiers and sailors, I detest the police!", he remarked disdainfully. "Take no notice of him—come!"

We stepped out into the sunlight. I suspect it was due to the good offices of the Naval Commandant that we were not asked about permits again and on the contrary were received with the utmost hospitality on all sides.

Dusk and the mosquitoes found our ship's company still luxuriating in the officers' swimming pool in which they had been immersed for the past two hours. The temperature was 87°F. That evening a black-bearded petty officer sat with the little girls while we dined in the very pleasant atmosphere of the mess.

Next day we replenished our supply of petrol—at 8/6d. a gallon—and Priscilla and Fiona bought a selection of brightly patterned traditional prints. One that the shopkeeper unfolded for Fiona's inspection bore the boldly printed slogan 'Celebrate Nigeria's Freedom'. He regarded it with shocked surprise and explaining that it should not have been in Angola at all, hastily bundled it up. It was evident that the Manchester cotton industry's salesmen had got their lines crossed!

Paulo, who like Amandio in Lobito was going out of his way to be of assistance, drove us in a military jeep to buy vegetables at the mission, which was situated a mile or so beyond the airstrip at the edge of the town. Half-way there he suddenly put his hand to his hip, felt about and then cursed under his breath on realising he had forgotten his revolver.

"It's all right though," he reassured us. "The mission is well within the five mile limit. It is beyond that where we need to go in convoy with armed escort."

It was only gradually in the course of a number of conversations that we were able to piece together some sort of picture of what was really happening and what emerged did not altogether fit in with official assurances that guerillas had been suppressed. The position apparently was that the only road linking Santo Antonio with the remainder of Angola could be forced by armoured units only; as far as all other traffic was concerned it was cut. Santo Antonio was held by the Portuguese as far as a perimeter five miles out. Beyond this their writ was uncertain and disputed. Sea and air communications were unaffected however, so the town was not in any sense in a state of siege. This was the second state we had visited where fighting was in progress; for an Ovamboland rising in South West Africa was currently being put down.

By way of atonement for having unwittingly given us such a scare, the Fina oil prospecting team invited us, children and all, to dine at their camp. In the bright glare of rows of electric bulbs slung from trees, poles and the eaves of huts, we seated ourselves round a table at the edge of the compound. The evening's great attraction was not the steaks despite their excellence, so much as making the acquaintance of a large and handsome monkey who boasted a topknot of bright red hair. Sitting back on his haunches and nonchalantly upending a bottle of beer, he drained it with evident enjoyment. Then very gently he nibbled everyone's fingers in turn, plainly gaining reassurance when we trusted them between his powerful jaws. Prior to this ceremonial establishment of mutual good faith he had been decidedly reserved and suspicious but afterwards he kept nuzzling and hugging us in the most affectionate manner, which even my cynical mind did not attribute to alcohol. The two girls were awestruck watching him showing off with spectacular acrobatics. These made such a lasting impression that both Susie and Vicky bruised themselves at sea later on, jumping down from the ratlines in an attempt, they confessed tearfully, to 'be like the red-headed monkey'.

Much as we wanted to prolong our stay, too much time had been lost at Walvis Bay. There was a good deal of head shaking over our intention to cross the river, for while no state of war existed between Portugal and Congo, neither did diplomatic relations and there was normally no contact across the closed river frontier. It is to the credit of the Santo Antonio authorities that far from putting difficulties in our way, they readily agreed to tow us far enough up river to obviate any risk of our being swept out to sea while we were crossing over.

On Good Friday morning, the 24th of March, we bade a reluctant goodbye to our kind hosts and their swimming pool, and after three hours under tow, headed out into the two mile wide river with our sails reassuringly filled by a fresh sea breeze. At the point we judged to be mid-stream we took down the Portuguese courtesy flag and hoisted to the starboard yardarm in its place the blue and gold of the Congolese Republic.

An awning-covered barge all fretwork and ballustrades so that it looked like a miniature Mississipi show boat, that was lying at a deserted landing was the only sign of life we saw as we slipped rapidly downstream. Beyond a headland matted with jungle there opened out an expanse of shallows two or three miles across and dotted with the stakes of fish traps. Two dugout canoes were crossing diagonally, the pair of standing paddlers in each maintaining their precarious balance with the skill of tightrope walkers. This still sheet of water was bounded on the far side by a midnight-green shadowed wall of mangroves, broken only by the dark mouths of two channels, the Crique du Banane and the Crique du Pirates—these 'pirates' in reality had been slavers; corroded copper fetters can still be dredged out of the mud there.

BANANA

Skirting the thinly covered mud flats, we turned into Banana Creek, up which the flood bore us rapidly towards a cluster of dilapidated official looking buildings near a concrete wharf. Here we made fast, tossing our warps to a group of startled looking soldiers in white sleeveless shirts, khaki shorts, toe sandals and berets.

What would be our reception? A public holiday is not the day to choose for expeditious port clearance at the best of times. In a few moments the Harbour Master, a slightly built quiet man named Joseph Simba, arrived with a group of colleagues. All wore the universal white shirt and sandals but had on slacks in place of shorts. Gathering up the ship's papers, we accompanied the delegation back to M. Simba's office.

Priscilla's proficiency in French was of the greatest assistance, being supplemented on this occasion by the English of an Army major who had served in a Welsh ship out of Cardiff. Everyone was courteous and very curious about us. A wall map enabled our route to be demonstrated. Then an odd coincidence was revealed and had to be explained. Why did our boat have a Congolese name? 'Moana' it turned out, meant 'little girl' in Congolese. Why were we flying the flag of the superseded Congolese Republic which two years since had become the 'Congolese Democratic Republic (Kinshasa),' whose flag was red and blue not blue and gold any longer? So that was the explanation why none of the public buildings had been sporting a flag like ours! Our error caused considerable amusement and the atmosphere at once became less formal and even more friendly.

We could not help overhearing one of the officials, who was shouting into a radio telephone in an effort to make himself heard in the distant capital Kinshasa above the crackle of static. He was insisting in carefully enunciated French that even I could follow.

"*Ils sont des visiteurs*, no, no, there is not a commercial ship, not at all. They must not be asked to pay harbour dues, *pas une centime*—they are guests!"

The English speaking officer had been reading through our crew list while this conversation was in progress. Now he looked up and regarding my grey hairs—a cliché I am afraid but the only phrase appropriate—with evident respect, he enquired:

"You got two wife?"

I hastily disclaimed any such good fortune, upon which an expression of resigned disillusionment replaced the admiration in his eyes.

The formalities having been completed, M. Simba bade us officially welcome and we adjourned with the major to the officers' mess. Alas, there was no swimming pool attached to this rather bleak concrete structure furnished only with circular metal tables and tubular framed chairs. Afterwards we did bathe in fresh water, in the sea on the outer side of Banana peninsula. Meanwhile we sat down to cold beer.

"Chin chin," said the Major as we lifted our glasses. After absorbing a very fair volume of lemonade, Vicky and Susie scampered off with a crowd of Congolese children to play on a roundabout, undeterred as far as could be gathered, by the difference in language.

Signs of the disorganisation that prolonged civil war had wrought were everywhere apparent, either immediately obvious, as with the neglected buildings or the small warship lying awash off the navigation school, or becoming so in the course of our stay, like the shortage of consumer goods. We were approached repeatedly by men who wanted to buy watch straps, torches, soap, biscuits or English books. As to food, custard apples, avocados and coconuts were among the few obtainable vegetables. The most obvious indication that recovery might be beginning was an oil refinery being built by the Italians on the high ground beyond the creek.

All this was much as we had expected but the absence of uniforms more elaborate than the plain shirts and shorts and the fact that no one appeared to be armed did come as a surprise, contrasting as it did with the position on the other bank. It appeared as if the Congolese were blissfully unaware of being, for the Europeans further south, the dread enemy!

Surprise has been expressed that we should have visited the

Congo at all while fighting was still in progress in the interior. This suggests a lack of appreciation of the scale of the country, for the Congo (Kinshasa) is only very slightly smaller than India. If we had been in London say, and a war had been in progress in Morocco, it would have been only *half* as far away as the nearest Congo fighting was from us in Banana.

Our main concern in Banana was the tremendous surge that developed on the ebb necessitating frequent shifts of berth along the quay. We eventually solved the problem by mooring bow and stern across the angle between the extremity of the pilot's jetty and the shore. It was then a simple matter to ferry ourselves in the Avon to and from the muddy foreshore over which amphibious fish scuttled.

Torrential rains fell for hours at a stretch (one morning we baled 35 gallons out of the rubber boat), and washed out so many roads that for some days the peninsula was virtually isolated. Combined effects of rain and Equinoctial Spring tides flooded Banana so effectively that we once rowed down the main road in the Avon. All our clothing grew furry coatings of mould.

The pleasantness of the inhabitants made up for the weather, though there was one rather alarming personality. This was the formidable majestically proportioned Madame Simba, wife of the quiet little Harbour Master. Our first encounter was when she for some reason dissuaded other garrison wives from being photographed. This was the more a waste because with their satin skins, slanted eyes and high cheekbones and above all, their grace of carriage, they made an attractive group. Most had their hair plaited *mayumbi* style on top of their heads and were wearing long draped patterned skirts and tight blouses.

We never ceased to marvel at the poise of African women, especially in Congo and Sierra Leone. Could it be from habitually carrying burdens on the head? Certainly gracefulness and feats of balance seemed to go hand in hand. We watched one slim woman bend forward to examine a heap of mangoes spread over a mat in a market without disturbing the bottle that rested *at an angle* on her head.

But even Madame Simba ultimately softened towards us to the extent of making an unforgettable dinner of *chicken moamba*—

chicken cooked in palm oil with spices, served with spinach-like cooked manioca leaves.

I have been forgetting to mention the nights as among the drawbacks of Banana. The oppressive heat would have been enough to discourage sleep without the deafening drumming of the downpour on deck, and once a splash and bump alongside that our imagination interpreted as a crocodile. Worse still, very much worse, were the droning hordes of anopheles mosquitos that forced us to wrap ourselves in sheets for protection, at the cost of mattress and sheet becoming wringing wet with perspiration. The only one not concerned was Vicky, who for some obscure reason cocooned herself in a blanket, alleging she was cold. We would unwrap her once she was asleep, fearing heat stroke. No one actually counted their uncomfortable itching bites except Fiona, on the second morning. They numbered *fifty eight!*

A dugout canoe drew up alongside one afternoon, its occupant addressing me in some obscure Congolese dialect. He clarified his purpose to some extent by indicating a heap of mangrove roots encrusted with tree oysters in the bottom of the canoe. As we attempted to barter—I had no wish to bargain but simply could not understand what he wanted in exchange—his exasperation at my incomprehension mounted. But whatever words he was using were not French and certainly not Swahili, *my* only African language. At last an intelligible phrase emerged, revealing what he had been speaking. He exclaimed in disgust. "You no spik English?"

While this comedy was in progress Priscilla had taken the children to a football match. The previous evening Susie had had one of her rare negative spells during which she had refused to greet or shake hands with anyone and had reacted to censure with stubborn defiance. Just how much the little girl must have pondered over this and determined to make amends was made clear when Priscilla told Fiona and me what had happened at the match. Susie had solemnly sought out every child in the crowd, shaken hands and said *"Bonjour."* Upwards of fifty children had been there.

There is a large hotel called the 'Mangrove' at the edge of the red cliffs at Moanda, where we were taken after the floods had subsided. The guests were in about equal proportions Belgian and Congolese. One highly extrovert Belgian with a Congolese wife, who told the most outrageous tales with the utmost good humour, laughed at the mention of Banana.

"That place is a punishment centre. Have you met their celebrities?" To our puzzled enquiry, he explained. "Remember the twelve Italian airmen who were eaten in 1961? Well, four of the men responsible are still on restriction in Banana!"

At this point a Congolese woman coming up to the table put an end to further revelations. Vivacious and voluble, her French was too staccato for us to follow. Certainly her manner was devoid of any embarrassment. After she had departed flirting her great ear rings, our companion explained. "That was the wife of the Chief of Police. She was asking for money to buy beer!"

A strange country the Congo, but never a dull one!

No less of a character in his own manner than our friend of the 'Mangrove' was Father Jean Martin. He was ruddy faced, bursting with energy despite the near intolerable heat and snowy white of hair and beard. His excitement about our voyage was so great that he bundled us into his car and drove at once to the mission where his fellow priests were sensibly enjoying a siesta. The irrepressible Father Martin thumped on their doors to announce the glad news of our visit to his unenthusiastic brethren, who had little option but to emerge, glaring at their innocent tormentor and ourselves with equal distaste.

Father Martin drove us through Cité Banane, the sprawling African civilian town where he was known to everyone. One could not help but be struck with almost biblical tableaux: a fisherman mending nets outside his hut while his soft eyed young wife suckled her baby and stirred a cooking pot over a tiny fire; a goatherd leading his flock—or he may have been a shepherd, for the lean, long legged African sheep cannot easily be distinguished from goats. Our little girls tried to make friends with the children of the Cité but we stopped too short a time at any one household for the barriers of shyness to be overcome. The pitiful sight of a sadly crippled little boy worried them and they stared at the fearfully distended belly of another child, that to me indicated only too plainly a malignant condition.

Driving on past the shacks of Angolian refugees—there are over a million in Congo, we came to the convent where we were to meet the English Sister Stephens. Later she returned our visit and once again we encountered earthy common sense, reasoned optimism without illusions, that was the more impressive by reason of the hardships and indignities she had suffered as a hostage.

As always, the time to depart came much too soon. The next leg of our voyage promised to be a weary one on which we must pay the penalty for venturing so deep into the great concavity of Equatorial Africa. Instead of the Trades of the sailing ship routes far out in the Atlantic we must expect an infinity of doldrums, head winds and foul currents.

Our usual plan of stocking up with fresh food before putting to sea would have been unrealisable had it not been for Captain Ameels the Senior Congo Pilot, who roared down river from Boma with his speed boat loaded down with fruit and vegetables, a bottle of Scotch Whisky, a carved wooden head, decorated gourds and a splendid basket that Fiona still uses for her shopping. For all these gifts we could only express our thanks, since there was no other way he would allow us to repay him.

ACROSS THE EQUATOR

On 29th March we cast off on the ebb which swirled us off down Crique du Banane into the main river, where we continued to be borne along more by the current than the intermittent breeze. We were soon sailing above a unique phenomenon, a trench that has been scoured out in the course of millenia down the middle of the shallow bed of the estuary to form an underwater canyon nearly *a mile* deep.

By noon the land had receded until the southern shore had long been lost to view and only the red cliffs of Moanda thirteen miles away on our starboard quarter still broke the horizon. Sceptical of accepting the word of the *Africa Pilot* without confirmation, we dipped up some sea water in the children's bucket. Yes, even so far from land it was still drinkable.

Abruptly at 10.30 that night, the yacht gave a sudden lurch

and veered sharply to port. Astern was the sharply defined ripple of the overfalls we had just crossed and farther behind us floating islands were silhouetted in the moonlight. We had left thus abruptly, we suspected, the river water for the salt sea proper. Next morning certainly the sea was salt enough, no more of the floating islands were to be seen and glassy swells rode the light green ocean to an unbroken horizon.

As indicated earlier, the Cape Verde Islands, our next objective, promised to be difficult of attainment. We must keep well south of the Equator to regain the South East Trade winds and make use of the South Equatorial Current. Even so, breezes would be light and the way long since we must hold course until past the bulge of Africa. By then we would have sailed westward two thousand miles, *two thirds* of the way to the longitude of Brazil, yet be barely clear of Africa! This brought home to us the sheer bulk of this continent that is bigger than Europe and South America combined.

But our real troubles would begin when we turned north round the 'bulge'. Having traversed the Doldrums, we must beat to windward along the 20th meridian, to the left of which the N.E. Trades predominate and to the right, the N.W. Monsoon. Worst of all, we should be stemming the powerful Canary Current.

The choice of the Cape Verdes had been dictated by the need for a convenient spot to receive mail—always a problem—and because reaching them would complete our circumnavigation as we had called at these islands after leaving the U.S.A. It was an ill judged decision; leaving aside a tactical error that I made, the group was virtually unattainable under sail without making a wide detour half-way across the Atlantic.

The mistake in tactics was to steer a hundred miles too far north in the second week, thus prematurely encountering the squalls and calms of the Doldrums. This aberration, and the resulting need to turn back southwards to the Trades again, added 250 unnecessary miles. Back once more on a westerly heading, we continued with the Southern Cross still visible well above the horizon to the left, and the Great Bear standing on its nose on our right hand.

It was the middle of the fourth week before we finally headed north-west across the Equator.

For a short time navigation was simplified. In temperate latitudes, something like four hours must elapse between successive sun sights to allow the sun to move far enough for position lines to make a good cut. When the sun passes directly or nearly overhead this period is considerably shortened. For now the sun remains east of the ship until noon, when for brief moments only it is north or south or in the zenith, after which it bears due west. The navigator is in the happy position of being able to obtain a 90° cross between his noon meridian sight and another taken ten minutes before or after.

Our progress up to this point had been disappointing, not only by reason of my ill advised zig-zag but also because of the absence of any appreciable South Equatorial Current, described in the pilot book as 'One of the most constant currents of the world'. If only the unfavourable Canary Current were to follow its example!

The passage of the Doldrums was enlivened by the sight of numerous satellites but little else that was not unpleasant. The heat and oppressive humidity meant that the children, who still did not complain of thirst, needed routine re-fuelling every hour. Calms alternated with black squalls that seemed to be marching away safely, when they would turn and attack viciously—the wind coming from any direction. To a constant accompaniment of growling thunder, the jib would be hurriedly lowered; invariably damage to the sail was the price of delay. Staysails would have to be changed while pelting rain lashed at us and the near-gale whipped and flailed the rebellious canvas. Perhaps a gallon or more of rain water would collect in the bucket suspended beneath the boom, only to be spilled as someone stumbled against it.

It might be an hour, or five minutes, before the downpour eased and the gusts abruptly died down, a gentle breeze from some quite different quarter or else a calm, taking their place. At night, the darkness rendered the task of foreseeing the next move of the elements doubly difficult.

There were two days when the squalls were so unpredictable

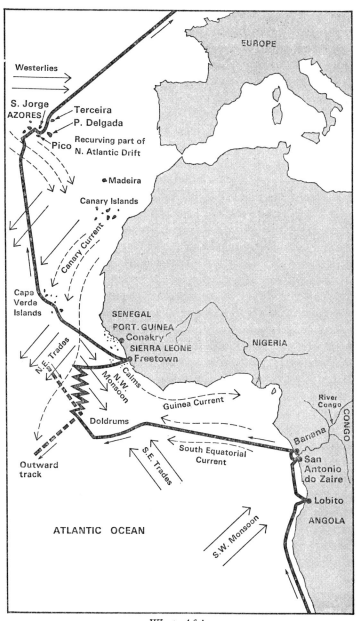

Westerlies

S. Jorge
AZORES
Terceira
P. Delgada
Pico
Recurring part of
N. Atlantic Drift

Madeira

Canary Islands

Canary Current

EUROPE

Cape
Verde
Islands

N.E. Trades

SENEGAL
PORT. GUINEA
Conakry
SIERRA LEONE
Freetown

N.W. Monsoon

Calms

NIGERIA

Guinea Current

Doldrums

S.E. Trades

South Equatorial
Current

River
Congo

Banana

CONGO

San
Antonio
do Zaire

Outward
track

ATLANTIC OCEAN

Lobito

ANGOLA

S.W. Monsoon

West Africa

and violent that we remained undercanvased all through the lulls, making but negligible progress in consequence. One period of 25 hours' continuous rain was followed by a night when the light of the full moon was so bright that the cloud shadows showed blue against the gleaming obsidian of the sea.

The more conveniently timed of the rain storms provided popular fresh water showers. Their only drawback was their tendency to be cut off abruptly, at a moment when one's face and eyes were smothered in soap suds.

To make matters more difficult, I was having bouts of vague feverish illness that left me lethargic and disinclined for days at a time to turn my hand to anything at all strenuous. So while I succeeded in typing an article and forty-seven long letters, more and more of the sail changing, night watches, navigation and general running of the vessel devolved upon Priscilla. Not only did she carry this heavy load with undiminished enthusiasm, she also found time to practise her photography until she was getting results of a fully professional standard.

Perhaps this is a suitable place to answer some of the questions so often asked me about sailing with women as crew, on the doubtful assumption that I should know something about them after three years. Any generalisation would, I am sure, be invalid and futile. My speculations are but random ones. For instance, women do seem particularly conscientious and trustworthy; then again few qualities are more valuable aboard a yacht than house-wifely order and method.

On the other hand, a girl often resents orders, so that an abrupt command may make her argue, slap your face, burst into tears, or all three, and the more intelligent and competent she is, the more accustomed to making her independent decisions. It says much for such high spirited young women as Fiona and Priscilla, that they did make an enormous effort to do things the way I preferred—witness Fiona moving the children that night at Walvis Bay.

Of course there have been times when I wondered, in the words of *My Fair Lady*, 'why couldn't a woman be more like a man?' Nevertheless I have a shrewd suspicion that my nervy skippering was to blame for most minor difficulties—there were none major because Priscilla and Fiona left to themselves, could change sail or reef with far less friction than if I were present. Moreover they seemed to be managing perfectly well now that I was so often ill.

One should not forget that *Rehu Moana* was also feminine. She showed this most plainly by shooting off course the moment I appeared from below, although the girl who was on watch would insist through tears of angry frustration, "The spiteful thing has steered perfectly for hours!"

A discussion of my illness at this point may save having to refer repeatedly to such a dreary subject. The reader will have realised as I should have done, that the cause was a dental abscess. Antibiotics had suppressed the acute phase but the chronic condition that remained produced increasingly disabling and ever more frequent toxic manifestations until the tooth was finally extracted in England. Up until then, the nature of the complaint remained so much in doubt as to require hospital investigation after our return. Amoebic dysentery in all probability thought my colleagues, while I was secretly convinced it was cancer!

If I was a skipper with little energy, the ship was tired as well. The analogy only holds so far as equipment and fittings were concerned, as the catamaran's structural soundness was, with one exception, beyond doubt. Apart from the deteriorated sails, there were other things that could only be replaced or reconditioned conveniently in England. Thus the fresh water (galley) and the salt water (bilge) pumps had all become temperamental and the long-suffering outboard, run for hours in the heat when overdue for major overhaul, was steadily losing efficiency.

This exhausting medley of doldrums and head winds coming after more than two and a half years of voyaging, was a trial to Fiona. Once she snatched away a paper on which she had been sketching something, before I could see what it was.

"What on earth is the matter?"

Rather shamefacedly she held out the plan she had been drawing of a house.

"It's all just day dreaming," she reassured me. I cannot remember ever hearing a more touching remark. Heartily sick of the sea as she was, she had consented to set off half-way round the world to Australian waters after our present long cruise was ended. Yet she was apologising for dreaming of having a home of her own!

Fortunately Priscilla and the children suffered no diminution of health or spirits. In fact Priscilla might never have lived on shore at all, so contented and at home was she on the ocean. She cheerfully continued doing far more than her share.

More frequently than formerly, either Fiona or I would feel an urge to shut ourselves off for a while in the privacy of a cabin or even a bunk, sometimes becoming lost in the lightest of paperbacks, or simply drawing comfort from being among our own belongings. I suspect that Priscilla had a similar desire more often than she admitted but was too busy to indulge it. The possession of a fragment of living space, of a personal retreat where you can leave your things as untidily as you like, seems to me to be an absolute necessity in the crowded solitude of a yacht on the ocean.

For Vicky's fourth birthday Fiona baked a cake in the Rippingilles oven; a cake complete with icing and candles. She and Priscilla had both made birthday cards, and Fiona a pair of doll's cots, one for each girl, complete with bedding. These she carved with a razor blade from wafers of delaminated plywood, gluing them together and painting one pink and the other lilac. The mattresses and pillows were made from petticoat net stuffed with cotton wool, sheets from trimming left over from dresses, blankets were from a dish cloth and the bed covers pieces of velvet ribbon joined together and quilted. The cots were 4 inches long.

I find the occasion easy to recall by reason of an incident early that morning. The darkness was as yet unbroken when I became aware that water was sloshing about in the port hull. The probing torchlight lit up a jet of water hissing in through a sprung seam as the boat pitched; a memento evidently of Walvis Bay that had opened up in recent beating to windward. Six hundred strokes cleared the bilge, but if we did not wish to continue pumping 250 strokes an hour something had better be done. A number of impractical ideas were put forward, mainly by the skipper.

"Why not simply jam a piece of wood across the hull to push

the frame out against the skin seam?" Fiona suggested, and this proved to be the answer. When a batten cut from the end of a Cape Town fruit box was hammered into position, the jet subsided to a moist oozing. For a time the person on watch could not refrain from examining the batten every half hour or so, but as it continued to hold we gradually lost our anxiety. In fact though I repaired the seam with fibreglass in Plymouth, the fruit box brace remains in place to this day.

A time came when the bilge pumps finally broke down, obliging us to remove a floor-board to be able to bail out by bucket such water as still oozed in. The children soon discovered that this had the makings of a splendid paddling pool, of which they proceeded to make the fullest use. The place became littered with toy boats and plastic ducks.

A second celebration was held on 29th April, three days after the birthday, to mark our crossing of our outward track and so the complete circumnavigation of the world. Two years, seven and a half months before *Rehu Moana* had been at that identical spot; in the interval she had sailed 29,400 nautical miles, reason enough for having a 'Round the World party'. The globe was duly brought out and the last section of track ceremoniously inked in. The remaining bottle of wine from Lobito and the last of the Fiji canned chicken had been saved for the occasion.

Watching the little girls spinning the globe as they dipped into bowls of popcorn, brought home to us how grown up they were becoming. A small matter on land perhaps, but not at sea; they could now be trusted to observe water discipline and fill their own mugs at the fresh water pumps without needless waste. More adult questions were entering their minds.

"What is dead?" Vicky had queried. "Is it like the kitten in Granny's house? Will it grow again?"

Then for the first time they, or Susie rather, had noticed that people varied in colour. It is said that prejudice is never innate but absorbed unconsciously in very early childhood from parents and companions. I think this is so. Certainly Susie's, "Why are the people in the country that we left dark?" was a straightforward request for information. Had there been charged undertones the question would undoubtedly have cropped up very much earlier.

The best explanation we could manage was in terms of how skins must fade over the centuries in countries deficient in sunshine.

Regular reading and writing lessons had been in progress since the Congo, mainly conducted by Fiona, who made illustrated word and number books; she offered a reward of one raisin for correct answers. Susie tried consistently; Vicky did very little at all, but took in enough to learn to write her name nearly as soon as her sister—albeit backwards.

Priscilla tried to teach them to coil ropes and tie easy knots. She was often the one to sit on deck watching the girls as they jumped, skipped and swung from the rigging with furious energy and wild abandon. The palms of their small hands grew daily more calloused.

Two weeks' continuous tacking to windward followed the 'Round the World' party. The sails' poor condition precluded us from carrying sufficient canvas to give *Rehu Moana* the power she needed to burst through the steep crested waves. Her speed was also greatly diminished by the marine growth thickly coating every inch of the bottom. We had shirked underwater scrubbing in the turbid and turbulent Congo, assuring ourselves that the barnacles would be destroyed by the fresh water. It appeared to have acted as a stimulant instead.

The catamaran was thus in poor shape to overcome the combined effects of surface wind drift and Canary Current, that between them carried us backwards an estimated 30-40 miles every day. As this mileage had to be made up before there could be any progress at all, it is not surprising that one week, the sixth, was productive of only 150 miles northing.

The time had come to re-consider our objective. Another fortnight and there would be anxiety, possibly a search; this at all costs must be avoided.

Sierra Leone, 250 miles to the east, was the obvious alternative, being nearer than the Cape Verdes and across the current. Arguments against were the extra 500 miles this would add to the distance to England, entering another major area of calms and the temporary loss of our mail. Then there was the scale of our one chart, that covered not only all Sierra Leone, but also the coasts of Guinea, Portuguese Guinea, Gambia and Senegal as well.

This promised to add spice to the landfall; we altered course for Freetown, Sierra Leone.

In spite of light winds we made satisfactory progress, crossing patches of agitated water where the powerful upwellings of the Canary Current created an appearance of tidal overfalls, though the sea was a mile deep. More than once we watched a swordfish hurtle from a swell and skip across the surface like a skimming stone, before plummeting down in a burst of spray.

A light north wind was blowing; the time was 4 a.m. We practically knew by heart the passage in the Pilot on West African Tornados. They were not to be confused with the entirely different American whirlwinds; the African storm would approach from the eastward as a dark bank of cumulo-nimbus cloud towering up to '20,000 feet or more.' The barometer gave no warning. A sudden easterly squall, that could 'reach fifty knots,' coincided with the passage of the roll cloud overhead, and was accompanied by very heavy rain and lightning. It only remains to add that this was the middle of the Tornado season.

Priscilla who had the watch, called me immediately the black mass shot with lightning appeared in the east. It was rapidly swallowing up the stars while we took in the jib, but the extraordinary ferocity of the 45 knot blast took us so much by surprise that seven feet of the mainsail had torn before it was secured. The continuous play of the lightning showed nothing beyond the yacht itself, so heavy was the downpour. In ten minutes it was all over.

In the ensuing calm we started the Seagull only to find that the copper cooling water pipe had fractured. After I had tried ineffectually to mend it, Fiona took a hand. She made the join with plastic tube that she softened with boiling water to bend into position and wired the sharp edged cooling water jacket to the clutch to hold it clear of the delicate plastic. The gears could no longer be changed, but this was of little moment as the forward one was all that was needed. Meanwhile Priscilla began to repair the mainsail, a task that occupied her and Fiona for five and three monotonous hours respectively.

Late the following forenoon we overhauled a Bullom boat, a 35 foot narrow fishing vessel, setting a great spritsail. Shortly afterwards Cape Sierra Leone floated into view through the heat haze. When we eventually neared the Cape we noticed the remains of a steamer rusting on a reef beside the fairway. She had been a Clan Line boat so the story ran, whose owners instructed the crew of another of their ships to paint out the wreck's funnel markings. Apprentices from the rival British India Line promptly painted them back again, and the game was kept up right until the funnel rusted through and fell down fifteen years later.

Afternoon calms held us back, so it was at 10 p.m. that we brought the Cape abeam, and after altering sharply to avoid an outgoing steamer, slipped silently up the estuary to the Quarantine anchorage, where we let go an hour later in eight fathoms. There were freighters lying half a mile off on either hand.

What a passage it had been! Forty-six days—six and a half weeks—for 3,130 miles, only 68 a day. My mistake in the second week had accounted for 250. Had we headed for Sierra Leone from the outset another 700 miles would have been saved, and the voyage from Congo to Sierra Leone would have taken under four weeks. Eighty-eight gallons of fresh water had been used, just under two gallons a day between us. The successful night approach with anything but an ideal chart, was all that redeemed us. The sea breeze stilled; the night was clear; we could relax.

The tremendous thunderheads stood out in the livid glare of the lightning, as barely an hour after our arrival, the tornado swept upon us. The suddenness of its onset equalled the last, but this surpassed the other in violence and lasted for hours instead of slackening in a matter of minutes.

In a moment it seemed, the flat calm was whipped into whiteness and *Rehu Moana* was plunging her bows under. The rain drove horizontally. We had dragged a quarter of a mile before managing to pay out the Walvis Bay gift warp to which we were riding to its full scope of 90 fathoms, but then the bearings of shore lights steadied. The second anchor joined its companion and we ceased dragging altogether. We had best try to make ourselves visible lest some vessel charged down upon us—if we could—for the hurricane lamp riding light had long since blown out. We lashed the Aladdin pressure lantern to a stanchion, where it miraculously stayed alight despite the gale-lashed rain that hissed on the hot glass, and the frenzied bucking of the deck.

Only slowly did the storm abate, so gradually in fact that not only the anchor watch but all of us, remained tense and watchful until morning. All that is except the children who had not woken once! At least there could be no residual trauma from the night in Walvis Bay.

It was only that afternoon, when we were securely moored off the Moslem quarter of Freetown, that we saw by the *Freetown Times* how exceptional the storm had been.

'Heavy Damages as Tornado Hits Freetown', ran a banner headline. 'More than three dozen boats, barges, lighters and launches were sunk in the estuary of the Sierra Leone River by the turbulent storm.'

Chapter 8

SHARK'S TAIL ON OUR BOWSPRIT

SIERRA LEONE

OUR unscheduled visit to Freetown delighted us all. Apart from an item of information gleaned from the Pilot which we suspected to be out of date, that 'the manufacture of cutlasses was engaged in', we were entirely ignorant of Sierra Leone. We had not anticipated the ubiquitous mosques whose onion domes outnumbered church spires, nor the degree of Moslem influence in clothing—men in blue or white loose sleeved gowns, for instance. Neither did the middle-aged members of the Bundo Society dress like what I suppose would be their English equivalent, a Church Ladies Guild. Bells tinkled around the hems of their skirts and each carried an umbrella, all most decorous—except that above the waist they wore nothing at all. In such an exotic setting, it was amusing to come across place names like 'Hastings' or 'Waterloo'.

"Hello Dr. Loos, Mrs. Loos!" Only the second time we had landed, but already every cheerfully grinning small boy seemed to know us. The narrow street was lined with stalls and booths and small wooden family shops. The atmosphere was animated, probably vulgar, and noisy, neither wealthy nor yet poverty-stricken. There were no beggars.

The unexpected prolongation of the voyage had rendered restocking our larder a main preoccupation. Canned goods, biscuits, dried fruit, cereals and fruit squash would soon be running low if not replenished. Fiona as usual was the one to draw up lists of requirements and spend hours going to and fro in airless stores and loud jostling markets, with the inexhaustible energy feminine women display when out shopping. The fact

A Force 10 gale
off the Azores

REHU MOANA

The last leg

of our being rather less solvent than usual did not make her task any easier.

The groceries were obtained from a young Lebanese, Victor Hakime, a keen dinghy sailor whose nautical vocabulary did not quite run to terms like 'The Trades', which he charmingly referred to as the 'Commercial Winds'. There was nothing at all commercial however about his failure up to the present, to cash a cheque I gave him to cover the balance of our purchases after we had exhausted our supply of local currency!

The circumstance that Sierra Leone's official language is English was certainly a help to Fiona in the shops. (Her greatest triumph on the voyage had been when she had scoured Lobito for three afternoons looking for a portable tin pump, of the type used to draw paraffin out of drums. She did not know the Portuguese name for it, and was directed to an assortment of garages, industrial pump stockists and bicycle dealers, before finally running one to earth.)

Not that there were no problems of communication in Sierra Leone. While correct English was usually spoken in shops, matters were sometimes different in the markets and dialect was not always easy to follow. A local proverb, for instance, runs somewhat as follows.

'De troke wan' box but 'een am shot.'

Discerning readers will no doubt realise though I did not, that the meaning is, 'The tortoise wants (to) box but his arms (too) short.'

Often a person's meaning would be plain enough, as when *Rehu Moana* was hailed from a dugout with the enquiry, "You speak banana for your chop?"

And only too plain was the implication, when an old charlatan selling herbal remedies, looked me over with a professional eye and enquired:

"You speak man medicine?" My Sierra Leonian companion shook with suppressed laughter. Irritated by his amusement, I asked, "Why does the old fool think I need medicine?"

"For impotence!" His mirth could no longer be restrained.

A fair proportion of our time was spent in the water beneath the catamaran. Removing weed for an arm's reach below the waterline using a length of board or a child's spade was relatively easy, since you could breathe through the snorkel the whole time. The skegs and bottom were another matter. Diving down, we would scrape away feverishly until the hull was lost behind clouds of severed goosenecks and coral fragments, and then surface with bursting lungs, clearing the snorkel with one explosive exhalation. Fiona was far and away the best deep diver, but all three of us had to spend hours in the water before the bottom was cleared from stem to stern. It seemed that nothing would grow there again—a pious hope but a doomed one.

In the course of the scraping Priscilla discovered a 3 inch bloated caterpillar-like creature tufted with bristles, that she carried aboard on her scraper held gingerly at arm's length. Placed in a bucket with a dozen or so gooseneck barnacles, this Sea Mouse at once proceeded to consume, or absorb, the lot. Suggestions for retaining it to browse on the catamaran's hulls were half-hearted so repulsive was its appearance, and we tossed it back in the sea.

Our anchorage at Freetown was over a mud flat, on which we grounded at low tide. This was the time that groups of women and girls went fishing. Throwing out a net to encircle the fish, they caught them with their toes, then bent down and grasped the catch and deposited it in a basket on the head. Looking at these fisher girls who were dressed 'Bundo' style, I thought how becoming would be a combination between relatively bottomless mini skirts and the fully topless Sierra Leonian style! "The fashion would suit you!" I said. Fiona was less enthusiastic.

Sierra Leone Yacht Club was attractively sited on a peninsula overlooking rocky headlands and indented palm shaded coves off which Priscilla went racing in an Enterprise sailing dinghy. A fair sprinkling of the members were African, who seemed to mingle on the friendliest terms with the European majority. This numerical proportion was not remarkable, as yachting is hardly the first sport to attract an undeveloped community. In the Pacific for instance, a man accustomed to sailing a fishing canoe generally finds a 40 h.p. Evenrude more congenial than an Enterprise. Similarly the Sierra Leone African yachtsmen tended more towards motor boating than sail.

The hospitable members could not do enough for us. One arranged for his firm to send us two cases of beer and sundry bottles of gin and Martini, and on my enquiring the cost, replied,

"I give you for dash!"

One evening a barbecue was organised, mainly at the instigation of the secretary, a New Zealander. It was a particularly happy evening, and those grilled steaks and sausage and chops were remembered with a nostalgia that increased in proportion to the shrinkage of our food supplies on the long journey north.

On the eve of departure, while Fiona was laying in mangoes, papaya, avocado and various fresh vegetables, I took the opportunity to film the busy market scene. One of the by-standers however became so resentful that I had to desist. This was the only even mildly unpleasant incident during our stay. A taxi was needed to convey our bulky purchases back to the boat. The driver enlivened the trip with an account of his plans and the doings of the rest of the family. One of his brothers, it transpired, was studying law in Moscow, another was tackling the same subject, but in the Middle Temple. It was all rather typical of emergent Africa.

It was customary in the days of sail, for a vessel to sport a shark's tail at the end of its bowsprit as a sign it had been round the world. *Rehu Moana* had now earned this distinction, but the nearest I got to catching a shark had been a buckled fish hook. Thanks to the M.F.V. *Playa de Baquio* of Vigo which was landing its catch in Freetown, this deficiency was now made good.

We left Sierra Leone on 20th May, with *Rehu Moana*'s new emblem lashed firmly in its place of honour.

TOWARDS THE AZORES

A flock of sailing dinghies and a motor boat or two from the Yacht Club kept us company as far as Cape Sierra Leone. The anticipated calms materialised before the Cape was low on the horizon, and persisted over the next nine days to much the same degree (two thirds of the time without effective wind) as they had approaching the Congo.

We tacked northward parallel to the coast to within sight of the lights of Conakry, the capital of Guinea. Then we turned north-westward away from the land, to work our way round the extensive labyrinth of shoals that fronts Portuguese Guinea to a depth of more than fifty miles. A curious incident occurred one night when we were lying rocking gently, almost becalmed, off Conakry. Fiona was awakened by a noise underneath the hull; it was less noticeable in the centre cabin and on deck was barely audible. We were puzzled and rather alarmed. However we were somewhat reassured after checking the echo sounder reading by sounding with a makeshift lead which confirmed that there were four fathoms, twenty-four feet, beneath the ship. The actual cause however, remained in doubt until Fiona thought to place an ear against the inside planking below the water line. The sound that was then transmitted as clearly as if its source were a yard away, was unmistakably the noise of pebbles being rolled along the sea bed by the sluicing tide.

The outboard motor had to be pressed into service over and over again in this area of coastal calms. How it kept running at all was rather a mystery, since it now clanked like a riveting hammer though more erratically, backfiring with a loud report and a shower of sparks at every second or third stroke. But it neither exploded nor disintegrated as we were half expecting, and only refused to run finally when we no longer needed it, having wind again to drive us.

The rich and varied marine life of the West African continental shelf was everywhere apparent; the black dorsal fin or two that cruised by with deceptive slowness; the booby bird that perched on the bowsprit and turned its head obligingly to show its profile for a photograph and a sketch by Fiona; the baby dolphin playing tag with its own phosphorescence. The patches of bright yellow plankton that littered the surface of the sea off Guinea looked so like foam that at the first encounter we recorded it in the log as such.

Tornados approached on two occasions but both missed the ship and passed harmlessly by. But the third did not miss. No more than a dark smudge on the south-east horizon at one thirty a.m., it expanded rapidly into a black rainbow, which advanced at express speed to arch over the whole sky, engulfing us like the mouth of some vast cavern. Simultaneously a howling force 9 gust fell upon the yacht. The time then was one forty five, only a quarter of an hour since the distant squall had been first sighted. We had succeeded in lowering jib and mainsail before this storm's arrival leaving us snugged down to the staysail. Though the gust was of brief duration, this headsail was still damaged.

Every shipping lane to the Cape or anywhere in West Africa, as it rounds the African bulge, converges to seaward of the shoals off Portuguese Guinea. One evening we counted the lights of thirteen vessels, then gave up enumerating in favour of concentrating upon keeping out of their way. There was comfort in the glare of the pressure lamp which was tied to a deck stanchion and bedded down firmly on a pad of Plasticine to prevent the base from slipping. We were listening to the radio reports of Sir Francis Chichester's arrival in England at this time, and thought how nearly his problems with the congestion of vessels in Plymouth Sound resembled ours in this West African shipping lane.

The well deserved acclaim of the Chichester voyage seemed oddly to overlook what it was that had really made his achievement so outstanding. This was less the passage of the Horn which, while always a major achievement, has been accomplished single-handed in far smaller yachts, but the *speed* of the voyage. I, who know a little of the problems, can only marvel at Chichester's heroic determination in keeping his yacht moving at her fastest month after solitary month, with all the effort of sail changing, discomfort and exhaustion involved.

Ten days after setting out from Freetown, we had reached a point opposite the southern boundary of Senegal, whence we could bid the calms farewell and turn decisively north westward out into the Atlantic. From here until near the Azores, consistent head winds would be our portion, the North West Monsoon at first and later the North East Trades, while every inch of the way would be contested by the Canary Current and the recurving portion of the North Atlantic Drift farther north. Essentially our problem was the same as before Sierra Leone—to make adequate headway while conserving our wretched sails; and it remained insoluble, because we dared neither spread an adequate area for hard driving, nor fail to reduce even this at the slightest gust. The endless succession of sail changes these circumstances demanded did not pass unnoticed by the children. On a day that saw no less than seven times consuming major substitutions of headsails or reefing of the main, I overheard this exchange between Susie, suspended upside down from the ratlines, and her sister on the deck below.

"I'm a sail," announced Susie. "What does Daddy mean by fouled?"

"Stuck," I supplied.

"I'm a fouled sail, Vicky. Pull me down!"

Beating to windward gave opportunity for another amusement. As *Rehu Moana* corkscrewed over oncoming rollers and pitched forward into the troughs hurling up spray from the bows, the girls discovered the joys of lying prone on deck, peering through the safety net waiting for splashes. When one came, they would dodge away with such a chorus of shrieks and giggles that Fiona muttered disgustedly, "You would think the waves had designs on them!"

Towards nightfall on 1st June, a tiny bird—a swift we thought, since it was too small for a swallow—flew into the cabin to perch on Priscilla's shoulder. After some fidgeting it finally settled on a small shelf under the front of the Perspex dome, and having dined on breadcrumbs and water served by Fiona using Vicky's egg cup as a plate, fell asleep. The girls were fascinated, being only dissuaded from trying to pick it up, play with it or wake it up to make sure it was really asleep, by the sternest admonitions. They were up only just in time in the morning to watch the self-possessed little bird, not apparently confused by the transparency of the Perspex, fly unerringly out of the hatchway to resume perhaps, a migration towards Europe.

The day before this 'bed and breakfast visit', the North East Trades had set in strongly—except that they blew from the far less favourable quarter of N.N.E. The violent pyramidal confused wave conditions that Fiona calls 'the sea being full of holes', and which would seem more appropriate to Portland Race than the open ocean, became even more prevalent than before Sierra Leone. The phenomenon, believed connected with vertical water movements, had been seen by Fiona and me on our outward voyage in this same area between the Cape Verdes and the Equator, and for that matter had been noted by the buccaneers Woodes Rogers and Dampier 250 years earlier. So violent was the impact of one of these aberrant waves, that part of the cockpit floor was torn free. Priscilla lashed it back into place with Terylene cord, an unconventional repair that was so successful that it has never been replaced.

The serrated outline of Sao Tiago, southernmost of the Cape Verde Islands, came into view on the starboard bow after nearly a week of steady winds. Heavy overcast to port hid the much higher Fogo, an active volcano, but just before dark the clouds opened a window in the west which framed Fogo's perfect cone against the red stained sunset sky.

A hundred miles beyond those first two islands we were drawing away from Sao Antao, the last of the group, when a northerly gale set in without warning other than a high mackerel sky. In a few hours it died down almost to a calm, but the next day and the one after, the weather followed a similar sequence. In spite of our care with the sails, two hour long sewing parties had to assemble on successive days. These thoroughly unseasonable conditions continued, though with rather less violent extremes of wind strength.

Fiona was the one to suggest a simple method of avoiding such frequent damage to our canvas. (It says little for my own seamanship that during close on 40,000 miles logged since leaving Plymouth, the idea had failed to strike me.) Seeing that the sails were torn virtually only when we grasped hold to pull them down, said Fiona, why not fit downhauls? Then no strain would come directly onto the cloth. The mainsail downhaul consisted merely of a line from the headboard down to the deck; the jib arrangement was only slightly more complicated in that its line passed round a sheave at the tip of the bowsprit and thence aft to the foot of the mast. To lower a sail with dispatch and without damage, it was only necessary to let go the halyard and pull in the downhaul smartly.

So heartened were we by this successful innovation, that we found energy enough to embark on the investigation of no less a question than which tack, port or starboard, was most favoured by the Portuguese man-of-war jellyfish, whose bladder 'sails' were so common a sight. It was only after some days of conscientious note taking, that it occurred to us that the project was invalidated by our ignorance of which end was the front, and hence which way they were going!

Soon after daylight on 12th June, the unexpected blast of a siren aroused Priscilla and Fiona abruptly and sent them hurrying to the hatchway. (Such a din was not enough to awaken me, though I did come to life in time to see our visitor disappearing over the western horizon.) The cause of the disturbance was the M.F.V. *Fregata* of Williamstad in the Dutch West Indies. What she was doing on this side of the Atlantic was as much a mystery as the westward course she took on departure. In Priscilla's words, "She looked too small to be out"—being no more than twenty feet longer than ourselves! A sequel to this encounter that cleared up the puzzle, was a photograph of *Rehu Moana* in 19°.48′N. 29°.21′W. sent us by one of *Fregata*'s crew. She had been built in England and was on delivery voyage to the Caribbean. They too had been rather concerned at seeing us so far out at sea!

A second early morning incident was ushered in by excited squeals of pleasurable alarm from the girls. "There's a big wriggly thing in the water following us," announced one sister. "Yes, and I think it's biting the rudder," supplemented the other. Priscilla's more prosaic identification of the fifteen foot undulating object that was indeed fast to the port rudder, was that it was a fishing net. Before we could free it I had eventually to dive down. While the detached net was being hauled aboard with a boat hook to serve as a new safety net, I took the opportunity of looking at the bottoms of the hulls. To my dismay they were thickly studded with young gooseneck barnacles, which while small as yet would very soon grow into a carpet an inch or more thick.

Steady though quite unspectacular progress continued, and it was already clear that we were in for another very long haul. Once again there was no diminution in Priscilla's keenness and enjoyment. Rather pathetically, she reminded Fiona and me. "It's all right for you two, going back to sea again soon, but this is my last trip for ages. I will have to teach for a very long time to earn enough to be away for another voyage!"

The children were contented as always. There were red letter days like 3rd July when an excited Susie awoke me to exhibit the first tooth she had shed, and which she proposed to keep as a present for her Granny. This worthy project seemed doomed to fail when at breakfast Susie announced tearfully that the tooth was lost. "Poor Granny will be so disappointed," she sobbed. Though we rather doubted this, a search was instituted which resulted in Fiona unearthing it under the girls' mattress and putting it away safely in a matchbox.

I have mentioned that it was Fiona's custom to bring out new or forgotten toys on at least one occasion during long passages. This time she produced pipe cleaners that she showed the girls how to twist into figures of people and animals; then there were new picture books, beads for threading and a plastic cooking set. Priscilla found some puzzles that the girls adapted to games of their own devising. (All the thoughtless father could find for them was bunches of Gulf weed that he had been able to scoop out of the water. This seaweed which contained small crabs, was much in demand.) Fiona made dolls' clothes and repaired the cots she had constructed earlier. On a more ambitious scale she began making up rhymes and doing sketches for what was to become a story book called *Snap the Dragon*, attractively illustrated in colour.

The reading lessons continued with fair regularity until Susie at any rate could write simple sentences. A new departure was Susie being taught to sew. She was enthusiastic and stitched away diligently. I see, however, that the next day's log has the laconic entry, 'Susie blooded finger.'

In the realm of seamanship, both girls mastered the overhand knot under Priscilla's expert tuition, and the elder the reef knot as well. A fresh generation of cockroaches had grown up to provide Vicky with practice in dexterity and speed of movement. Nowadays, instead of squashing the insects she caught in her hand, she adopted the more refined and ladylike procedure of throwing them over the side.

The adults found themselves turning more towards books for

relaxation as the weeks dragged by. Since we keep paper backs we have read, to exchange when opportunity offers with other yachts or people on shore, the character of our collection is subject to considerable fluctuation. H.M.S. *Protector* for instance gave us detective stories almost exclusively, Australian yachts Westerns, and the U.S. Peace Corps in Sierra Leone American classics. These latter now made up the bulk of our current reading matter, which was thus weighted rather more towards literary excellence than light entertainment.

As the dots of our daily positions crept out of the tropics, and then beyond the Trade Wind belt into the zone of variable winds described on the chart as the Horse Latitudes, the nights grew colder. I took to wrapping up my face in a jersey, secured by knotting the sleeves on top of my head, before going on deck or even looking out into the windy darkness. Neglect of this precaution, which I was assured unkindly made me look like the bearded lady, resulted in a throbbing ache in my infected jaw that sometimes lasted for days.

It was 1st July and we had been six weeks at sea, before the Horse Latitudes obliged with the first westerly wind. The outstanding characteristic of this area, as its alternative name implies, is variability in both strength and direction of the wind. At one minute we were watching the frantic efforts being made to race us by a three inch crab with sporting instincts. Then in a flash he had been lost astern, as *Rehu Moana* accelerated in a sudden wind from abeam. More memorable of those latitudes, because so wearisome, were the 42 major sail changes we had to make in the final fortnight at sea—though thanks to the downhauls, the sails were not torn once.

It took us a day under seven weeks to complete this passage of only 2,620 miles; 200 hours of calms and our difficulties with the sails to windward being the main factors responsible for the delay.

For two weeks before reaching land, we had felt it prudent to ration our food lest the voyage be prolonged unexpectedly even further. That this was necessary, was a reflection of my faulty estimate of our probable time at sea; it was the only occasion such measures were ever necessary. Priscilla was the one to suffer most from short commons and to lose weight, no doubt because she was undertaking so large a proportion of the physically exhausting deck work.

We first caught sight of the pyramidal cone of Pico at dawn on 5th July when, because it lay in the eye of the wind and we were tacking, it appeared tantalisingly on the beam instead of ahead. Next morning we were vouchsafed another glimpse of Pico much nearer this time, and also of the lower Faial our objective, before clouds billowed over them. It was Fiona who next saw Faial late that afternoon, appearing as a group of white squares floating suspended in haze that the binoculars revealed as houses standing out against an unsubstantial loom of land. Up until 1958, she would have first seen a prominent lighthouse on a cliff. It was still there, but a volcanic eruption in that year had thrown up two miles of sea bed into scoria hills around it, so that the lighthouse now hid in a valley.

Horta, the port of Faial, faces Pico and so was on the opposite side of the island from the one we were approaching. It took us most of the night to coast along the southern shore and tack up the channel between Pico and Faial, eventually coming to anchor in Horta harbour at 4 a.m.

The first mail for six weeks would be awaiting us here. How many hours must pass, we wondered, before all those endless Portuguese formalities were completed and we could land and collect it? The time that did in fact elapse between the arrival even before our sails were stowed of a solitary Port Official and his departure having cleared the ship, was exactly ten minutes! "Our letters?" we had asked him, "in the Post Office no doubt?"

"No, not there, Peter will have them—see that small blue building—Peter of the 'Café Sport'."

We were beginning shrewdly to suspect that the friend to yachtsmen who must surely reside in this town, would turn out to be this same Peter. The assumption was quite correct.

HORTA

We examined the island with interest as the daylight became complete. We were back in Europe! No matter that they lie far out in the Atlantic, the Azores have that European air of permanent intensive cultivation. If the blue hydrangea hedges separating the little fields look exotic, the green and golden fields themselves are not, the woodlands are tame, the brick or stone stuccoed houses are solid as if they had grown out of the land. The red cliffs, laced with waterfalls, are reminiscent of Devon. Yet Faial had been the scene of volcanic violence less than ten years before; the Azoreans share with the Tongans the distinction of being the last to hunt Sperm and Right whales by oar and sail with the hand harpoon. So perhaps the resemblance of the Azores to the mainland is in part a mask for their own individuality.

We found Peter as charming as he and his father's little café, whose visitors' book went back to Alain Gerbault. The Café Sport was like some private house so hospitable that the moment you crossed the threshold (the mat was labelled, if I remember correctly, 'New York Yacht Club'), a glass of Pico wine was pressed upon you. During the hours that I spent there in a vain effort to put through a telephone call to *The Times* in London, I am sure that more than once I ate Peter's own lunch or dinner. He acted as a kind of unofficial yachtsmen's consul. Due to his efforts formalities had been waived, moorings were available, fresh water was laid on at the quay side and the price of diesel fuel had been reduced.

Peter helped with Fiona's shopping. He also introduced us to his friend Mario, in charge of the Naval radio station, who overhauled our radio transmitter. This last was very necessary to us, as my agent in London had signed a contract with *The Times* by which we were bound to communicate with them every day for the rest of the voyage to England. A trial transmission failed. Mario re-examined the set but could find nothing whatsoever amiss. *Rehu Moana*'s crew then spent twenty-four hours waiting in relays at the café for a telephone connection with London. When none eventuated (not audible at any rate), we posted a long letter to the newspaper giving the background of our story, and suggested that in the event of radio failure we would request ships to report our position to Lloyd's (the course skirted several shipping lanes), so that *The Times* would at least be able to follow our progress. I assumed, however, knowing how powerful was the

Marconi Kestrel, that the high islands had blocked our trial transmission, and that all would be well in the open sea. Our other preoccupation at Horta was with barnacle encrusted hulls. Now the water temperature may well have been tolerable by English standards, but to us fresh from the equatorial zone it was icy, almost freezing. Fiona, who dislikes cold water at the best of times, carried on feeling literally faint; Priscilla worked stubbornly on; I dived and scraped, dived and scraped again, until my ears rang and my body felt numb. By the second afternoon the hulls were clean once more.

THE LAST LAP

There was time only for a drive to the central crater and along the coast of Faial but for no other sightseeing before, at noon on 12th July, we put to sea bound for England. After tacking up the channel between Faial and Pico, we were becalmed from mid-afternoon onwards, and drifted all night close under the terraced fields of San Jorge Island. At the appointed radio schedule at 4 p.m., we could hear G.C.N.3, London perfectly, but once again the catamaran failed to come through to them. As before we blamed the high surrounding islands.

The first day's run was inevitably a very poor one—only 37 miles from Horta, because the calm did not break until midday. But then a fair south-west breeze sprang up that sent us racing into the tidal heave and cross swell off the point of San Jorge, and three hours later past Terceira, twenty-five miles farther on. Then the islands, each one under its separate roll of cloud, vanished in the dusk and were not seen again. A hundred and thirty miles were logged the following day, and though winds are never uniformly favourable, they were far kinder than they had been of late, so that by the end of a week Rehu Moana had covered 660 miles, more than half the distance to England.

Meanwhile, every day we ran the generator for half to one hour to ensure that batteries were fully charged, prepared a report to be read over the air to The Times and tuned in the radio. And each afternoon, punctually at four o'clock, the voice of the London operator filled the cabin.

"G.C.N.3, G.C.N.3, London, calling M.G.O.Y., Catamaran *Rehu Moana*, on 8805 K.C.s, listening for you on 8255. Come in please. Over."

"This is M.G.O.Y., M.G.O.Y., answering G.C.N.3, London. Receiving you loud and clear, can you hear me? Over." So the one sided conversation would continue for thirty minues, leaving me hoarse with shouting and all of us depressed, until the resigned voice of the G.C.N.3 operator advised us to try at the same time next day and signed off. Not once did we succeed in making contact though we persisted until almost the end of the voyage. Only when the Scilly Isles were almost in sight, did we get through, not on short wave to London, but to the medium wave station at Land's End.

Naturally we did not readily acknowledge defeat. While still in the neighbourhood of the Azores, we attempted unsuccessfully to call up the medium wave station at Punta Delgada. We then tried passing ships on the 2182 K.C. International Distress frequency, but none was apparently keeping a listening watch. Fiona, who has far more mechanical aptitude than me, studied the Marconi handbook for an hour, after which she proceeded to dismantle the transmitter to check that the correct crystals were in place. Everything was in order.

To anticipate by some months, the solution of the mystery was that the twelve square feet of copper earth tacked round the bottom below the water line, had become detached from both the hull and connection with the radio set. Marconi's found everything else to be in order—a salutary lesson on the need for a transmitter to be well earthed.

On board *Rehu Moana*, while continuing our radio efforts, we also turned our attention to another means of communication. The signal flags M.I.K. flown one above the other mean, 'please report me to Lloyd's.' The signalling ship's name can be read on side or stern and her nationality will be indicated by her ensign. The only difficulty was that we lacked the signal flags. Fiona overcame it by making them. The colour designs were done in oils on both sides of quarter portions of a sheet making very creditable flags indeed, larger and more readily distinguished than those usually carried by yachts.

The first opportunity to put them to use occurred two days later when we closed a British tanker. She circled several times round the yacht, the officer of the watch examining us through binoculars, but after arousing such hopes, the ship resumed her course without having hoisted an answering pennant to acknowledge our message. A similarly disappointing sequence of events took place later the same afternoon with a Greek freighter. After these two encounters, though we passed almost within hail of several more vessels, not one of them appeared to have noticed *Rehu Moana* at all.

Failure to communicate apart, however, this passage was proving a welcome relief after the preceding ones. The second week was ushered in by light airs that backed a little from S. by W. to S. by E. and freshened the first evening, until by ten o'clock as the log put it rather picturesquely, 'phosphorescence was streaming along the racing hulls.' The barometer, though still very high, had been falling slowly since two that afternoon. 'Blinding rain,' reads the log entry at midnight. At three in the morning the wind fell away to force one to two and remained very light, continuing to back to E.N.E., while the glass went down more rapidly.

THE GALE

That morning, 24th July, our position was some 400 miles southwest of Land's End and a little outside the Bay of Biscay. The little girls were having breakfast when the N.E. gale struck furiously through the rain. The downhaul could not prevent the mainsail fouling, when a great gap immediately opened in the leach before it could be secured. Having hove-to under boomed staysail we went below streaming water, to be informed by the children—it seemed to amuse them—that their cabin was 'all sogging wet'.

"It's such a *big* drip of rain," commented Susie with self-evident truth, adding cheerfully, "This is the biggest storm we ever had." Indeed so violent had been the onset, that the gale had quickly reached force 9 and often force 10, between which it continued to fluctuate about a mean of 50 knots or so. This is a very severe gale indeed and the seas built up with frightening rapidity, curling over and tumbling with increasing frenzy—long lines of foam ran, streaking the sea at first, but ultimately coalescing until the whole surface was one sheet of driven spume.

Not wishing to lose more ground than necessary, for the wind was dead ahead, we did the same as we had off Cape of Good Hope, lowering the remaining sail and streaming an anchor chain, a warp and our two motor tyre fenders over the stern, and so adjusting the helm that the catamaran's quarter was presented to the seas.

I went below with relief out of that howling wind where you could hardly breathe. But not for long. With an appalling crash, the hatch cover blew open and was torn from its hinges, luckily to land in the cockpit where it could be retrieved. The girls, who were sitting on the floor cutting out pictures, looked up.

"What a big bang!" was all Susie's comment, while Vicky contented herself with giving a throaty chuckle, before they became absorbed in their pastime once more. The next disconcerting discovery was thoroughly shameful. Chain, warp and fenders had all disappeared, having been made fast inefficiently in the first place by someone—who regrettably had been the skipper! In their place I streamed our remaining two warps in bights, including the enormously long Walvis Bay one, adding the third anchor and chain when these failed to slow the catamaran sufficiently. Back once more in the relative peace and quiet of the cabin, the peace was quickly shattered by a breaking sea that swept us violently. The crash of cascading cutlery, bottles and tins from the galley, followed almost instantaneously upon the deafening roar of the cascade and the shock and jar of the impact.

Steering by hand became necessary to hold *Rehu Moana* at the desired attitude to the wind to avoid on the one hand being swept around broadside and on the other flying off 'downhill' in the direction from which we had come at a rate of knots. We did in fact lose ground in this gale at something like one and a half knots.

With the whole gale at its height, Fiona cooked a lunch of chipped potatoes with fried bread and tomatoes, something that would have been impossible on a single hulled vessel.

Nearing Plymouth

The first slight lull in the gale came at about 4 p.m. after the wind had been mostly force 10 for six hours. Patches of blue sky appeared, the wind backed further to become north and blow itself out. We would have liked to have relaxed then, but forced ourselves to take advantage of the increasing sunshine and slackening spray to take some ciné film. Before long there was a new subject for photography—and a fresh cause for watchfulness. Three, six, then a dozen tiny dots came into view far to leeward. As the catamaran drifted slowly down upon them and they came equally slowly to meet us, for they were hove-to, steaming dead slow head to wind, we recognised them as French tunny fishermen by the enormous curved tunny rods sprouting from each side like the antennae of an insect. The nearer the first rank approached, the more were tossed into view on the crests of far off waves, making it clear that we would still be among them after dark, and for most if not all of the night.

"Oh, what poor little boats!" exclaimed Susie, as the nearest ones drifted by. They certainly presented an impressive spectacle, rolling their scuppers under, pitching onto their noses and swept by volleys of spray and occasional white water. It was no use trying to reassure Susie that they were all quite safe. We explained that the smallest must be nearly twice our boat's length and many times her bulk, and that *Rehu Moaha* while maintaining a relatively even keel, was herself being borne up onto the crests and was swooping down into the troughs with all the agility of a demented kangaroo. The little girl still watched them with anxious concern. Before darkness had hidden all else save the bobbing lights of the Tunnymen, I was able to screw back the hatch cover, and Fiona to produce an even more impressive meal than the last, consisting of fried sausages, savoury rice and salad.

The gale was over save for an occasional half-hearted gust, well before midnight and I could feel waves of tiredness sweeping over me after the physical and nervous strains of the last few hours. But the fishermen's lights that were still visible on all sides, clearly demanded that a careful watch be maintained all night. Priscilla volunteered to take the first spell; I went to my bunk and fell asleep instantly. When I awoke the sun was shining. Seeing my exhaustion, Priscilla regardless of her own equal weariness, had remained on watch for ten hours—the whole night!

It is a sign of moral weakness in a yachtsman to delay unduly making sail after a gale is over—I invariably display it. On this one occasion I had the excuse of having been asleep, and it did take Priscilla and me one and a half hours to bring in and stow away the warps and the anchor, to mend a steering line and make adjustments to the self-steering, before we could hoist the staysail and get under way at 10 a.m.—only then did Priscilla have an opportunity to rest.

There remained endless small repairs to be seen to as a result of the gale, but only one major one—the sail. Fiona had begun the day badly by dislocating a little toe, but had reduced and strapped it herself. It was about eleven when she ensconced herself in the cabin surrounded by festoons of mainsail and set to work to triple stitch eight feet of 11 oz. sailcloth. She only broke off once, and that was to deal with the staysail in which an ominous rent had appeared, so it was little wonder that the afternoon was well advanced before she was done. Not content with having done so much for the ship, she turned her attention to me and cut my hair. One result of the battering the yacht had received had been to loosen the leak batten, so with the bilge pump out of action, forty-two buckets full of water had to be bailed out and emptied via the galley sink into the sea.

Day by day now, as the wind steadied increasingly in the south-west, we made better progress, often running goosewinged with headsails boomed out on either side to catch more wind.

Still no radio contact! We had had little success at keeping faith with *The Times*, but there remained the long article I had agreed to write for *The Sunday Times*. This had been begun soon after Horta, but the gale had delayed its completion. It was not an easy piece to write being nothing less than a review of the last three years—neither was it rendered less difficult by the need to reach up from the typewriter time and again to grasp the steering wheel and put the boat back on course.

THE SUMMARY

A great deal of totting up distances from the log was necessary before the article was finished. In cold figures (adapted to the end of the voyage in Plymouth), *Rehu Moana* had covered 41,609 nautical miles in the 3 years and 2 months that had elapsed since she had sailed down Plymouth Sound—not far off twice the distance round the earth at the Equator, which is 21,600 nautical miles. The last 4,700 after the 'Round the World party' off West Africa had been the most wearisome; since leaving the Congo *four months* before England, we had been on land only *ten days!* (Five in Sierra Leone and the same in Horta.) In the course of the whole circumnavigation, however, we had spent 43% of our time ashore—in 37 ports of 18 countries. The voyage had been unusual by reason of the type of vessel, the route and the little girls' ages. Its success had been a team effort to which each of the adults had contributed an essential part without which it would not have been possible.

THE SEAGOING CATAMARAN

Rehu Moana was the first multi-hull yacht (that is catamaran or trimaran) to sail round the world by any route, and hers had not been the easiest possible. This seems therefore to be a suitable opportunity to generalise about what our experiences taught us about such a craft. All that I will try to do is to suggest lines of thought; emphatically not asserting absolute opinions—there is still too much to be learned about all types of craft, and my own experience is too limited. In any case the ocean abhors the dogmatic.

Should non-technically minded readers wish to skip this section, the story proper resumes at the subheading, 'Arrival'.

There has been no need to modify any of the conclusions set down in the appendices of my last two books *Daughters of the Wind* and *Dreamers of the Day*, both of which are about *Rehu Moana*. I am afraid there is not space enough to re-state them here. The catamaran's performace since New Zealand has been so much conditioned by the state of her sails, that her best 24 hour run remained 198 miles and the highest speed recorded on the log 15 knots. (We had no speed recording log after Auckland.) The advantages of a well built and designed catamaran like ours should have come out in the narrative itself, so my purpose here is to enlarge on some points that have been but cursorily dealt with.

Let us leave aside some very important cruising characteristics; level, upright sailing (we could usually stand full mugs on the table when sailing to windward in force 6), shallow draft and spacious accommodation, and concentrate for the moment solely on performance.

Why is it that catamarans are faster and/or more easily driven than normal yachts? Douglas Phillips-Birt points out in *Ships and Boats* that wave making resistance (that limits the speed of non-planing hulls) is reduced by making a vessel slimmer. He cites figures for two ships of the same weight, one 400 feet long and of normal beam, the other 600 feet and very narrow. At 22 knots the wave making resistance of the narrow one was one quarter that of the other. For obvious reasons this process cannot be carried very far in ordinary craft, but a catamaran can combine fineness of hull—*Rehu Moana*'s length to beam ratio at the waterline is 13:1—with stability from great beam.

As stability is such a primary necessity in cruising yachts, what factors, other than the obvious one of beam, affect it in a catamaran? Weight is often forgotten. In the 1967 Crystal Trophy offshore race for multi-hulls, the heavy Prout boat *Pelican*, loaded with cruising gear, had the heels of wider craft a quarter of her weight. Why? Because the initial righting moment so important in a catamaran, is half the beam times the *weight*. No wonder the 8 ton *Rehu Moana* has never lifted a hull in 41,000 miles, even when struck by a force 7 squall with 1,000 square feet of canvas spread, or when clawing to windward close under the land inside Magellan Strait in a wind speed of 50 knots gusting to 60. We gave away our automatic sheet release in New Zealand as redundant.

Another stability factor; there have been capsizes off both England and New Zealand in catamarans whose hulls were not only narrow, but so sharply vee-ed as to approach the shape of hollow keels in section. In such cases when the weather hull

276

begins to come up, the other has not sufficient buoyancy to support the vessel and 'knifes' down deeply, sharply reducing the righting moment. Incidently, our hull sections are semi-circular. Strength need be no problem with modern materials and methods (I am including stressed skin plywood techniques), provided the scantlings are adequate. This last proviso does mean some weight, but a little added momentum is no bad thing if a boat is to burst her way to windward through offshore seas. *Rehu Moana*'s strength and resilience were amply proved in Walvis Bay.

The thorny problem of ultimate stability; undoubtedly any yacht would be likely to overturn if struck by the 70 foot wave recorded by automatic devices aboard *Weather Reporter* in a North Atlantic hurricane in 1961. Once over, there seems little likelihood of getting a multi-hull back. One solution would be inflatable buoyancy bags on cabin top and aloft. The size required to render any particular craft self-righting can be worked out. Obviously a good deal of research would be necessary to develop a practical system—and this would cost a great deal.

But I would myself consider that the risk of a well designed cruising catamaran in *any* conditions would be more than offset by her ability to stay afloat even when waterlogged—the enormous practical advantage possessed by a vessel that is lighter than the sea she floats upon. (In this as in the other characteristics touched on, I am including trimarans, which in my opinion differ not at all in principle from catamarans.)

Would I modify *Rehu Moana* in any respect? Only in very minor ones. An extra six inch depth on the after part of the skegs, without increasing the draft of the vessel herself, would enormously improve her self steering ability down wind. Raising the after part of the centre-section six inches would obviate the bumping we experienced in conditions such as those south of the Cape Verde Islands. Headsails properly designed to fit her own fore triangle (our jib was a gift from another yacht), would much improve windward performance.

Though we will be putting to sea very shortly in a single-hulled yacht for reasons explained earlier, I hope to make further catamaran voyages in the future, for I can only conclude from our experiences that a well designed catamaran is faster, roomier, much more convenient and spacious and probably safer than a conventional yacht.

ARRIVAL

The next two days brought numerous signs that we were coming into soundings over the European continental shelf. There was the trawler trudging her five mile circle, her working lights illuminating the sea all around her; gannets had begun to join the familiar storm petrels and fulmars; ships were starting to converge in increasing numbers. Attempts at calling Land's End Radio had as yet been unsuccessful. Our excitement slowly mounted at each new indication, as when Round Island Radio Beacon in the Scillies began to come in on our port bow.

On the third morning, 26th July, we found the sea had changed colour to a lighter shade of blue-grey and the birds were all different, seagulls having entirely replaced the petrels. The sky was overcast and a low mist hung over the sea. We came on cautiously now, for this was not ideal visibility for making a landfall on the Scillies, at which we had determined to call to establish communications. Then at 10.30 the pencil shape of Bishop Rock Lighthouse detached itself from the horizon, and soon afterwards everything began to happen at once. Half an hour after sighting the Bishop we did raise Land's End Radio and in ten minutes were talking with *The Times* in London. They advised us to come straight on to Plymouth, so we hastily altered course round the south side of the Scilly Isles and ran on eastward through the Chops of the Channel. At midnight we had brought the Lizard abeam—and ourselves into a danger as great as any we had ever experienced.

Ships were converging on the headland from all directions at speeds up to 17 knots (nearly 20 m.p.h.) or so, through the fog that had suddenly shut down. Engines were thumping up ahead and others behind us, the sound of some dying away while others grew ominously louder. Twice a minute other noises were drowned by the raucous long and short blasts of the Lizard fog siren, and though we could have been no more than a mile and a half away, not even the loom of its light, that normally has a range of 21 miles, pierced the fog bank. Little reassured by the pressure lamp on deck or our navigation lights, we turned away to seaward in an attempt to escape from the traffic. Nor did we dare to turn inshore across that lethal stream of shipping until full daylight. No matter that we had told *The Times* to expect us off Plymouth Sound about 9 a.m., and that the detour out into the Channel would put back our arrival until well past noon, for had we remained jostling among that radar confident throng, our friends might have waited far longer—and in vain.

All that morning, the 27th of July, was spent closing a dim line of land, out of which familiar landmarks progressively took form. First Dodman Point emerged from the grey overcast, then the Eddystone Light and last of all Rame Head at the entrance to the Sound itself came up right ahead. Two weeks and a day for the 1,290 miles from Horta; we had in fact arrived a whole week sooner than we had told people to expect us, and the only warning anyone could have had of our approach would be the previous day's radio message.

The Times correspondents and photographers, who were waiting off Rame Head, came aboard in a series of perilous leaps from the foredeck of a pitching launch. We were delighted to welcome them, though we could have wished that their exclusive interview rights might have been exercised a little less drastically towards the other press men and camera crews who headed out to us.

Then a splendid white beard streaming in the breeze announced the arrival of Capt. Shaw, secretary of the Royal Western Yacht Club in a launch carrying my daughter Anna, Sir David and Lady Cairns, (Priscilla's parents), and Merton Naydler, veteran of *Rehu Moana*'s Iceland voyage. Fiona's mother, Terence Shaw shouted, was waiting at the yacht club, and my son Barry was on his way.

The rest is, I fear, a jumble of impressions—of making fast off the club, a press conference followed by a belated lunch at the Royal Western where Granny duly received the gift of Susie's tooth, and finally of locking into the quiet of Millbay Dock.

But in all the welcoming excitement there was none of us, I think, whose mind did not stray over the last eventful years. The enterprise had at times demanded all our courage and endurance

—but at the end we had the satisfaction of having accomplished what we had set out to do.

Aboard ISBJØRN at
Plymouth Feb. 1968

POSTSCRIPT

Rehu Moana now lies forlorn and deserted in the yard at Cremyll, a shell stripped of all those personal belongings and familiar things that had made her not only a home but an entity to which we entrusted our lives. Her accommodation being less suited to coastal cruising than extended passages, she remains unsold.*

The unavoidable necessity of having a heavy diesel engine and fuel capacity for the Pacific research project made a different vessel imperative. *Isbjørn*, a thirty year old ketch on Scottish fishing boat lines, with a 44 h.p. Kelvin diesel and an impressive Arctic record under her former owner, has been the answer. But how we miss the spaciousness of *Rehu Moana*, her absence of heel, shallow draft, that thrilling acceleration in a breeze and the comforting knowledge that no matter how badly she might be holed, she could not sink!

Preparing the new venture leaves us little time for nostalgia. Fiona encouraged by the knowledge that she can rely on hyoscine to prevent seasickness is already looking forward to seeing the Café Sport in Horta again and new islands in the Caribbean and the Pacific. The children are very happy in school but equally ready for fresh adventures. My nineteen year old son Barry is part of the ship's company now, splicing the rigging with the proficiency I could never have equalled and making himself familiar with every detail if *Isbjørn*'s engine and rig.

Priscilla has gone back to teaching as she predicted she would have to. She shows slides and films to yacht clubs and sadly contemplates the prospect of at least another year on land. For her the element of anti-climax has been greatest, a particularly unjust sequel since it was her capacity for restraint that made such a big contribution to our harmony. I wonder if she realises yet how

*Since this was written *Rehu Moana* has been sold.

281

unquestionably she has established herself as a yachtswoman and navigator whose experience and ability are equalled by few.

If the account were to close at this point it might leave an impression that all that remains of those three years is a lonely red catamaran drawn up on the shingle. This would be totally misleading.

None of us is quite the same person, though I doubt whether either of the young women realise this. They take for granted the rare quality they showed of rising to an emergency. Nor are they conscious of their enhanced poise and a confidence that was not theirs before. Fiona simply says that 'she carried on so as not to let me down, but felt she often had'. This book, I think, is comment enough!

As to the children, their own opinions are quite forthright.

"I like living on a boat better than a house," said Vicky firmly in a radio interview. Equally definite was Susie.

"We like the gales, they are fun, they are the best part." They have an odd conception or two such as the idea that land floats on water, an obvious analogy with boats. "I have seen it," Susie insists vehemently, probably referring to the floating islands of the Congo. But in general they are very normal happy little girls. What they have gained from it all is something that seems to me beyond price—the ability to live fully with gaiety and confidence and to live unafraid.

Their formative years, and our more mature ones for that matter, have been enriched by many experiences. There have been the awe and majesty of many a full gale, the romance of watching the palms of an atoll climb up over the horizon of a white flecked ocean or the sun rise through steaming mists above the vast brown face of the Congo in flood.

It seems to me that, in place of being observers of life reflected through the medium of the arts, we have been living the actual raw material of poetry.

ACKNOWLEDGMENTS

LITERARY SOURCES
I am indebted to the following authors and publishers of the following
works for much information, either paraphrased or directly quoted:

Hydrographic Office, Ministry of Defence, London:
Quotations from *Ocean Passages for the World* and
from *Africa Pilot* Vols. II & III.
Douglas Phillips Birt: *Ships and Boats*, Studio Vista, London 1966.
Harold Gatty: *Nature is your Guide*, Collins, London.
Corney, B. G. 1913: *The Quest and Occupation of Tahiti by the
Emissaries of Spain during the Years* 1772-6, London, Hakluyt
Society. Andia y Varela's account of voyaging.

OTHER
Already Acknowledged in Other Books
In *Dreamers of the Day* I thanked firms and people who contributed to
the original building and fitting out of *Rehu Moana*. I would like to
thank them again, for their workmanship and products have stood the
sternest tests of the sea.

In *Daughters of the Wind* I acknowledged our debt to a number of
firms and individuals mainly in England and New Zealand. Thus the
greater part of those who helped us to refit in New Zealand were
thanked in that book.

New Zealand
Sir Bernard Fergusson, then Governor General of New Zealand, for
his kindness and the introductions he gave us.

To all the people and firms listed in *Daughters of the Wind*, I would
like to reaffirm my thanks.

ACKNOWLEDGMENTS

Tonga
Mr. A. C. Reid, British Consul
Kaloni Kienga, Inter-island skipper
Graeme and Judith Wells

Fiji
My cousin and his wife; Justin and Kathleen Lewis
Royal Suva Yacht Club

Port Moresby
Ron and Marjorie Crocombe
Dr. John Gunter, Vice-Chancellor, University Papua and New Guinea
Peter Lalor, Clarissa de Derka, Mr. and Mrs. Hagon
Port Moresby Yacht Club. The Navigators: Loheia Lei
                                              Frank Rei
                                              Joseph Tonnaku

Hogar
The Stephens Family

Thursday Island
Bruce Gillison

Darwin
Arthur and Helen Swain   Alan Wilson   Glen Whom
Carl Atkinson   Arthur Beckenham, Bank Manager
Doctors and Nurses of Darwin Hospital

Durban
Wolfie Reiche Ltd.   James Brown and Hammer Ltd.
L. M. Jennings Ltd.   Fast Sails Ltd.   The Manager and Staff of
Royal Natal Yacht Club   Barclays Bank
Point Yacht Club   Hamish Campbell   Bruce Dalling   Bianca Lavies

Capetown
Oldham & Son Ltd.   Royal Cape Yacht Club
Bob Hining   Jean and Brian Quail   Colin Allen

ACKNOWLEDGMENTS

Johannesburg
Fiona's mother and stepfather, Nancy and Eric Sunderland
Fiona's uncle, Arthur Aiken
Noisy and Arne Cilliers

Walvis Bay
Ovenstones Ltd., Gearing Ltd., Walvis Bay Yacht Club
Jens and Hanelore Von de Fecht, Ian Simpson, John and Stephanie
Canner, Viggo Lund, Rudi Allers, Bill LeRoux, Thys and Pat Mool-
man, Dave Owen, Tom Lund, Tworek Fagan.

Lobito
Capt. Melo Cristino, Amandio and Olivia da Silva, Evaristo Guedos,
Lobito Sports Club.

Santo Antonio do Zaire
Commandante and Officers of the Garrison, Fina Company personnel,
Lt. Paulo Marques.

Banana
M. et Mme. Simba, François Ntela, Victor Ameels, Le Père Jean
Martin, G. van Lerbier.

Sierra Leone
Sierra Leone Yacht Club. Victor Hakime, Brian Leyland, Keith and
Audrey Meecham, Alan Breese.

Horta
Jose Azevedo (Peter), Henrique Azvedo, Mario de Almeida, Antonio
Praceres.

Plymouth
Royal Western Yacht Club, and Capt. and Mrs. Shaw.
Jim and Eileen Stephen, Martin and Jill Minter Kemp, Val and June
Bailey, Roy and Barbara Hamilton, Neil Beaton, Mashford Brothers,
The Earl and Countess of Mt. Edgcumbe.

ACKNOWLEDGMENTS

England generally

I wish to renew my thanks to the many firms who provided so many items of equipment who have already been listed in *Daughters of the Wind*.

This also applies to peoples and organisations.

In addition, Margaret and Tony Law, Eric and Florence Llewelyn, Merton Naydler, Nicholas Thompson.

Royal Burnham Yacht Club whose burgee we flew.

In conclusion, I would like to apologise to those whom I must inevitably have unintentionally omitted.

The journey to New Zealand

as described in _Daughters of the Wind_

NORTH PACIFIC OCEAN

UN

● Port Moresby

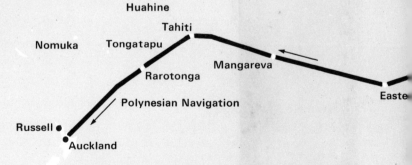

Huahine

Tahiti

Nomuka   Tongatapu

Mangareva

Rarotonga

Polynesian Navigation

Easte

Russell ●

Auckland

NEW ZEALAND

SOUTH PACIFIC OCEAN